That's Entertaining
Celebrations for All Seasons

Yvonne Young Tarr

Photographs by Yvonne Young Tarr

SIMON AND SCHUSTER

NEW YORK · LONDON · TORONTO · SYDNEY · TOKYO

Copyright © 1987 by Yvonne Young Tarr
All rights reserved
including the right of reproduction
in whole or in part in any form
Published by Simon and Schuster
A Division of Simon & Schuster, Inc.
Simon & Schuster Building
Rockefeller Center
1230 Avenue of the Americas
New York, New York 10020
SIMON AND SCHUSTER and colophon are registered
trademarks of Simon & Schuster, Inc.
Designed by Levavi & Levavi
Manufactured in the United States of America
10   9   8   7   6   5   4   3   2   1
Library of Congress Cataloging in Publication Data

Tarr, Yvonne Young.
    That's entertaining.

    Includes index.
    1. Entertaining.   2. Menus. I. Title.
II. Title: That is entertaining.
TX731.T37   1987   641.5   87-4884
ISBN: 0-671-52320-1

I dedicate this book to my parents, Margaret and Elwood Young, my husband, Bill, my sons, Jonathon and Nicolas, and my mother-in-law, Hannah Tarr, all of whom I love very dearly.

A special word of thanks to my assistant and friend, Ruth Grossman, my editor, Carole Lalli, my agent, Christine Tomasino, and to Steve Manville and Leslie Segal for their friendly advice.

Contents

Autumn   141

Winter   175

Foreword

My earliest memory is of a green room lit by the cold flash of sparklers set in a pink birthday cake. No one else in my family recalls the event, but for me it signaled the good times and good food to come. As a matter of fact, that portion of my brain devoted to things past seems inordinately preoccupied with foods I have known and loved. I have no idea what character, or lack of it, this may indicate, but while I often forget who I dialed by the time the receiver reaches my ear, I can recall with vivid accuracy most of the meals I have enjoyed in my adult life, as well as many from my childhood.

Although I have dined willingly and well in exotic places to celebrate many joyful occasions, the meal I remember most fondly was served close to home and honored a serious event rather than a happy one. The "Dutch" openhouse that welcomed weary relatives following the funeral of my sweet Grandfather Nicholas in Lewistown, Pennsylvania, was a feast as plain in its surroundings as it was fancy in taste.

On a twelve-foot cherrywood table, polished over several generations to a winey glow, a baker's dozen Amish aunts and cousins piled bowl after bowl of homespun treasures. As more friends and distant relatives crowded in, bearing gifts of "eats," a second table was drawn up and set end to end with the first. Brown and tan and blue crockery were reflected in the wood beneath, so that scarlet spiced crabapples, cranberry sauce, and berry jams seemed to double in quantity.

A mammoth ham with crumbly brown sugar glaze rose like Everest on its stippled platter, and two wild birds, a turkey and a pheasant (each roundly stuffed), shone majestically in the mirrored wood beneath them. Of the potatoes there were four varieties—mashed, roasted, glazed-sweet, and dumplings. The mashed potatoes were not merely mashed but folded with whipped cream until they were nearly light enough to levitate; the roasted ones were basted with ham drippings until the outsides were burnished while the insides remained as white as milk; the sweet potatoes were not simply glazed but simmered to caramelized nuggets that glistened like amber; the dumplings were so fleecy they seemed in danger of floating out of the bowl.

Naturally there were autumn vegetables fresh from the garden: fat knobs of sprouts, parsnip pudding, pureed butternut, and rutabaga; jars of pickles of all kinds, crunchy cucumbers, green and yellow string beans, beets and onions, relishes as colorful as confetti. From the orchards there were pear, apple, and peach butters; from the fields, dried corn and crusty brown and black breads. Desserts waited shoulder to shoulder on the sideboard: apple cakes and apple cookies, pumpkin tarts, devil's and angel food cakes, lattice-crusted black berry, cherry, and gooseberry pies, and a steamed pudding added for good measure.

Nicholas Young was a good man who lived a long, rich life and who was loved by all. With treasures of good food and drafts of sweet, clear apple cider, we celebrated the joy of his having lived among us. In every society the sharing of food and drink underscores the importance of all sorts of occasions. Of course a stunning location also adds luster to any entertainment. It's impossible not to respond well to dinner before a crackling fire in a glass chalet nestled beneath a fringe of mountains or lunch beside a pool suspended over the Aegean. Even though I don't always include it, I think background music—a touch of Vivaldi or a dash of Cole Porter—brightens a party as much as a sprinkling of fresh herbs adds dash to a salad.

And I confess to having an obsession for unusually beautiful table appointments. To me they are essential in setting the tone of an entertainment. Even a simple Sunday night supper might be counterpointed with hand-painted linens sugared with lace, china as delicate and colorful as Easter-egg shells, stemware with the look of carved ice, chunky silver or shaped ivory flatware, plus a variety of vases, bottles, sculpture, trays, baskets, or any interesting mix of antique, contemporary, or ethnic objects that increase the drama, elegance, or sense of fun.

When I'm designing a table setting and can't locate the ideal assemblage of napery and china, I create them myself. Many quiet winter's evenings I paint my own designs on linen napkins and tablecloths by candlelight so I know that the colors will be precisely right. My mother, a potter, introduced me to the secrets of her potter's wheel, glazes, and kiln when I was a child, so it seems simple and practical for me to paint and fire exactly the dishes I need. This may seem an extreme measure

to some, but no setting is as satisfying to me as these intricate and delicately colored linen damask cloths set with their matching porcelain, napkins, and stemware.

As conducive to pleasure as delicious food, drink, and exquisite decoration may be, the guests themselves are the element without which any party would be meaningless. Come to think of it, without you to read it, a book like this one would also lose its purpose. You are the guest without whom the party would lose its fizz. I've created these menus just as I would if you were expected to dinner. I've picked out the china, linens, and flatware you see here—some borrowed treasures, most right from my closet shelves. I've tested, tasted, and prepared all of the food in my own kitchen as well and have photographed it as you would see it if you were about to sit down at my dining table or in my nice, shady garden.

The dishes you see here are not make-believe foods, manufactured in a chemist's laboratory, sprayed with varnish, gussied up with glycerine, stuffed with cotton, set out on a shovelful of sand to represent a beach under an orange gel to take the place of the sun. I felt it was important for you to see these dishes just as they would arrive at your table. This is real food, meant for real people to enjoy—and enjoy it they did in real surroundings immediately following the last click of my camera. Delicious food is not always perfectly round or square, high or low. If a cookie crumbled, I photographed it anyway—and ate it, too, just as you probably would.

As a matter of fact, many of the recipes here harken back to those old-fashioned, bountiful days of full cookie jars. Then again, quite a number present the contemporary in a variety of ways. What this book is about then, is creating good, wholesome, seasonal party foods in interesting preparations and harmonious combinations; in other words . . . taking good care of those you care about with a dash of spontaneity, a splash of color, and a flash of ingenuity. I hope you enjoy using it as much as I have enjoyed putting it together.

10

Introduction

I live in a place that is known for its parties. In summer it's dazzling here. The beaches stretch out languorously, pale and golden, embracing both the land and the sea. There's a haze in August that filters the sunlight so that it falls softer than gauze against the skin. The fields are flat and verdant, and edge up to the dunes tentatively, without infringing on their rolling beauty. Because the land is low, the sky dominates the landscape, blazing at sunset, luminescent by moonlight. But what is really precious in the New York Hamptons—more priceless even than its magnificent farmland and world-class beaches—are its inhabitants.

The rich, the famous, even the infamous come here. The beautiful, the elite, especially the talented, come here. The titled come here, from kings and queens, princes and princesses, to Miss America. The sports come here from every sport. You name it! Members of the press congregate in droves. In fact, given the chance, almost everyone from everywhere in the world comes here. And the favorite Hampton recreations are giving and going to parties. Beach parties. Theater parties. Lawn parties. Charity balls. Save the Whale parties. Political parties. Pool parties. Buffets. Caviar parties. Fireworks parties. Publishing parties. Little sit-down dinners. Rites of Spring parties. Celebrate Summer parties. Traveling parties. Torchlight picnics. Costume parties. Tandem parties. Wine tastings. Every conceivable sort of cocktail party. Memorial Day parties as the high season commences and Labor Day parties as it closes.

And so, since the world in effect comes to the Hamptons, it follows that the best place to observe the finer points of going to and giving parties is right here in my own backyard. And observe I have . . . some of the most gracious hosts and hostesses and accomplished caterers in the world. It's not unheard of in August, at the peak of the summer season, to be invited to several gallery openings and four or five parties in one twenty-four-hour period. But then, going to parties is the easy part . . . giving them is quite another.

Still, there comes a time, perhaps while you're weeding in the green of your country garden, or sipping a sherry and drinking in the flicker of city lights at sunset, when a certain madness seizes you, and you know you're about to embark on that adventure called entertaining. Even after all these years I never quite know what influence makes a party inevitable . . . masses of June roses begging to be picked . . . a full moon backlighting our neighbor's palomino in the meadow by my husband's studio-barn where we often entertain . . . a rack of lamb hanging in a butcher shop window . . . the fragrance of strawberries as I pass the "U-Pick-Em-3-Boxes-for-$3" sign. Never mind. I know I am lost, caught in a frenzy that doesn't release me until, after bingeing on the wine of human contact, after bidding the party's last good-byes, I fall asleep as satisfied as a child after a birthday celebration.

I realize now that my parties are entertainments designed to give me the pleasure of seeing and caring for my friends, as much as to please them. Perhaps that's why, no matter how much work remains to be accomplished, no matter how many snags develop, I feel joy rather than apprehension as party day approaches. Once, a scant hour before a buffet party for three hundred, our electricity failed, a common occurrence in the rural Hamptons. I transported giant pans of Bobotee (an African curry) to friends with gas stoves, along with specific baking directions. What I hadn't taken into account was that some had fast ovens, others had slow ones.

When the bubbling trays of curry were returned, all were sufficiently baked, but a few had a rather sickly pallor. I brushed the pale ones with melted butter mixed with meat glaze for an instant brown, sprinkled all with minced parsley, and served them forth. I could have had a nervous breakdown, but I decided instead to put an old "La Conga" record on the player as a distraction. As the party rose to a crescendo, some guests "conga-ed" to their cars with wild cries of "best party ever!" Well, maybe. Maybe not. But since everyone seemed to have had a great time, at least *I* was satisfied that it was the best party it could have been, given the unfortunate circumstances.

To my mind that's what this book is really all about: taking the panic out of entertaining. Whether the occasion be formal or homespun, the information here will help you decide what kind of party you want to give and how to cook, deco-

rate, and present the menu you choose.

Great party-giving is a social sport which the party-giver can only practice in public, under fire and in front of guests where mistakes are glaringly visible. Since most hosts and hostesses are only occasional entertainers, it should help to have a kind of party coach lessening the risks by building into each menu all of my sure-fire methods, shortcuts, tricks, and secrets gained through two decades of party-giving—on a realistic level. I selected the parties for this book rather than any others because they are based on principles that work for me, principles that to my mind encompass the important "yesses" that make an entertainment work.

While this book does visually concern itself with entertaining—flowers, tablecloths, china, candles, and the like—it is really about food that makes guests feel taken care of. Nurturing food: hot soup on a frigid day; custard that slips down sweet and easy. Food for soothing the savage beast in you: gooseberry fool; crusty, cracker-dipped fried chicken; goat cheese and grits. Satisfying food: fresh vegetable gumbo with nuggets of smoked salmon and fat slices of baby okra in a silky yogurt base; deep, dark cheesecake filled with chocolate mousse; garlicky eggplant-rice pudding; lentil soup with osso bucco right in the bowl; melty white chocolate fondue.

These and all the thousands of other recipes I've developed and tested in the process of writing twenty books and two syndicated columns reflect the influence of my father's Pennsylvania-German background and my mother's Kentucky heritage. Both of these life-styles embraced the virtue of sharing with neighbors, friends, relatives, and, often, with strangers. There was never too little; there were never too many who needed feeding. These good folks practiced a natural style of planting, cooking, and eating that anticipated so many of today's trends. Their pantry shelves reflected the natural bounty that blossomed around them. Their plain wooden tables sagged beneath farm-smoked hams, lusty sausages, sauerkraut

fresh from the barrel, still bubbling in the throes of fermentation, dozens of relishes that shone like jewels in their plain white saucers, spicy dried-apple pies, and hickory nut cakes.

From this background, that sanctified simplicity, I came to maturity and eventually began to entertain at my own table. But those early impressions left their imprint—my mother's warmth and her dedication to Southern hospitality, my father's straightforward charm.

While there is certainly a place for the formal meal, and I have presided over many, I have a preference for spur-of-the-moment entertaining. Often I, and I suspect my guests as well, haven't the slightest notion of how two-weeks-from-Thursday will turn out. Who knows? On that evening I might prefer to go twilight snapper fishing or take in a film. But when a fisherman surprises me with ten pounds of sand shark that might otherwise go begging at market, visions of parties dance in my head. Shall I serve shark's fin soup? Seviche? Kebabs? Who's in town? Who adores Oriental food? What's ready in the garden today? Shall I sprinkle that new plum wine over fresh raspberries? Are the tea roses my neighbor dropped off yester-

day still beautiful? Before I know it, I'm on the phone. Suddenly it's dinnertime tomorrow, and familiar faces smile across a table scattered with rose petals, sparkling with silver, aglow with candlelight. That's the ideal way, it seems to me, to put together an evening's festivities.

But, in addition to the relaxed little dinner party, sometimes other, more complex entertainments are called for. Looking for quick, easy, low-cal nibbles for twenty? Picnicking, tailgating, or sailing parties? Intimate entertainments for two? A salad-bar party for two hundred of your closest friends? After-theater sweets? A holiday open house? Each of these can be created with confidence using the specially designed menus in this book.

If you have twenty upstairs-downstairs helpers in your manse in Newport, if you are a prestigious caterer with dozens of elves to carry out a party plan as logistically intricate as the invasion of Normandy, if you are a film star with a movie studio to finance, direct, and produce your latest bash, you probably won't need this book. However, if you are not so blessed but nevertheless hanker to entertain with style, assurance, ease, and originality, read on.

Spring

Rites-of-Spring Sit-Down Dinner for Eight

The first dinner party of spring has a freshness unlike any other season's. The sun's frail brilliance warms and awakens my napping garden and beacons last autumn's neglected arugula and lettuce seeds, green and bronze and red, to offer up the first salad of the season. Young and tender vegetable and animal edibles are at their peak of perfection everywhere. It's time to bring forth the most succulent specialties of the vernal equinox.

Spring lambs, born in February or March, can be found in the markets by April or May and on through the end of September. These young creatures graze on the delicate new grasses of the season, and as a result yield moist, high-quality, sweet-tasting meat with no hint of the mature taste that develops in older animals.

The noisettes featured here are cut from extra-thick rib chops trimmed of excess fat and flattened slightly. If the chops are not minuscule, one is ample to satisfy a small appetite, but for guests with more hearty inclinations you should plan on two apiece. Since the meal is fairly rich and quite satisfying, most often I compromise and prepare an even dozen to serve eight. But to be on the safe side, prepare sixteen.

TABLEWARE, TIFFANY AND CO., NY, NY

Menu

Herbed Clam and Cucumber Bisque

Lamb Noisettes with Sorrel Sauce

Frittered Fiddleheads

New Potatoes in Garlic-Flavored Olive Oil

Rites-of-Spring Salad

Soufflé of Rhubarb with Candied Grapefruit Rind and Grapefruit Syrup

Herbed Clam and Cucumber Bisque

Here on Long Island, surrounded as we are by climate-tempering bay and ocean waters, **spring and herbs** are practically synonymous. Even through the winter months, it's easy **to keep** pots of these treasures in a cool, sheltered, indoor or outdoor nook, handy for **harvesting.** Once another frost seems unlikely, out they go on a full-time basis to thrive for early spring until late-summer pruning. For this soup, **be sure to include dill, tarragon,** thyme, and chives, or **whatever compatible combination is available in your own garden.**

(SERVES 8)

> *1 large cucumber, peeled, seeded, and sliced*
> *3 scallions, including 2–3 inches of the green tops, chopped*
> *6 tablespoons mixed fresh herbs (as noted above)*
> *1 quart homemade or good-quality prepared chicken broth, skimmed of all fat*
> *3 cups ice-cold juice from fresh clams*
> *1½ cups very cold light cream or half-and-half*
> *2 tablespoons Pernod*
> *8 shucked, raw littleneck clams (optional)*
> *White pepper*

Simmer together the cucumber, scallions, herbs, and broth until the scallions are tender. Puree and chill well. Combine the clam juice and cream; add the Pernod. Chill until ready to use.

Just before serving, place the clam-juice mixture in the freezer—for about 5 minutes. Combine the two mixtures and pour into small porcelain or glass bowls; slip one clam into each bowl if you are using them. Sprinkle with white pepper, and, if desired, a bit of additional finely minced herbs.

Lamb Noisettes with Sorrel Sauce

(SERVES 8)

> *12–16 thick-cut lamb chops*
> *2 tablespoons fruity extra-virgin olive oil*
> *3 pounds fresh sorrel, well washed and drained*
> *3 tablespoons butter*
> *½ cup heavy cream*
> *½ cup plain yogurt*
> *Salt and freshly ground white pepper to taste*
> *Sprinkle of nutmeg*

Remove the small round filet from each chop and trim away excess fat. Rub the filets with oil and pan-fry or broil them to suit your taste—rare, medium, or at the very least, pink. Do not let them dry out.

Discard the stems of the sorrel. Finely chop the leaves in a food processor or by hand and simmer in the butter until soft. Add the cream and cook until the sauce is slightly thickened. Off the heat, stir in the yogurt and season with salt, pepper, and nutmeg. Serve the sauce warm, not hot, with the meat.

Frittered Fiddleheads

These prettily coiled young shoots of the ostrich fern look a little like the scrolled head of a violin and have a flavor somewhere in between those of artichoke and asparagus. Fiddleheads have had a rush of popularity in food circles, but I remember as a child gathering them in the cool shade of Canadian forests on fishing trips. They are interesting, whether tossed in salads, stir-fried in hot oil for a minute or two, or as in this recipe, quickly fried in a delicate batter. What's important is to expose them to as little heat as possible so that they retain their unique taste and nice crunch. If you can't find really fresh fiddleheads, don't bother. The canned variety is fit only for making soup. (Substitute asparagus heads, baby okra, cattail shoots, or squash blossoms.)

(SERVES 8)

> 40–50 *fiddleheads, depending on size*
> 1 *egg*
> ½ *cup each milk and water*
> 1 *cup all-purpose flour*
> 1 *teaspoon baking powder*
> *Oil for deep-frying*

Rinse the fiddleheads, drain them well, and then dry them between paper towels, lightly pressing out all water. Beat the egg, milk, and water together. Sift the flour with the baking powder. Fold the dry ingredients into the egg mixture 1 tablespoon at a time. Do not overmix. The flour should be barely moistened and the batter thick and lumpy.

Dip several fiddleheads at a time into the batter and fry in deep, hot oil (350–370 degrees F.) until golden. Drain on paper towels. Repeat the process until all the fiddleheads are fried. Line a baking sheet with several thicknesses of paper towel, arrange the fried fiddleheads on top, and put into an oven that has been preheated to 200 degrees F. to keep warm until the potatoes and lamb are ready to serve.

New Potatoes in Garlic-Flavored Olive Oil

As delectable as extra-virgin olive oil is, I often flavor it with a branch of fresh thyme and a clove of unpeeled garlic scored with a sharp knife. Why unpeeled garlic? When garlic remains in its papery wrapping, less of its oils are released. The flavor is more mellow, not nearly so dominant; nutty rather than sharp or bold. This is particularly important if you are serving fiddleheads, which should have less competition to allow for the full pleasure of their distinctive flavor.

(SERVES 8)

> 32–40 *tiny new potatoes, well scrubbed*
> *Garlic-flavored olive oil (see above; infuse about ½ cup extra-virgin olive oil*
> *with one garlic clove for at least one hour)*
> 4 *tablespoons sweet butter*
> *Coarse salt to taste*

Parboil the potatoes for 3 minutes in water to cover. Drain them and dry them well. Discard any loose skin. Fry the potatoes in the oil until they are tender. Add the butter and continue frying until the potatoes are golden brown all over. Sprinkle with coarse salt and serve very hot.

Rites-of-Spring Salad

When you live in the country, as I do, part of the fun is to assemble the evening's salad by gathering crisp infant greenery from your own garden and foraging bits of wild edibles from surrounding fields. (For the latter to be safe, of course, you have to know exactly what you are looking for.) I deliberately plant more seeds in the spring than necessary so that I may enjoy the tiniest shoots of salad greens when I thin out the rows later on. In the fields I pick only those findings I know to be safe—dandelion greens, wild onions, violets, borage, and the like. City dwellers might forage exotic vegetables and greens from ethnic markets and vegetable stands. Use your imagination *and* a wonderful dressing to create a younger-than-springtime salad.

(SERVES 8)

> 2 *quarts mixed salad greens, well washed and dried*
> 1 *quart other salad fixings (sprouts, dandelion greens, etc.), well washed and*
> *dried*
> 2 *hard-cooked eggs, shelled and finely chopped*
> 3–4 *tablespoons chopped mixed fresh herbs*
> ⅔ *cup olive oil (the fruity extra-virgin is nice for this)*
> 3 *tablespoons wine vinegar*
> *Salt and freshly ground black pepper to taste*

Chill the greens and other salad fixings well. Mix the chopped eggs and herbs, and keep them chilled. Whisk the oil into the vinegar until well mixed, then season with salt and pepper. Chill the dressing until serving time, then whisk in the egg mixture and toss with the salad at the table.

Soufflé of Rhubarb with Candied Grapefruit Rind and Grapefruit Syrup

The lovely, slightly tart edge that adds dimension to this soufflé is heightened by slivers of your own crunchy-with-coarse-sugar candied grapefruit rind and clear grapefruit syrup. If you haven't the spare minutes needed to prepare the candied rind, you may substitute store-bought orange or lemon rind and flavor the soufflé with Grand Marnier rather than with Grapefruit Syrup. The taste combinations will be different but also very interesting. If making the candied rind, try to prepare it the day prior to your dinner party if possible. The soufflé itself will hold up in the dish for an hour or so before baking.

(SERVES 8)

Rhubarb Soufflé

2 tablespoons sweet butter
Sugar
1 cup cold milk
⅓ cup flour
5 egg yolks
½ teaspoon vanilla extract
1⅓ cups Rhubarb Puree (recipe below)
2 tablespoons Grapefruit Syrup (recipe below)
     or Grand Marnier liqueur
Pinch of salt
8 egg whites
¾ cup granulated sugar

Wrap a 5-inch-high collar of aluminum foil or parchment paper around a 2-quart soufflé dish and tie with string so that 3 inches extend above the edge of the dish. Butter the inside of the dish and the collar, and sprinkle with sugar.

In a small, heavy saucepan whisk the milk into the flour a few tablespoons at a time to make a smooth mixture. Continue whisking over medium heat until thick and smooth.

Beat the egg yolks until the mixture is creamy and pale yellow, then beat in the vanilla, Rhubarb Puree, and Grapefruit Syrup. Add a pinch of salt to the egg whites, whip them at high speed until they froth up, then whip in the remaining granulated sugar, 1 tablespoon at a time, until this meringue is very firm, high, and glossy.

Preheat oven to 375 degrees F.

With a spatula, fold about 1 cup of the egg white into the egg yolk mixture, cutting gently down through the whites, across the bottom of the bowl, then up and over until the whites are fairly well mixed in. Pour this mixture over the rest of the whites and gently repeat the folding-in process, turning the bowl as you go, until the mixture is light and well incorporated and no chunks of white are left whole. Do not overmix.

Pour the mixture into the buttered and sugared soufflé dish. After you've served the entree, slip the soufflé into the oven and bake it for 25–30 minutes or until it is nicely puffed and lightly browned. If you prefer the center fully cooked rather than moist, leave it in the oven 5 minutes more. Sprinkle with granulated sugar just prior to serving. Top with bits of slivered rind and spoonfuls of Grapefruit Syrup.

Candied Grapefruit Rind and Grapefruit Syrup

> *1 small pink grapefruit*
> *1¾ cups granulated sugar*
> *Coarse sugar*
> *2 tablespoons grenadine syrup*

Peel the zest, or colored part, of the grapefruit's skin off and cut into 2-inch lengths (include none of the white pith). Squeeze the pulp and reserve the juice. In a small stainless-steel or enamel saucepan, bring the rind, ½ cup of the granulated sugar, and ¼ cup of grapefruit juice to a boil and continue boiling until the syrup reaches the soft ball stage (234 degrees F.). Remove the zest with a slotted spoon, arrange it on waxed paper that has been sprinkled with half the coarse sugar, then sprinkle the remaining coarse sugar over it and let it stand for at least one hour or overnight. Add the remaining sugar and grapefruit juice and the grenadine syrup to the grapefruit syrup and boil until syrupy. Set aside. When the zest is cool, cut it into strips ⅛ inch wide.

Rhubarb Puree

A sure sign of spring is the appearance of this ruby-stalked vegetable—yes, vegetable. Choose slender, bright red, young rhubarb ribs that will need no peeling and little cooking to be tender. The grenadine is used mostly to brighten the color.

> *6 slender young rhubarb ribs*
> *1 cup granulated sugar*
> *⅓ cup lemon juice*
> *2 tablespoons grenadine syrup (optional)*

If the rhubarb turns out to be neither young nor tender, you will have to peel off and discard the skins or "ribbons" from the stalks along with the bitter, poisonous leaves. Cut the peeled rhubarb into ½-inch slices. Bring the sugar and lemon juice to a low boil and boil for 3 minutes, then add the rhubarb and cook about 5 minutes or until the pieces are tender and most of the liquid has evaporated. Cool slightly and puree. You should have 1⅓ cups. Stir in the grenadine and cool the puree to room temperature.

Picnic by a Watercress Stream

My favorite warm-weather hideaway is a not-to-be-believed half acre of watercress rooted in the icy trickle of a freshwater brook with a split personality. Only a few hundred feet downstream, this idyllic location becomes a languid saltwater inlet populated with friendly, feathered, Hampton residents.

Lunch in the great outdoors needn't be make-shift. Well thought out and properly packed, picnic food can be sublime. The secret lies in defying convention and knowing what you're about. Here, each item was chosen for good reason. Elongated hard rolls are strong-shouldered enough to retain their crunch through hours of travel time. Smoked meats can hold their own flavor-wise, even when encased in a roll, and they possess splendid keeping qualities. Wild mushrooms and sweet pepper slices retain their unique textures and actually increase in flavor as they marinate, something no lettuce leaf can do. Creamy Stilton needs neither refrigeration nor warming to taste terrific. Flaky Curried Biscuits are wonderful nibbles, especially when partnered with that East Indian hot-weather standby, chutney. And finally, enjoy a sweetly tart Tomato Marmalade Cake based on my grandmother's prized jam cake recipe famous for retaining its nectarous moistness long before the advent of plastic wrap.

This repast was served in compartmentalized Korean wooden lunch boxes—an inexpensive find at a local charity flea market—but plastic tackle boxes with large and small cubbyholes will also serve admirably.

Watercress garnish, anyone?

Menu

Hollowed-Out Hard Rolls Filled with Layers of Smoked Breast of Chicken, Marinated Wild Mushrooms and Sweet Pepper Slices, and Blue Cheese

Curried Biscuits

Mixed Vegetable Chutney

Grandmother's Tomato Marmalade Cake

Gingered Iced Tea

Watercress Garnish

Hollowed-Out Hard Rolls Filled with Layers of Smoked Breast of Chicken, Marinated Wild Mushrooms and Sweet Pepper Slices, and Blue Cheese

Here in the Hamptons, so near the Atlantic shore, our favorite picnic sites are within minutes of home, so refrigeration is not really a problem. It's easy to tuck a generous lunch into two compartmentalized Korean Bento Boxes, a basket, and one small cooler bag. No plates are needed either, since the small wooden drawers not only hold the food, but serve as dishes, then slip back into place when they're empty. Thermos tops serve as cups, the chutney can be dispensed from a wide-mouthed container, and finger pickin' is the rule of the day. A stack of linen napkins and an attractive luncheon cloth add a luxurious touch.

If yours is a larger party, and you will be traveling in cars for a longer distance, you may want to pack ceramic plates and a bigger cooler with wine, Gingered Iced Tea, glasses, and other utensils.

Smoked foods are gaining in popularity and luckily are more available and higher in quality than ever before. If you can, there is no reason why you shouldn't purchase the birds already smoked and save a little time. If not, it's an easy matter to smoke them yourself in one of those small, inexpensive home-smokers. Surprisingly, they are more convenient to use and are actually less work than your backyard barbecue. Home-smoked foods are usually superior to their store-bought counterparts, and the savings are considerable. Remember, though, this process is really smoke cooking, not dry smoking, which is a difficult, time-consuming procedure that preserves foods for protracted periods of time without refrigeration. Smoke cooking imparts excellent flavor and does provide some protection against spoilage, but foods must still be kept chilled, especially in hot weather. Therefore, the only ingredient in this lunch that will have to be kept cool is the breast meat of the birds. I am especially fond of Pintelle Guinea Fowl smoked in apple wood, but use what you prefer.

(SERVES 6 TO 8)

> 6–8 *smoked breasts of chicken, thinly sliced*
> 1/3 *cup fruity extra-virgin olive oil*
> 1 1/2 *cups coarsely sliced wild mushrooms (morels, shiitake, chanterelles, or, if*
> *these are not available, cultivated tame ones)*
> 1 *large clove garlic, unpeeled*
> 4 *sprigs of fresh Italian parsley, coarsely chopped*
> 2 *tablespoons lemon juice*
> *Salt and freshly ground black pepper to taste*
> 1 *each sweet red and golden pepper, seeded and cut into strips*
> 6–8 *hard rolls, each about 7 inches long*
> 1/2 *pound creamy blue cheese cut in 1/2-inch-thick slices*

Brush the breast meat very lightly with the extra-virgin olive oil. Wrap in plastic wrap and refrigerate until needed. Rinse the wild mushrooms only if they are sandy and blot in paper towels to absorb all the excess moisture. Slice any large pieces of mushroom and set aside.

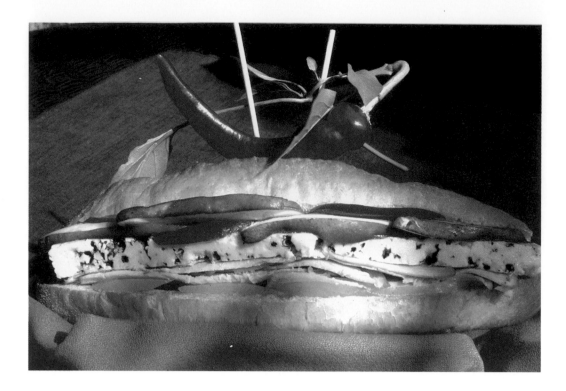

Heat 2 teaspoons of the olive oil in a small skillet and sauté the unpeeled garlic clove until it is lightly browned on all sides and softened. Peel the garlic and pound in a mortar along with the parsley, adding enough of the remaining olive oil a drop at a time to make a nice paste. Mix in the lemon juice, salt, and pepper to make a dressing. Place this and the pepper and mushroom slices in a wide-mouthed glass or plastic container, cover, and shake them well.

Just before you start off to the picnic site, place the rolls in your basket or plastic box, and the wrapped chicken slices and marinated mushrooms and peppers in your cooler bag. When you're ready to serve lunch, carefully break open the rolls, pull out some of the soft insides, and layer in the smoked chicken slices, peppers, mushrooms, and cheese.

Curried Biscuits

These flaky biscuit pies are filled with chopped pecans and served with a tangy chutney of simmered fruits and crisp mixed vegetables.

(SERVES 6 TO 8)

2 *cups all-purpose flour*
1/2 *teaspoon salt*
1 *teaspoon mild curry powder*
2 *teaspoons baking powder*
6 *tablespoons butter*
Milk
2 *tablespoons softened butter*
1/2 *cup chopped pecans*

Sift together the flour, salt, curry powder, and baking powder. Use a food processor with the steel cutting blade or 2 knives to cut the 6 tablespoons of butter into the dry ingredients until the mixture has the consistency of a very coarse meal. Lightly mix in just enough milk to make a soft dough, then knead it gently on a lightly floured surface for about 30 seconds. Roll out to a thickness of ¼ inch and cut into 2-inch rounds with a floured biscuit cutter (do not twist the cutter). Spread half the rounds with the softened butter and sprinkle the remaining half with pecans, taking care not to flatten the dough. Place a buttered round on top of a nut-covered round but do not press it down. Bake on a greased baking sheet for 15 minutes or until nicely browned. These are also terrific just slathered with the chutney.

Mixed Vegetable Chutney

Chutney is child's play to prepare and heightens and enhances the distinctive flavors of a wide variety of dishes—meats, fish, eggs, pastas—and, as here, it is terrific with biscuits. As long as you're at it, you might as well simmer up a few pints; guests are invariably in awe of the homemade variety. This combination of fruits and vegetables is unusual and particularly versatile.

(MAKES 3 TO 4 PINTS)

1 cup each coarsely chopped onion and celery

¾ cup each chopped and whole golden seedless raisins

3 hard green pears, peeled, seeded, and cut into slices ½ inch thick (or substitute firm, tart apples)

1 underripe papaya, peeled and cut into ½-inch cubes (reserve 1 tablespoon of the seeds)

1 cup each yellow and green runner beans, snapped into 1-inch pieces

1 sweet red and 1 green pepper, seeded, with pith removed, and cut into ½-inch squares

1 cup honey

2 cups granulated sugar

1 cup white distilled vinegar

1 teaspoon each salt, dry mustard, curry powder, and ginger

¼ cup each cayenne pepper and ground cloves

Bring all ingredients to a boil in a large stainless-steel or enamel pan. Cook at a low boil, stirring frequently, until the syrup is thick enough to cover the vegetables. In other words, until the mixture resembles chutney. There's no need to bother canning this, as it disappears too quickly. It will keep well for a month or so in the refrigerator.

Grandmother's Tomato Marmalade Cake

Fresh and fruity, with a delicate difference you won't quite be able to put your finger on. In fact, that elusive flavor is the old American love apple, lending its fragrance, color, and all-around panache to a down-home favorite . . . loafcake.

(SERVES 8 TO 10)

> 10 small yellow pear tomatoes or red plum tomatoes
> 1½ cups light-brown sugar
> ¾ cup white granulated sugar
> 1 orange and 1 lemon
> ½ cup (1 stick) sweet butter
> 4 eggs, separated
> 2 cups all-purpose flour
> 1 teaspoon each baking soda and ground cinnamon
> ½ teaspoon each ground nutmeg, cloves, and allspice
> 1 teaspoon lemon juice
> 3 tablespoons milk
> Coarse sugar

Preheat oven to 450 degrees F.

Arrange the tomatoes on a baking sheet (one with sides at least ½ inch high) and bake in the preheated oven for 15 minutes. Remove the tomatoes from the oven and lower the heat to 375 degrees F. When the tomatoes are cool enough to handle, cut off and discard the stem ends and the skins.

Place the tomatoes and their pan juices in a heavy stainless-steel saucepan and cover them with ¾ cup each of light-brown and white sugar. Squeeze the juices from the orange and lemon, and pour over the pan ingredients. Bring to a high boil, stirring constantly. Immediately lower the heat, maintaining an even low boil, and continue cooking, stirring frequently, until the tomatoes turn translucent and the mixture resembles jam. Be careful that the mixture does not scorch. Remove the jam from the heat, cool it slightly, then coarsely chop up any remaining large tomato pieces.

Meanwhile, cream together the butter and the remaining ¾ cup of brown sugar until the mixture is light and fluffy. Beat in the egg yolks, 1 at a time, incorporating each before the next is added.

Sift together the flour, baking soda, and spices. Mix together the teaspoon of lemon juice and the milk, and stir into the tomatoes. Add the dry ingredients to the creamed mixture alternately with the cooled tomato mixture, stirring well after each addition. Beat the egg whites until they are stiff but not dry, and fold them into the batter.

Butter a 10-inch ring pan, and pour in the batter to no higher than 1 inch from the top; if there is any batter left over, bake some cupcakes for breakfast. Sprinkle the top of the cake with coarse sugar and bake in the preheated oven for 35–45 minutes or until the cake begins to pull away from the sides of the pan. Cool on a wire rack.

Gingered Iced Tea

1 tablespoon peeled and minced fresh ginger
3 tablespoons dried, black tea leaves
Boiling water
Sugar to taste
Ice

Steep the ginger and the tea in 1 quart boiling water for 5 minutes. Stir in sugar until dissolved. Add additional water until the tea is the strength you prefer. Pour over ice.

Flowers for All Seasons

There is a splendid clarity to the air after the season's first warm, drenching rain. Every bud, leaf, and field has the freshly laundered look of spring. Winter's shallow streams swell with mossy tidbits that entice passing waterfowl to drop in for lunch. In Nature's carelessly tended garden, flowers and vegetables shoot up through last year's tangle of broken leaves and twigs. To celebrate the season I, too, love to mix blossoms with tender young vegetables and herbs in natural-looking armfuls rather than in self-conscious, overly worked arrangements. In the spring, I combine lilacs, herbs, tulips, hyacinths, slender young asparagus, and remnants of winter leeks; in the summer, sunflowers, goldenrod, and broccoli that have gone to flower; in the fall, colorful autumn leaves, branches of cherry tomatoes, and bright golden mums; and in the winter, stark, interesting tree branches with dried and fresh arrangements.

Flowers are their own reward. They enrich the senses and add a deeper dimension to your table, your pleasure, your life.

Great-Aunt Katie's Southern-Kitchen Dinner

My great-aunt Katie's kitchen dinners were not of the hamhocks-awash-in-greens variety. Aunt Katie had definite illusions of grandeur. Her mother's small family hotel that once nestled beneath oak trees hung with wisps of blue-gray moss had vanished when she was a girl, long before my birth, but her dinners revived its legend. Even when we dined alone, this aging aunt and teenaged niece sipped her celebrated bourbon-bound mint juleps from slender, silver julep cups that dated back to great-great-grandmother's trip to the Washington White House for President Grant's inauguration.

Aunt Katie's kitchen philosophy was straightforward: "Never serve food with really good, strong drink." "Don't cook the same dish in the same way more than once." "Always take chances." In retrospect, I find it as difficult to quarrel with her approach to food as I did to disagree with her unique self. The following menu is a collage of several of the many dinners I had the pleasure of experiencing with Great-Aunt Katie.

Menu

Katie's Mule-Kick Mint Juleps

Katie's Cracker-Crusted Spring Chicken

Fried-Chicken Biscuits

Fresh Carrot and Grits Pudding

Katie's Own Turtle Pie

Katie's Mule-Kick Mint Juleps

Aunt Katie's juleps were brassy and sure-footed, with sharp, clean strokes of bourbon and mint vying for attention. She swore that hers was the authentic article, identical to those served at Churchill Downs in Louisville. Her julep-making rituals were carried out with precision. First, chopped mint was muddled with sugar to produce a thick paste and then a sticky syrup of blue-grass green, then fresh mint sprigs were cut exactly to the height of the two straws (always two) to assure that the mint aroma was inhaled just as the jolt of mint-enhanced bourbon electrified and then soothed the taste buds. For Aunt Katie, only her silver julep cups were exalted enough to embrace this sacred essence, and these she touched only by their handles once the drink was poured, so that frost would form on them without blemish as they chilled.

I treasure Aunt Katie's recipe and have followed it without change for thirty years. This is a drink that should be sipped, not gulped. It slips down like satin but packs quite a wallop.

(MAKES 1 DRINK)

> 1½ teaspoons superfine sugar
> 1 tablespoon chopped fresh mint leaves (about 4 to 5 medium leaves)
> 1½ ounces Kentucky bourbon whisky
> Finely crushed ice
> Sprigs of fresh mint, cut 2½ inches higher than the cup or glass

Place the sugar and chopped mint leaves in a small ceramic mortar or bowl and bruise the leaves with a muddler or pestle until a thick paste forms. Add the bourbon one tablespoon at a time, and continue muddling until the paste becomes a syrup. Fill a silver julep cup half full with crushed ice, then push in the mint sprigs (and 2 straws cut to the same length) along the side of the cup. Add the syrup and bourbon and in the freezer chill the drink for 10 minutes, or until it's well frosted. Be careful not to touch the sides of the cup with your fingers or frost won't form evenly.

To prepare 8 juleps at once, place about 40 medium-size mint leaves and ¼ cup of superfine sugar in a food processor fitted with the knife blade, and whirl until the mixture forms a thick paste. Add ½ cup of water and continue the whirling until you have a smooth green syrup. Prepare the drinks as directed above, dividing the syrup equally among the 8 julep cups or whatever suitably elegant glasses are available—champagne flutes, for instance. Transfer the drinks by their handles from the refrigerator to a tray and serve them immediately.

Katie's Cracker-Crusted Spring Chicken

This is Aunt Katie's own recipe, and for it she was justifiably famous. Her secret? There were several. For one, she chose only the tenderest two-pound spring chickens and soaked these in a buttermilk bath for half an hour. Then, to seal in the juices, she dredged the pieces in sage-perfumed flour and egg-dipped them. Next, to give them crunch, she rolled them in coarsely crushed soda crackers and quickly fried them to golden in smoking-hot lard. Finally, to tenderize them (and to give guests time to relax), she kept the chicken in a very slow oven until serving time.

After a round (or two) of Katie's Mule-Kick Mint Juleps (recipe just given), the "birds" were brought forth on a platter surrounded by Fried-Chicken Biscuits with a pitcher of silky Brown-Crumb Milk Gravy alongside.

(SERVES 8)

3 2-pound (or less) young spring chickens, cut into quarters
Buttermilk or sweet milk for marinating, plus ⅓ cup
1½ cups all-purpose flour
1 tablespoon each minced fresh thyme and sage, or 1 teaspoon each dried and powdered
2 eggs
4–5 cups coarsely crushed soda crackers
1 cup peanut oil or enough to fill a medium-size skillet to a depth of 1 inch
Salt and coarsely ground black pepper to taste

Marinate the chicken pieces in buttermilk for 30–40 minutes. Shake off the excess milk, then dredge each piece in a mixture of flour and herbs and shake off the excess flour. In a fairly large but shallow bowl, beat the eggs lightly with ⅓ cup of buttermilk or sweet milk. Dip the pieces, 1 at a time, in the egg mixture, then roll each in cracker crumbs, thoroughly coating all surfaces. If it's more convenient, prepare the chicken pieces up to this point several hours early, and refrigerate them until just prior to your guests' arrival. Then fry the pieces, 1 at a time, in smoking-hot peanut oil until golden brown on both sides, turning them once. Carefully transfer each piece as it is done to a shallow ovenproof dish. Do not break the crusts. Sprinkle with salt and pepper. Bake at 200 degrees F. for 1 hour, or until ready to serve. Chicken pieces fried directly from the refrigerator should be baked at 275 degrees F.

Brown-Crumb Milk Gravy

Aunt Katie made her milk gravy with light cream. Perhaps that's why she lived to be only ninety-three.

(MAKES ABOUT 2½ CUPS)

> 1½ tablespoons all-purpose flour
> 2 cups rich chicken broth
> 1 cup light cream
> Salt and coarsely ground black pepper

Pour off all but 3 tablespoons of fat from the pan. Using a fork, loosen the golden brown bits in the bottom of the pan and crush them if they are larger than ¼ inch. Sprinkle in the flour and stir over medium heat until lightly browned. Pour the broth in all at once and continue to stir until the gravy thickens, pressing out any lumps with the back of the fork as you stir. Mix in the cream and cook at a low boil for 2 to 3 minutes or until the gravy has a nice consistency. Serve steaming hot.

37

Fried-Chicken Biscuits

If you haven't tasted biscuits fried in the same fat that chicken was fried, you have a treat coming. These flaky baking powder nuggets are cut square instead of round to provide extra surface for crisping up on the outside, and the brown crumbly bits left over from the chicken add a batch of extra flavor. Aunt Katie was "Dixie-trained," as she called it, to work the fat into the dry ingredients with her fingers rather than cutting it in with knives. I must say, the results here seem to prove her right. One thing, though, when the weather is sizzling, the warmth of your fingers may cause the butter to melt rather than to merely soften. In this case begin with chilled, not room temperature, butter and work quickly.

(MAKES ABOUT 2 DOZEN 1-INCH-SQUARE BISCUITS)

> 1 cup all-purpose flour
> 2 teaspoons baking powder
> ¼ teaspoon salt
> 2 tablespoons butter, at room temperature
> ¼ cup milk

Sift the dry ingredients together and work or cut in the butter until the mixture is the consistency of small peas. Stir in the milk slowly, mixing only enough to just moisten the dough. Roll out to a thickness of ½ inch and with a sharp knife cut into 1-inch squares. Fry to golden in smoking-hot oil for 2 minutes on each side, turning the biscuits only once. Serve on the same platter as the chicken.

Note: For softer biscuits cut the dough into 1½-inch squares.

Fresh Carrot and Grits Pudding

This is a custardy concoction, somewhere between carrot pudding and grits soufflé, that offers the finest qualities of each.

Fair warning: A dollop of this should be ample, given the old-time richness of the meal. However, if you prepare two batches, both will rapidly disappear.

(SERVES 8)

> 1 cup quick grits
> 2½ cups boiling water
> ¾ teaspoon salt
> 3 tablespoons butter
> Salt and coarsely ground black pepper to taste
> 3 eggs, beaten
> 1 cup minced cooked carrots
> 1 cup real buttermilk, preferably fresh-churned, with bits of butter floating in it
> ½ teaspoon baking soda
> 4 ounces soft goat cheese or other soft cheese
> ¼ cup grated Parmesan cheese

Preheat oven to 325 degrees F.

Sprinkle the grits into the boiling salted water a bit at a time, stirring constantly to keep lumps from forming. Take care with this procedure: If lumps do form, they must be strained out. Cook, stirring, until the grits return to a boil, then lower the heat and stir until thickened. Remove from the heat and immediately stir in the butter, salt, and pepper. Beat the eggs, carrots, buttermilk, and baking soda together, then beat this into the grits until well incorporated. Transfer to a large, well-greased soufflé dish or casserole. Crumble on the goat cheese, pat down lightly with the back of a spoon, sprinkle with Parmesan, and bake in the preheated oven for 30–40 minutes, or just until the mixture stops quivering in the center when you shake the dish. Serve at once.

Katie's Own Turtle Pie

When the time came to choose a dessert recipe for this menu from Aunt Katie's vast collection, I found it very nearly impossible to decide among President Tyler's Pudding Pie, General Lee's Favorite Cake, Transparent Pie (in all of its variations), Chess Pie, Pecan Pie, or Stack Pie. Finally, I settled on Katie's Own Turtle Pie, the candy kind, not the creatures. By rights I should have opted for a plain dish of Jell-O to make amends for the super-richness of Katie's other recipes. But this pie, with its layer of pecan halves and caramel and milk chocolate sauces is so dangerously delicious that it could almost make a dessert lover faint.

If you like chocolate turtle candies, you'll go mad for this.

(SERVES 8)

> *5 eggs*
> *1½ cups light corn syrup*
> *¾ cup granulated sugar*
> *2 tablespoons all-purpose flour*
> *3 tablespoons light rum*
> *2 cups pecan halves*
> *3 tablespoons melted butter*
> *2 teaspoons vanilla extract*
> *1 recipe Pastry for a One-Crust Pie (page 259)*
> *1 recipe Caramel Sauce (see below)*
> *1 recipe Milk Chocolate Sauce (see below)*
> *Whipped cream (optional)*

Preheat oven to 325 degrees F.

Beat together the eggs, corn syrup, sugar, flour, and rum. Stir in the nuts, butter, and vanilla. Pour into the prepared pie shell and bake for 1 hour or until a knife comes out clean when slipped into the middle of the pie. Cool to room temperature and then lightly chill. Serve topped with warm Caramel Sauce and Milk Chocolate Sauce and a dollop of whipped cream.

Caramel Sauce

> *20 Kraft caramels*
> *¾ cup light cream*

In a small, heavy pan, stir the caramels and cream over low heat until the sauce is thick and smooth. Serve warm.

Milk Chocolate Sauce

> *6 ounces best quality milk chocolate*
> *¾ cup light cream*
> *2 teaspoons sweet butter*

In a small, heavy pan, stir the chocolate and cream over low heat until the chocolate is melted and the sauce is thick. Beat in the butter. Serve warm.

Spring Wine Sampling with Streamlined Hors d'Oeuvres

"Ahhh," a small inner voice whispers. "It's spring! We've all survived the winter. Let's celebrate!" With a variety of exquisite, light-and-lovely spring wines! May wines, Botticelli-sweet . . . precocious young wines . . . exciting, inexpensive wine "finds" . . . heady wine and champagne punches. With these let us serve quantities of fresh-tasting, low-cal nibbles for guests to "hunt 'n' peck" their way through: rounds of pattypan squash spiraled with Seafoam Cream . . . zucchini blossoms, crunchy snow pea pods, asparagus as slender as grass blades . . . all rolled in coarse herb-spiked salt . . . tawny wild mushrooms or tiny tame ones . . . a

rainbow of flawless sauces for dipping . . . deep, dark caviar, ruddy lobster, golden saffron. "Remember, this is a wine sampling, not a wine tasting. These wines and punches are meant to be sipped, consumed, and enjoyed along with the hors d'oeuvres."

Menu

Spring Hors d'Oeuvres with Seafoam Cream
Asparagus, String Beans, and Sugar Snap Peas with Herb-Spiked Salt
Smoked Fish-Filled Ravioli
Golden Saffron Cream
Twisted Bread Branches
Your Own Herbed Cheese
Deep, Dark Caviar Sauce
Sun-Dried Tomato and Lobster Sauce

Spring Hors d'Oeuvres with Seafoam Cream

Nothing says "spring" like miniature vegetables topped with this delicate cream. If you can't locate these tiny specialties, buy the smallest young vegetables available and cut them into bite-size pieces. Most of these small-fry are picked and packed with extreme care and require at the most a wipe with a damp cloth. Since there is such a large variety of hors d'oeuvres included, I've figured only one of each vegetable per guest, but if you favor a larger quantity of a particular tidbit, prepare additional ones.

(SERVES 30)

> 10 *pattypan squash, 1 1/2 inches in diameter*
> 30 *squash blossoms*
> 30 *nasturtium flowers*
> 30 *mushrooms, 1 inch in diameter, or 10 2-inch mushrooms, quartered*
> 30 *fiddlehead ferns, 1 inch in diameter*
> 1 *recipe Fresh Curd Cheese (page 87)*
> 2 *tablespoons Lobster Butter (page 252)*
> 1 *teaspoon unflavored gelatin softened in 1 tablespoon water*
> 2 *tablespoons orange juice, heated*

If the pattypans are very small, simply cut them in half across the middles and cut away and discard a slice on each of their rounded sides, so that the halves won't topple over. (Follow this same procedure for slightly larger pattypans, but in addition, cut off a thin slice from the middle of each side so that each pattypan provides 4 usable pieces—2 evened-off ends and 2 center slices.)

Taste a squash blossom, a nasturtium blossom, a mushroom, and a fiddlehead to determine if they are gritty, and rinse them only if they are.

Prepare the Fresh Curd Cheese and the Lobster Butter. Soften the gelatin in 1 tablespoon of water, add the hot orange juice, and stir to melt. Stir the melted gelatin into the Lobster Butter, then mix in the cheese. Chill the mixture until it just begins to stiffen, then fasten a fancy nozzle to your pastry tube and pipe spirals, stars, and so forth, onto the sliced pattypan and the fiddleheads, and into the mushrooms and flower blossoms. Refrigerate immediately and chill well. Pass on trays while still cold.

Asparagus, String Beans, and Sugar Snap Peas with Herb-Spiked Salt

I prefer asparagus with heads unconquered by contact with hot water, and so I stand them upright to flash-cook only the stems. Neither am I particularly fond of those little tips on green beans—and so off they come. To me, snow pea pods have a metallic taste and are a nuisance to relieve of their strings when they're too large, and so I substitute tiny sugar snap peas. These prejudices of mine need not prejudice you. It's your party. Consider what I suggest . . . then do as you like.

(SERVES 30)

> 30 slender asparagus spears
> 30 thin green beans, with tips removed
> 30 very small sugar snap peas
> 3 tablespoons each very finely minced fresh red basil, oregano, and chives
> Coarse salt
> 2 egg whites
> 1 tablespoon water

Tie the asparagus in 2 bunches so that the heads are even, then cut the stems to equal lengths. Measure the stems (without including the heads) and measure the same depth of water into a tall, narrow pot. Bring the water to a boil, stand the asparagus upright in the pot, cover with foil, and boil for 2 minutes. Drain off the water and immediately plunge the asparagus into cold water to halt the cooking. Drain, dry, and arrange on paper towels on a foil-lined tray. Refrigerate.

Drop the green beans into boiling water, cook for 3 minutes, drain, and plunge into cold water.

Place the sugar snap peas in a strainer and dip them in scalding water for 1 minute. Drain, dry, and arrange on paper towels on a foil-lined tray. Refrigerate.

Shortly before party time, mix the herbs and the salt. Beat the egg whites with 1 tablespoon of water and, using a pastry brush, brush the mixture lightly over 1 side of the asparagus (the side facing up), the beans, and the sugar snap peas. Sprinkle with the herbed salt and let dry. Arrange on serving trays salt-side up.

Smoked Fish-Filled Ravioli

Miniature ravioli filled with smoked fish and capers make wonderful finger foods, particularly when passed with Golden Saffron Cream. Any kind of smoked fish filling is excellent here. For years I've utilized whatever variety I've caught and smoked myself. Now, fish shops and appetizing stores in many areas of the country feature smoked shark, weakfish, eel, sea robin, and other delicious oddities that I've used to prepare an inexpensive and extremely tasty filling. But of course, if money is no object, don't hesitate to use smoked salmon. (Sun-dried tomato and smoked mozzarella are also terrific in these.)

(YIELD: ABOUT 60 RAVIOLI)

2 pounds pasta dough (fresh, store bought, or homemade)
1 pound boned smoked fish, finely chopped
2 tablespoons drained and minced capers
1 tablespoon minced chives
1 recipe Golden Saffron Cream

Prepare the pasta dough by following a recipe for making ravoli. Mix the smoked fish, capers, and chives, and use this mixture to fill the ravioli. Cover the stuffed ravioli lightly with towels and refrigerate. Just prior to party time, cook the ravioli as directed, brush them with oil, and cover with damp towels until time to serve. Pass with Golden Saffron Cream.

Golden Saffron Cream

(MAKES 2½ CUPS)

A large pinch each of saffron threads and ground turmeric
¼ cup hot, rich chicken broth or canned, undiluted condensed broth
1 tablespoon sesame oil
½ cup onion, coarsely chopped
8 ounces cream cheese, at room temperature
1 cup Crème Fraîche (page 253)
Salt and cayenne pepper to taste

Steep the saffron and turmeric in the hot chicken broth for 10 minutes. Whirl the saffron mixture, sesame oil, onion, and cream cheese in a food processor or blender until the onion is minced and the cream well mixed. Stir in the Crème Fraîche and season to taste. Serve cool, not cold.

Twisted Bread Branches

Somewhat thicker than breadsticks, much more slender than conventional loaves, these twisted bread branches are just right to accompany elegantly understated hors d'oeuvre. Cut some branches into thin slices. Leave some intertwined like an eagle's aerie around the large, low-cal, Boursin-like cheese, for guests to cut or break for themselves.

(YIELD: 8 LONG, THIN LOAVES)

1 package dry active yeast
1 cup lukewarm water
3 tablespoons butter
1 cup hot water
6 cups sifted all-purpose flour
4 egg whites, beaten until stiff

Dissolve the yeast in the lukewarm water. Mix together the butter and hot water, and when the mixture has cooled to lukewarm, add to the yeast. Beat in 2 cups of flour until the dough is smooth. Fold in egg whites. Add the remainder of the flour and knead until

(continued)

the dough is smooth and elastic (5 minutes by hand, 2 minutes with an electric dough hook). Place in a large, greased bowl, turn it over, and cover it with a damp towel. Let the dough rise in a warm, draft-free place until doubled in bulk, about 1 hour. Punch the dough down, cover, and let it double in bulk again in a warm, draft-free place, about 45 minutes. Punch the dough down once more and let it rise for 15 minutes.

Cut the dough into 4 equal portions and, on a lightly floured surface, roll each out to a rectangle about ½ inch thick. Cut each rectangle into 4-inch squares. Roll each square between your palms to form a long, snakelike shape, about 1 inch thick. Twist the loaf once or twice into roughly the shape of a tree branch (slit the last 3 inches of each end and twist slightly askew to enhance the effect if you like), and place on a greased baking sheet. Cover with a damp towel and let the sticks rise in a warm, draft-free place for 30 minutes. By the time you have finished forming the loaves, the first tray will be ready to bake.

Bake in a preheated 350 degree F. oven until golden brown, about 15 minutes. Cool on racks. To store bread overnight, wrap in foil and then warm for a few moments in a moderate oven just prior to serving. If you must store the bread for longer than 24 hours, wrap it in foil and freeze. Unwrap and warm in a moderate oven just prior to serving.

Your Own Herbed Cheese

Would you believe that a mellow, herb-freshened cheese with a decidedly French accent could be low in fat and calories? And that you could make it yourself with very little effort? One taste will make a believer of you. The farmer's cheese is included here to increase the quantity and cut down on the time required to produce enough cheese for a large party. For a smaller quantity it may be omitted, and the herbs and salt halved. The result will be a softer, more delicate cheese. If calories are no problem, you might want to substitute a cup of light cream for 1 cup of the buttermilk to enrich the cheese. Prepare this several days prior to your party to make sure the cheese has sufficient time to firm.

(MAKES ABOUT 2½ POUNDS)

> 1 *pound farmer's cheese*
> 1 *quart buttermilk*
> 1 *quart unflavored yogurt*
> 1½ *tablespoons salt*
> ¼ *cup minced fresh herbs (be sure to include dill)*
> 2 *large cloves garlic, peeled and minced*
> *Coarsely ground black pepper*

In a large bowl, mash the farmer's cheese with 2 cups of the buttermilk. Thoroughly mix with remaining buttermilk and all the other ingredients except the pepper. Cover with cheesecloth, and let stand overnight. Line a large colander with several thicknesses of cheesecloth, and pour in the cheese mixture, a cup at a time. Fold the ends of the cheesecloth over the top of the mixture and let the cheese drain overnight into a deep bowl. If in the morning the cheese is too soft to hold its shape, let it continue to drain until it does. Unwrap the cheese and roll it into a ball. Sprinkle foil generously with pepper, then roll the ball of cheese in this to cover the surface. Serve slightly chilled. The whey, with its herb-garlic undertones, enhances the flavor of the Twisted Bread Branches (page 45) when one cup of it is substituted for the lukewarm water in that recipe.

Deep, Dark Caviar Sauce

(MAKES ABOUT 3 CUPS)

> 3 cups Crème Fraîche (page 253)
> 4 tablespoons black caviar
> 1/4 cup minced black olives
> 1/2 small onion, peeled, coarsely chopped, and pressed in a garlic press to produce
>   2 teaspoons onion juice

Mix all the ingredients and chill well.

Sun-Dried Tomato and Lobster Sauce

> 1 recipe warm Lobster Butter (page 252)
> 1/2 cup sun-dried tomatoes, coarsely chopped
> 1 tablespoon minced fresh basil
> A squeeze of fresh lime juice

Whirl all the ingredients in a food processor or blender until the tomatoes are minced. Serve warm.

Wine Punches

I love the freshness of fruit juice with wine or champagne . . . particularly in the spring.

Grapefruit Blossom

An outdoor party is the perfect setting for champagne with a splash of freshly squeezed pink grapefruit juice.

(MAKES 1 DRINK)

Fill a champagne glass three-quarters full with champagne. Add 1 or 2 tablespoons freshly squeezed pink grapefruit juice and a twist of orange peel. Serve immediately.

Sambuca Spritzer

Offbeat but beautifully icy.

(MAKES 1 DRINK)

Shake glass three-quarters full with sparkling white wine and a generous dash of Sambuca with ice. Pour into a wine glass. Add 2 coffee beans if desired.

Three-Curry Buffet Dinner

Are three curries two too many to present at one dinner? Not if the guests are curry aficionados and the curries are, respectively, Fresh Fruit, Red Vegetable, and White Seafood, served with a variety of delicious condiments including your own piquant Date and Apricot Chutney. This is a perfect buffet meal—a little exotic, beautiful to look at, extremely tasty, and not difficult for guests to cope with. A leafy salad and a fruity dessert round out the meal. Easy but elegant. And just as awe inspiring when served as a sit-down dinner.

With drinks before dinner, serve San Ton Pa, an Indonesian dish that is neither seviche nor mousse but an interesting combination of both. With this, offer small dishes of spiced nuts, raisins, and dried fruits. If yours is to be a more elaborate party, you could also serve steaming stuffed breads, Parathas Stuffed with Black Bean and White Radish Filling cut into thin wedges and passed on small plates with flavored sour cream.

At the buffet table, present each curry on a separate platter accompanied by its own flavored rice or set forth one large bowl of rice and three platters of curry: one sweet, one fiery, and one mild but with an unusual combination of mixed seafood. In either case guests help themselves to rice, portions of each curry, and a colorful variety of condiments.

Menu

San Ton Pa

Parathas Stuffed with Black Bean and White Radish Filling

Fresh Fruit Curry

Red Vegetable Curry

White Seafood Curry

Date and Apricot Chutney

Rice

Small Bowls of Condiments (Shredded Coconut, Dark and Golden Raisins, Diced Bananas, Spanish Peanuts, Cashews, Minced Scallions, Cubed Avocado, Grated Red Radish, Toasted Sesame Seeds, Red and Green Peppers, and Cold Yogurt)

Rum-Baked Bananas

San Ton Pa

This is a kind of piquant mousse made with sparkling fresh raw fish; impressive, but with none of the bother of cooking and deceptively simple to prepare. San Ton Pa is really superb with fried whole wheat paratha or other crisp bread or crackers.

(SERVES 10)

> 1 pound each very fresh skinless filets of salmon and flounder
> 1½ teaspoons each salt and sugar
> ½ cup each water and lemon juice
> 1 large sweet white onion, peeled and coarsely chopped
> 5 cloves garlic, peeled
> 1 sweet red pepper, coarsely chopped
> 3 tablespoons each coarsely chopped fennel and coriander leaves

Place the fish in the bowl of a food processor fitted with the steel cutting blade. Turn on and off to just mince the fish, taking care not to overprocess or you will end up with fish puree. Transfer the fish to a bowl. Mix together the salt, sugar, water, and lemon juice. Pour it over the fish and let stand for 15 minutes. Meanwhile, process the onion, garlic, sweet pepper, fennel, and coriander leaves until finely minced. Again, do not overprocess. Drain the juices from the fish and from the onion mixture. Boil these liquids together in a small pan until reduced to 3 tablespoons, then cool to room temperature. Mix all the ingredients, spoon into a mold, and chill well. Just before serving, unmold onto a lettuce-covered platter.

Parathas Stuffed with Black Bean and White Radish Filling

Serve these steamy, dark, beany beauties with cold sour cream flavored with grated white radish and minced scallions, or coriander and grated cucumber. An unusually winning hors d'oeuvre. The black bean filling can be made hours in advance, or even the day before serving.

Paratha

Traditionally, paratha are fried in melted butter, but their flavor does not seem to be diminished if you thin the butter with a little oil.

(YIELD: TWO 10-INCH PIES)

> 3 cups whole wheat flour
> ½ teaspoon salt
> 4 tablespoons cold butter
> Water
> ½ cup (1 stick) butter, melted
> Black Bean and White Radish Filling (recipe below)
> ⅓ cup each grated white radish, minced scallion, cucumber, coriander
> 2 cups sour cream

Sift the flour and salt together, and cut the 4 tablespoons of cold butter into it, using a food processor fitted with the steel blade or 2 knives. Sprinkle with just enough cold water to make a firm dough. Knead in 1 tablespoon of the melted butter. Cover and let stand for 1 hour. Knead again, working in a little water and melted butter if the dough is very stiff.

Divide the dough into 4 pieces and roll each into a circle about ¼ inch thick. Dust the surface of your pastry board with a little whole wheat flour if the dough sticks. Brush each circle of dough with melted butter, fold in half, and roll out to a circle again.

Spread Black Bean and White Radish Filling to within 1 inch of the edge, top with a sprinkling of the radish and scallion mixture, cover with another paratha, and pinch the edges together to seal them. Trim if necessary to neaten. Fry each filled paratha 1 minute on a greased, heavy, nonstick griddle, then add a generous amount of melted butter around the edges. Fry to golden on both sides, adding butter as necessary. Serve cut in thin wedges with very cold sour cream mixed with the remaining grated radish, minced scallion, cucumber, and coriander.

Black Bean and White Radish Filling

Black beans with an Indian accent. I can't resist flavoring them with bacon—blame the influence of my Southern cousins—but if you prefer a vegetarian approach, omit the meat.

> *1½ cups dried, picked-over black beans*
> *Water*
> *1 whole onion, peeled*
> *3 cloves garlic, peeled*
> *1½ teaspoons salt*
> *1 ½-inch piece of ginger root, peeled and minced*
> *1 tablespoon each chopped fresh marjoram and rosemary, or 1 teaspoon each dried*
> *4 strips bacon, minced (optional)*
> *1 tablespoon butter*
> *½ teaspoon each chili powder and Garam-Masala (page 96)*
> *2 tablespoons lemon juice*
> *¾ cup peeled and grated white radish*
> *¼ cup thinly sliced scallions*

Bring the beans to a boil in water to cover. Boil 2 minutes, cover, and let stand for 1 hour. Drain the beans well, add the onion, garlic, 1½ teaspoons of salt, and water to cover. Simmer until the beans are tender, then drain and mash them.

Meanwhile, sauté the ginger, herbs, and bacon for 2 minutes in 1 tablespoon of butter. Add the spices, lemon juice, and mashed beans, and fry, stirring, for several minutes. Set aside to cool. Mix in the radish and scallions.

Fresh Fruit Curry

In the typical Burmese fashion, this curry starts with a coconut milk base, flavored with an interesting combination of turmeric, chili, caraway, and Garam-Masala. If you choose to serve this curry on a platter with the rice you may add dimension to the latter by tossing it with clarified butter and rose water just prior to serving.

(SERVES 10)

> *3 tablespoons sweet butter*
> *1 large white sweet onion, peeled and coarsely chopped*
> *1 tablespoon minced peeled ginger*
> *½ teaspoon each caraway seeds, ground turmeric, Garam-Masala (page 96),*
>   *and chili powder*
> *2½ teaspoons arrowroot*
> *½ cup each chicken broth and light cream, mixed*
> *1 cup Coconut Cream (page 253)*
> *Salt and cayenne pepper to taste*
> *3 large bananas*
> *10 cups fresh fruits (any combination of the following) peeled, seeded, and cut*
>   *into 1-inch cubes: ripe papaya, peach, pear, mango, avocado, or honeydew,*
>   *cantaloupe, casaba, or cranshaw melons*
> *Grapes and pitted dates*
> *Candied fruits*
> *Mint leaves (optional)*
> *1 cup macadamia nuts, coarsely chopped*
> *6 cups hot cooked rice*
> *3 tablespoons clarified butter (optional)*
> *2 teaspoons rose water (optional)*

In a large, heavy skillet, melt 1½ tablespoons of the butter. Add the onion and ginger, and sauté until the onion is transparent. Stir in the spices. Mix the arrowroot with the broth and cream. Add to the pan with the Coconut Cream and stir over medium-high heat until the sauce thickens, reduces slightly, and has a nice consistency. Season to taste with salt and cayenne. Set aside—the sauce can be kept, refrigerated, for 24 hours.

An hour or two prior to serving sauté the bananas in the remaining 1½ tablespoons of butter until they are lightly browned but still quite firm, and set them aside. Heat the cream sauce with the assorted fresh fruits. When the fruits are heated, but not cooked, transfer the curry to a serving dish and decorate attractively with the banana pieces, grapes, dates, candied fruits, mint leaves, and nuts. Serve with the rice.

53

Red Vegetable Curry

What? A curry with sweet potatoes, carrots, and tomatoes as prime ingredients rather than chicken or lamb? When most Westerners think "curry," they automatically associate the food with the brilliant, yellow-gold shimmer of saffron and turmeric. Actually, many Indian curries are tomato-based, as is this sizzler, but this recipe carries the red curry theme a step further to include only red-vegetable ingredients. The result is a dish that glows on the plate while it incinerates the palate.

(SERVES 10)

1 *large sweet potato, peeled, quartered lengthwise and parboiled 2 minutes in*
   1 tablespoon lemon juice and water to cover and then drained
3 *tablespoons vegetable oil*
4 *large cloves garlic, peeled and minced*
3 *medium-size red onions, peeled and quartered and cut lengthwise into fine*
   shreds
2 *medium-size carrots, scraped and cut lengthwise into very fine shreds*
2 *tablespoons red basil, cut into fine shreds*
2 *teaspoons salt*
2 *teaspoons hot curry powder or paste*
1 *teaspoon each chili powder and Garam-Masala (page 96)*
8 *large, fully-ripe tomatoes, peeled, seeded, and coarsely chopped*
3 *tablespoons lemon juice*

Cut the sweet potato into strips ¼ inch by ¼ inch by 2 inches.

Warm the vegetable oil in a large, heavy skillet. Add the garlic, onions, sweet potato, carrots, and basil, and sauté for 2 minutes. Add the salt, curry powder, chili powder, and Garam-Masala, and stir-fry until the onions are transparent, but not browned. Remove from the pan with a slotted spoon and set aside. Add the tomatoes to the pan and sauté until soft, stirring occasionally, then mash them with a fork. Simmer until the sauce is nicely thickened; add the lemon juice. The elements of the curry may be made to this point a day in advance of your party and then tossed together and reheated just in time to be spread in a shallow bowl, topped with Dry-Curried Red Vegetables (see below), and edged with Dry-Curried Cabbage and Beets (see below).

Dry-Curried Red Vegetables

Not all the vegetables contained herein are actually red, of course, but all are "hot" in color as opposed to cool. All are also "dry curried" and arranged over the "saucy" curry just prior to serving. Since the red cabbage and beets tend to bleed color onto the other vegetables, these two are prepared last and then used as a garnish around the edge of the dish.

5 *large sweet red peppers, cut into quarters lengthwise, with pith and seeds discarded*
2 *large golden peppers, cut into quarters lengthwise, with pith and seeds discarded*

4 *medium-size carrots, scraped and quartered lengthwise*

2 *cloves garlic, peeled and minced*

1 *small fresh hot red chili pepper, with seeds discarded, minced (or more to taste)*

¼ *cup red basil, cut into narrow shreds*

1 *large red onion, peeled and coarsely chopped*

3 *tablespoons vegetable oil*

1 *teaspoon each ground turmeric and chili powder*

Salt to taste

2 *large sweet potatoes, peeled, cut lengthwise into strips ¼" by ¼" by 2", and parboiled 2 minutes (in 1 tablespoon of lemon juice and water to cover, and then drained)*

1 *teaspoon Garam-Masala (page 96)*

1 *teaspoon arrowroot*

2 *tablespoons mild red wine vinegar*

¾ *cup chicken broth*

Cut the red peppers, golden peppers, and carrots into strips ¼ inch thick by about 2 inches long. Sauté the garlic, red chili, basil, and onion in the oil until the onion is transparent. Stir in the turmeric, chili powder, and salt. Add the vegetable strips, sprinkle with Garam-Masala, arrowroot, and vinegar, and toss with the seasonings in the pan. Pour the chicken broth over all, then bring to a boil over medium heat while you continue to toss the vegetables for about 3 minutes. Do not overcook. Arrange the hot red vegetables over the center of the red curry sauce and edge with the Dry-Curried Cabbage and Beets.

Dry-Curried Cabbage and Beets

4 *medium-size beets, steamed until barely tender and then peeled*

2 *medium-size red cabbages, quartered, cored, and with limp outer leaves discarded*

2 *medium-size onions, peeled, halved lengthwise, and cut into fine shreds*

2 *tablespoons vegetable oil*

1 *teaspoon chili powder*

1 *tablespoon salt*

2 *teaspoons Garam-Masala (page 96)*

Steam and trim the beets, and then run them through the coarse grater of a food processor or cut them into matchstick julienne. Cut the cabbages into long shreds, each no more than ¼ inch thick. Fry the onions in the oil until golden, then stir in the chili powder and salt. Add the cabbage all at once and cook it over medium heat for 5 minutes without stirring. Slip a spatula under the cabbage and turn it over so that the uncooked portion is nearest the heat. Continue to cook a minute or two until the excess moisture is absorbed, then lower the heat, cover, and cook several minutes until the cabbage is barely tender. Finally, remove the cover once more, raise the heat slightly, and stir-fry until the vegetables lose most of their moisture but not their color. Toss them with the Garam-Masala. Immediately arrange the cabbage and the beets around the edge of the shallow bowl containing the Red Vegetable Curry.

White Seafood Curry

Although golden Fresh Fruit Curry and fiery Red Vegetable Curry may attract more immediate attention, this ivory seafood curry is full of complexities that belie its pallor. The sauce echoes the richness of its ingredients: lobster, mussels in their shells, shrimp, squid, and three varieties of fish, all cooked in order in the same ever-deepening stock, from the most delicately flavored to the strongest. This clever broth is then reduced to an elusive sauce waiting to be puzzled out.

(SERVES 6)

> *3 1–1½-pound filets from fish varieties that do not fall apart easily, each no*
> *less than ½ inch thick. Blackfish, salmon, scrod, striped bass, and swordfish*
> *are among the best choices, but snapper, mackerel, monkfish, mako, and*
> *tilefish are fine, too.*
> *1½ pounds large shrimp in their shells*
> *2 small live lobsters*
> *¾ pound scallops*
> *2 pounds plump mussels*
> *2 cups good-quality dry white wine*
> *½ cup peeled and chopped shallots*
> *¼ teaspoon minced dried thyme*
> *1 small bay leaf*
> *3 quarts water*

Rinse the fish and scrub the shellfish if necessary. In a stockpot, bring to a boil the wine, shallots, thyme, bay leaf, and water. Lower the heat until the water is barely shivering; there should be no bubbles. Slip in the most delicately flavored of your fish filets and poach it for 4–5 minutes—the fish should *not* reach the flaking stage. Carefully remove the fish without breaking it and drain it well. Repeat this process with the other 2 fish filets, ending with the strongest in flavor.

Bring the water in the stockpot to a boil—add a quart or 2 more, if necessary, to bring the level to the middle of the pan. Reheat the water to just under a boil, add the shrimp, and poach for 3 minutes. Remove from the pot and drain well. Refresh under cold water. Place the scallops in a long-handled strainer and dip them in the "shivering" stock for 1 to 2 minutes or just until they become opaque.

Bring the water in the pot to a boil, add the lobsters headfirst, cover, and bring the water back to a boil. Boil for 8 minutes per pound (add 3 minutes more for every ¼ pound of extra weight). Remove and drain.

Discard any mussels that feel overly heavy (these may have sand or mud in them). Place the mussels in the pot, cover, and bring to a boil over high heat. Boil for 6–7 minutes. Remove mussels as they open. Discard any that remain closed.

Boil the stock over high heat until reduced to 4 cups. Carefully pour through a cheese-cloth-lined strainer into a smaller pan, without including any of the sand in the bottom. Cool.

4 tablespoons sweet butter
1½ cups peeled and chopped shallots
1 tablespoon each peeled and minced ginger and garlic
½ teaspoon each ground cumin and ground cardamom
2 teaspoons hot chili powder
Salt and white pepper to taste
1 tablespoon cornstarch
Heavy cream
3 tablespoons clarified butter
2 teaspoons mild curry powder
6 cups hot cooked rice

Heat the butter in a large, heavy skillet. Sauté the shallots in the butter until they are soft but do not let them take on any color. Stir in the ginger, garlic, and seasonings, and cook, stirring, 1 minute more. Mix the cornstarch with ½ cup of cooled stock and stir until well blended. Add this and 2 additional cups of reduced stock to the skillet and cook over medium heat, stirring constantly, until the sauce thickens. Thin with a little cream if the sauce seems too thick. Set aside in a warm spot.

Cut the fish into 1-inch cubes. Remove the meat from the lobster tails and cut it into ½-inch slices. Peel the shrimp, cut them in half lengthwise, and remove the black veins. Mix the clarified butter and curry powder, toss with the rice, and spoon around the edge of a warm platter. Place the fish in the center of the platter, top with the lobster meat and scallops, and pour the sauce over. Arrange the shrimp halves around the edges. Keep the mussels in their shells—wings upright—and place where the shrimp meet the fish cubes. Decorate the center of the platter with the whole lobster shells. Serve immediately.

Date and Apricot Chutney

(YIELD: ABOUT 3 CUPS)

    1 *cup malt vinegar*
    2 *cups orange juice*
    ¹/₂ *cup light-brown sugar*
    1 *pound pitted dates, coarsely sliced*
    1 *cup dried apricots, quartered*
    1 *1-inch piece ginger root, peeled and thinly sliced*
    3 *large cloves garlic, peeled and minced*
    ¹/₂ *cup seedless raisins*
    1 *teaspoon Garam-Masala (page 96)*
    ¹/₂ *teaspoon each salt and ground cinnamon*
    ¹/₄ *teaspoon each powdered nutmeg and cloves*

In a heavy saucepan, bring the vinegar, orange juice, and sugar to a boil until the mixture becomes syrupy. Add the remaining ingredients and cook over low heat, stirring frequently, until the mixture thickens. Serve at room temperature. This can be made in advance and will keep well, refrigerated, for several months.

CONDIMENTS: Small bowls of any or all of the following—shredded coconut; dark seedless raisins; golden seedless raisins; diced bananas; roasted peanuts (Spanish are best); cashews; minced scallions; chopped avocado tossed with lime juice; grated red radish; toasted golden sesame seeds; black sesame seeds; cubed red and green peppers; plain cold yogurt.

Rum-Baked Bananas

(SERVES 10)

> 1 *cup dark rum*
> 1 *cup light-brown sugar*
> 1 *cup water*
> 3 *tablespoons sweet butter*
> ¼ *teaspoon nutmeg*
> ¼ *cup heavy cream*
> 10 *ripe bananas, peeled and halved lengthwise*
> ¾ *cup coarsely chopped pecans*
> *Whipped cream or vanilla ice cream (optional)*

Preheat oven to 300 degrees F.

Boil the rum, sugar, and water until the mixture becomes a medium syrup. Stir in 1 tablespoon of the butter, the nutmeg, and the cream. Use the remaining 2 tablespoons of butter to heavily grease a large, flat, ovenproof dish. Arrange the halved bananas in 2 rows without overlapping them. Spoon the syrup over them to cover them completely. Sprinkle with pecans and bake for 55 minutes. Serve with or without whipped cream or ice cream.

Fresh Vegetable Gumbo with Fish and Shellfish

When the last sweet flush of spring melts into the hot sting of summer, a lunch or light supper centering around an unconventional, cool, and silky yogurt gumbo makes entertaining a breeze.

This soup is at its best refrigerated for twenty-four to thirty hours in advance. The garnishes will hold up beautifully overnight, the Peppercorn Doughrounds are even more fiery the second day, and the lush, toasty-with-oats Fruited Scottish Cranachan can easily be prepared several hours prior to your worry-free party. If you set the table in advance, you might even have time to take cocktails elsewhere before flying home and finessing your own supper party.

Menu		
Fresh Vegetable Gumbo		
Peppercorn Doughrounds		
Fruited Scottish Cranachan		

62

Fresh Vegetable Gumbo

This unique soup has flavor built in twice: first into its creamy, dill-flavored base enhanced by crunchy, unblanched almond bits; and then, more importantly, into its unusual garnishes, thin circles of red onion, fresh endive, and blanched squid; squares of fresh tomato, sweet red pepper, and buttery avocado; nuggets of smoked salmon, crab, poached flounder, or other fish, roe, and, of course, traditional baby okra with its tiny pearl-like seeds.

(SERVES 8)

> 3 each small cucumbers and dill pickles, peeled, seeded, and cut into 1-inch
>   pieces
> 1 leek, white only, split lengthwise, well washed, and cut into ½-inch slices
> ½ cup parsley, with tough stems removed
> ¼ cup fresh fennel, tender leafy tops only
> ¼ cup fresh dill, tough stems removed
> 1 cup unblanched almonds
> 5 cups unflavored yogurt
> 3½ cups milk
> 3 tablespoons lemon juice
> ½ pound cooked and flaked fish (drained canned tuna will do in a pinch)
> Salt and freshly ground black pepper to taste
> 3 hard-cooked eggs, shelled and coarsely chopped
> Garnishes: Thin slices of red onion, fresh endive, and blanched squid; squares of
>   fresh tomato, sweet red pepper, and avocado; nuggets of smoked salmon, crab,
>   flounder roe, and baby okra.

Coarsely chop the cucumbers, pickles, leek, parsley, fennel, dill, and almonds in a food processor or blender or with a sharp knife. Do not overprocess or puree. Transfer the mixture to a large glass, enamel, or stainless-steel bowl. Stir in the yogurt, milk, lemon juice, and flaked fish, and season to taste with salt and pepper.

Refrigerate the soup overnight, if possible, or for at least 4 hours.

Just prior to serving, add all but several tablespoons of the chopped eggs and stir thoroughly. Adjust the seasonings and, if the soup is too thick, thin it a little with a bit of milk. Transfer the soup to an attractive bowl or pitcher and garnish with the remaining chopped eggs and a grind or two of pepper. Fill cups or bowls and present the garnishes and the spicy Peppercorn Doughrounds with the soup.

Peppercorn Doughrounds

I suppose it's inevitable that we think of doughnuts as sweets. Actually, bread doughnuts are made from yeast and flour, like conventional breadstuffs, but they contain little, if any, sugar. To transform them into a bona fide savory, cut back on the sugar and add a few snappy herbs and spices. These particular, rather innocuous-looking rounds of fried dough explode on the tongue with a fiery burst of flavor that guests won't soon forget—a lovely counterpoint to the cooling shiver of the soup.

(YIELD: ABOUT 18 DOUGHROUNDS)

> 1½ packages dry active yeast
> 1¾ cups warm milk
> ⅓ cup butter
> 2 large cloves garlic, peeled and minced
> 1 large egg, at room temperature
> 2 teaspoons granulated sugar
> ¼ teaspoon cayenne pepper
> 1½ teaspoons salt
> 3 tablespoons green peppercorns, drained
> 3 cups sifted all-purpose flour
> Oil for deep-frying
> Coarse salt (optional)

Sprinkle the yeast over the warm milk and let it stand for 5 minutes. Melt the butter with the garlic. Place the milk, yeast, butter, garlic, egg, sugar, cayenne pepper, salt, and peppercorns in a food processor fitted with the steel cutting blade and whirl just until well mixed. Remove the top of the processor and add the flour. Replace the top and whirl until the dough forms a ball above the blades. Remove the dough, turn it over, and whirl it for 1 minute more. (If you do not use a food processor, follow directions for kneading given on page 260.)

Place the dough in a lightly oiled bowl, turning once. Cover and set it in a warm, draft-free place for 1 hour until double in bulk.

Punch down, then roll the dough out. Cut into 3-inch rounds with a doughnut or biscuit cutter or into strips 3 inches long by 1 inch wide. Arrange on baking sheets and allow to double in bulk again in a warm, draft-free place. Heat 1½ inches of oil to 370 degrees F. in a deep, heavy skillet. Fry a few rounds or strips at a time until browned on both sides, turning them once. Drain them on paper towels and sprinkle with coarse salt if desired.

Fruited Scottish Cranachan

A snowy mound of Scotch whisky-laced cream. Nutlike toasted oats slightly caramelized with light-brown sugar. Of all the divine desserts, this one definitely deserves the 3-E award: E for effective, E for elegant, and E for effortless. This Scottish sweet is not as American as apples in pie but a taste we owe it to ourselves to acquire. Scots eat cranachan straight, but I love it with fresh fruit and the tartness of yogurt to enhance the richness of the whipped cream.

(SERVES 8 IN COMBINATION WITH FRUIT)

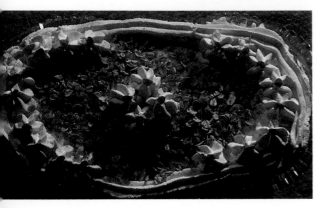

1 *cup quick-cooking (not instant) oats*
½ *cup light-brown sugar*
1 *cup unflavored or vanilla yogurt*
2 *cups heavy cream, beaten until stiff*
¼ *cup good Scotch whisky (or a little more to taste)*
6–8 *cups of the following peeled, pitted, and sliced fresh fruits, singly or in*
      combination: papaya, mango, peaches, apricots, greengage plums, and so
      forth, or small berries such as raspberries, blueberries, wild strawberries,
      and the like
8 *mint sprigs*

Preheat oven to 350 degrees F.

Sprinkle the oats on a cookie sheet and toast them, stirring twice, until they are golden (15–20 minutes). Remove the oats from the oven, sprinkle the sugar over them, and immediately use a fork to mash them with the sugar. Fold the yogurt into the whipped cream. Cool the oats and fold them into the whipped cream mixture. Fold in the Scotch and chill for 2–3 hours. Serve over the cold fruit in small, cut-glass bowls or in tulip-shaped ice cream dishes. Top with a mint sprig if available.

Note: The yogurt can be omitted and the heavy cream increased to 3 cups.

A Little Supper: Occidental Hodge-Podge

When old friends are passing through town unexpectedly or when there are new acquaintances I want to know better, the "Little Supper" is my favorite way to fit a nice, cozy get-together into a busy schedule. These informal occasions rarely include more than four guests and the menu is best kept simple. The one-dish entrée that follows, with a satisfying salad, and a rich dessert, either or both picked up at the local specialty-foods shop, is a perfect example.

Quantities here are based on the dish as I cooked it on one particular occasion. My ingredients list changes every time, as I'm sure yours will, too. There should be roughly two pounds of assorted vegetables, plus any other tidbits you may have on hand.

(SERVES 6)

1 1-pound flank steak, partially frozen and very thinly sliced across the grain
2 tablespoons each soy sauce and sherry, mirin, or Scotch
1½ tablespoons cornstarch
1 teaspoon powdered sugar
1 small Chinese cabbage (limp outside leaves discarded), cut into ½-inch slices
½ pound wild (or tame) mushrooms, cleaned and coarsely sliced
½ pound asparagus, scraped and cut into 1-inch pieces
1 cup small snow pea pods, strings removed
5 scallions, trimmed and cut into ½-inch slices
1 cup Jerusalem artichokes or fresh water chestnuts, peeled and cut
Safflower oil
3 generous slices fresh ginger root, peeled and minced
1 small clove garlic, peeled and minced
6 thin slices baked ham
4 marinated artichoke hearts, drained and cut in quarters
1½ cups rich beef broth or consommé
Salt to taste
8 cups hot cooked rice
⅓ cup minced scallions
Sesame oil

Toss the beef with the soy sauce, sherry, cornstarch, and sugar until well coated. Cover and marinate to room temperature for 15 minutes to 2 hours to tenderize. Stir-fry the vegetables in the order given, adding a tablespoon of oil as is necessary and removing each batch as it is done. Add 2 tablespoons more oil and when it sizzles, stir-fry the beef slices for a minute. Remove the beef from the pan, add the ginger and garlic, and stir-fry for a few seconds. Return all the ingredients to the pan except the beef, and stir over medium heat until the juices thicken slightly. Return the beef to the wok and stir for a minute or two until mixture steams. Do not overcook. Add salt to taste. Toss the hot, cooked rice with the minced scallion and sesame oil to taste (about 2 teaspoons), top with the meat and vegetables, and serve at once.

Let Them Eat... Cheesecake!

Talk about irresistible! Guests crumble when they find themselves in the presence of this richest of super-rich desserts. Along with chocolate, cheese-cake seems to be the delicacy most likely to bring fire to the eyes and a smile to the lips of even the most jaded epicure. A total cheesecake entertain-ment is perfect following the theater or as a Sunday evening treat. Because cheesecake has such a long shelf life, this is an especially easy party to organize. Cakes may be baked midweek for a weekend party with no significant loss of flavor or beauty. (To enlarge this to a charity fund raiser, assign each volunteer one cake to bake.) Serve the cakes in sliver-thin slices so that guests may sample each variety as they sip strong tea or spiked espresso.

<table>
<tr><td align="center">

Menu

</td></tr>
<tr><td align="center">*Devil's Food Mousse Cheesecake*</td></tr>
<tr><td align="center">*Apricot-Papaya Cheesecake*</td></tr>
<tr><td align="center">*Nougatine Cheesecake with
Orange Sauce*</td></tr>
<tr><td align="center">*Sweet Potato Cheesecake with
Pecan Crust*</td></tr>
<tr><td align="center">**Ginger Cheesecake with Poppy Seed
and Golden Raisin Toppings**</td></tr>
</table>

Devil's Food Mousse Cheesecake

A cake that is five ways chocolate! A crunchy chocolate-cookie crust, chocolate mousse nestled up to a chocolate cheese layer, spiky little horns of devil's food icing piped around the top, and, in case you're counting, a fifth layer of sweet German chocolate smack-dab in the middle.

(SERVES 20)

Crust

1½ cups chocolate wafer cookie crumbs
2 tablespoons granulated sugar
5 tablespoons butter, melted

Preheat oven to 300 degrees F.

Place the crumbs and sugar in a bowl and toss with the butter. Press over the bottom of a 9-inch springform pan and bake for 5 minutes. Cool in the pan.

Chocolate-Cheese Cake

12 ounces bittersweet chocolate
2 tablespoons strong coffee
3 8-ounce packages cream cheese, at room temperature
2 cups granulated sugar
1 5-inch piece vanilla bean, split lengthwise, or 1 tablespoon vanilla extract
4 eggs at room temperature
1 cup flour

Melt the chocolate and coffee in the top of a double boiler over hot, not boiling, water and cool to room temperature. Beat the cream cheese in a food processor or the large bowl of an electric mixer until very soft. Whirl in the sugar, a little at a time; stop once or twice to scrape the sides and bottom of the bowl. Scrape out the soft insides from the vanilla bean and beat it, or the vanilla extract, into the mixture, along with 1 of the eggs. Add the remaining eggs, 1 at a time, beating each egg until well incorporated before adding the next. Beat in the chocolate and the flour.

Pour the batter over the crust and bake for 1 hour. Turn off the oven, open the door, and cool the cake in the oven for 1 hour. Remove the cake from the oven, cool to room temperature, and chill overnight in the pan.

Chocolate Mousse Filling

½ cup granulated sugar
⅓ cup water
4 ounces bittersweet chocolate, finely chopped
4 egg yolks
3 tablespoons dark rum
1 cup heavy cream, whipped

Boil the sugar and water together, without stirring, until the syrup is clear and spins a thread when you pour a little from a spoon. Add the chocolate and stir until completely melted. Beat the mixture in a food processor or electric mixer. While it is whirling, add the egg yolks, 1 at a time, and then the rum. Cool to room temperature. Gently fold in the whipped cream and chill overnight, or for at least 4 hours.

Sweet Chocolate Layer

2 ounces German sweet chocolate, melted
1 3-ounce package cream cheese, at room temperature
1 cup confectioners' sugar
Heavy cream

Beat the melted chocolate and cream cheese in a food processor or mixer until creamy. Beat in the sugar, a little at a time, until well incorporated. Whirl in just enough cream to produce a stiff mixture.

Devil's Food Icing

4 tablespoons butter, cut in pieces
3½ cups confectioners' sugar
3 ounces bittersweet chocolate, melted in the top of a double-boiler over hot water
    and cooled to room temperature
1 tablespoon dark rum
Heavy cream

Whirl the butter in a food processor or mixer until creamy. Beat in the sugar, half a cup at a time, until well incorporated. Beat in the chocolate and rum and just enough cream to make a smooth, stiff icing. Chill.

To assemble the cake:

Spread the Sweet Chocolate Layer over the Chocolate-Cheese Cake and chill it in the springform pan. Top with the chocolate mousse and freeze until firm. About 10 minutes prior to serving, sift confectioners' sugar over the top of the cake (for an attractive pattern, dust the sugar through a paper doily). Pipe points of Devil's Food Icing around the outside edge of the cake and serve immediately.

Apricot-Papaya Cheesecake

An exceptionally fresh-tasting cake with tart fruit suspended in a rich honey cream. The peppery crunch of papaya seeds provides a nice contrast to the smoothness of the filling, and the black seeds themselves are marvelous for decorating the top of the cake.

Notice that the apricots take 24 hours to soften and plump up, so be sure to allow enough time. Don't substitute fresh apricots for dried ones; they can't provide the sharp tart flavor that dried ones do. If papaya is unavailable, substitute peeled fresh peaches.

(SERVES 20)

Crust

> 1½ *cups zwieback crumbs*
> ½ *cup (1 stick) butter, melted*
> 6 *tablespoons granulated sugar*
> ½ *cup finely chopped unblanched almonds*
> 2 *tablespoons heavy cream*

Preheat oven to 375 degrees F.

Whirl the zwieback in a food processor or crush them with a rolling pin. Thoroughly mix in the butter, sugar, and almonds, and stir in the heavy cream. Press the mixture firmly into the bottom of a 9-inch springform pan. Bake for 15 minutes. Cool in the pan.

Apricot-Papaya Cream

> 1 *cup dried apricots*
> 3 *cups apricot nectar*
> 5 *8-ounce packages cream cheese, at room temperature*
> ¼ *cup flour*
> ½ *cup each granulated sugar and honey*
> 4 *eggs*
> ⅛ *teaspoon ground nutmeg*
> 2 *cups peeled, seeded, finely chopped ripe papaya*
> 1 *ripe papaya, peeled and cut in half (remove but reserve seeds)*

Rinse the apricots, drain them well, then soak them in the apricot nectar for 24 hours.

Drain well, place on paper towels to blot dry, and finely chop the apricots. Cool. Whirl the apricots, cream cheese, flour, sugar, honey, eggs, and nutmeg in a food processor until well mixed. Drain the chopped papaya well, blot dry on paper towels, and stir into the batter. Pour the batter over the cooled crust and bake for 1 hour. Turn off the oven, open the door, and let the cake slowly cool to room temperature. Chill well.

To assemble the cake:

Just prior to your party, remove the cake from the pan and place it on an attractive serving dish. Cut six ½-inch slices lengthwise from the halved papaya and arrange them in pairs, curving toward each other so that they resemble touching parentheses. Pick over the reserved seeds to remove any bits of papaya flesh and use them to fill the spaces between the slices. If you like, place fresh or canned apricot halves between these decorations and pipe whipped cream sweetened with light-brown sugar around the bottom edge where the crust meets the plate. Serve at once.

Nougatine Cheesecake with Orange Sauce

Nougat is similar to praline except that it can be made with a mixture of nuts—walnuts, hazelnuts, pistachio, as well as almonds. I try to keep a small, air-tight box filled with this treasure on hand all the time, to dress up ice-cream desserts or to flavor whipped cream. The only drawback is that it is very nearly irresistible, and so the box is too often empty just when I need it most. The recipe below is for double the amount of nougatine you'll need, in case you're as easily tempted as I am.

Just for a change of pace, I've set the cake in a nutty sponge cake ring, the kind that will soak up some of the orange sauce to marry the flavors and textures. This is a refinement that you may not have the time to tackle. If so, omit the sponge ring and substitute the Kuchen Crust (p. 74).

(SERVES 20)

> 4 *8-ounce packages cream cheese (2 pounds for those who buy in bulk), at room*
>   *temperature*
> 1 *cup granulated sugar*
> 2 *tablespoons Cointreau*
> 1 *4-inch piece vanilla bean, or 1 tablespoon vanilla extract*
> 4 *eggs*
> ½ *recipe Nougat (recipe below)*
> 1 *cup sour cream*

In a food processor or the large bowl of an electric mixer, whirl the cream cheese until it is soft and smooth. Add the sugar, Cointreau, and vanilla, and process until well blended. With the motor still running, fully incorporate one egg at a time. Fold in the nougat and sour cream gently but thoroughly. Pour the batter into a 9-inch springform pan. Place the pan on a baking sheet and bake for 1 hour in a 350-degree preheated oven. Turn off the heat and allow the cake to cool in the oven until it reaches room temperature. Chill the cake while you prepare the Orange Sauce.

Nougat

1 cup mixed unsalted nuts (walnuts, hazelnuts, pecans, almonds, and so forth)
2/3 cup granulated sugar
1/3 cup water
Oil

Preheat oven to 300 degrees F.

Warm the nuts on a baking sheet for 3 minutes. Meanwhile, boil the sugar and water in a small, stainless-steel or enamel pan until it is light brown and syrupy. Stir the warm nuts into the syrup over medium heat until they are coated on all sides. Spread on an oiled baking sheet to cool and harden. Coarsely chop the nougat and store it in an air-tight container.

Orange Sauce

8 navel oranges
3 cups freshly squeezed orange juice
2 tablespoons freshly squeezed lemon juice
1 cup granulated sugar
1 tablespoon Cointreau

Cut away the peel and white pith from the oranges. Use a small, sharp knife to separate the flesh from the membranes. Coarsely chop the flesh and boil it with the orange juice, lemon juice, and sugar until syrupy. Off the heat, stir in the Cointreau and cool the sauce.

Sponge Ring

7 egg yolks
3/4 cup granulated sugar
1/3 cup ground blanched almonds
1/3 cup all-purpose flour
6 egg whites, beaten until stiff
1/8 teaspoon almond extract
1 medium-size lemon, squeezed

Preheat oven to 350 degrees F.

Cream the egg yolks and sugar until the mixture is light and fluffy. Stir in the almonds and flour. Gently but thoroughly fold in the beaten egg whites, then the almond extract and lemon juice. Spread the batter in a buttered 11-inch tart pan and bake for 25 minutes, or until the center of the cake springs back when lightly pressed with a finger. Cool to room temperature.

To assemble the cake:

Just prior to your party, carefully remove the Sponge Ring from the pan and place it in an attractive shallow bowl. Remove the cheesecake from its pan and place it in the center of the Sponge Ring. Decorate the top with orange slices and kumquats as shown. Spoon sauce around the edges of the Sponge Ring, or serve it on the side (or both). Remove the decorative orange slices from the top before cutting the cake.

Sweet Potato Cheesecake with Pecan Crust

This may be the creamiest cake ever! Sweet potato pie turned tony—laced with rum, smoothed with cream cheese, crusted with pecans, finished with lemon topping, and dressed with flowers of candied fruits.

(SERVES 20)

Crust

> 1½ cups zwieback crumbs
> ¾ cup finely chopped pecans (if using a food processor, don't chop the nuts beforehand)
> ⅓ cup granulated sugar
> ½ cup (1 stick) butter, melted
> 2 tablespoons heavy cream

Preheat oven to 375 degrees F.

In a food processor, whirl the zwieback, pecans, and sugar together to mix. With the motor still running, add the butter and then the cream. Press the crust into the bottom and over the sides of a heavily buttered 9-inch springform pan. Bake for 15 minutes. Handle with care so that the crust doesn't break away from the sides. Cool to room temperature.

Sweet Potato Filling

> 2 pounds sweet potatoes or yams, boiled or baked in their skins and then peeled
> ½ cup (1 stick) butter, melted
> 4 8-ounce packages cream cheese, at room temperature
> ¼ teaspoon each ground cloves, ginger, and allspice
> ⅓ teaspoon salt
> ½ cup each white and light-brown sugar
> 4 large eggs, separated
> 2 tablespoons lemon juice
> ¼ cup dark rum

Preheat oven to 350 degrees F.

In an electric mixer or food processor, blend the potatoes and melted butter together until smooth. With the motor still running, add the cream cheese, one-fourth of the package at a time, until it is all well incorporated. Add the seasonings and sugars, and process again until well mixed. Beat in the egg yolks, lemon juice, and rum. Whip the egg whites until stiff but not dry, and fold the potato-cheese mixture gently into them. Spoon the filling carefully into the crust, taking care not to damage the sides. Bake for 1¼ hours, then turn off the heat and allow the cake to remain in the oven for 2 hours. Remove the cake from the oven and cool to room temperature. Meanwhile, prepare the topping.

Lemon Topping

> 4 tablespoons butter, at room temperature
> 3 cups confectioners' sugar
> 2–3 tablespoons freshly squeezed lemon juice

Cream the butter and sugar together until well mixed, then beat in just enough lemon juice to make fairly firm icing. Chill well.

To assemble the cake:

Just prior to serving, carefully remove the cake from the pan, keeping the crust intact, and place on an attractive serving plate. Use a spatula to ice the top of the cake. Decorate with flowers made from candied pineapple and cherries, kumquats, and orange rind. Chill. Remove from the refrigerator 10–15 minutes prior to serving (depending on the heat of the day). The topping should not be melty.

Ginger Cheesecake with Poppy Seed and Golden Raisin Toppings

No one who loves desserts should miss this nippy ginger cake set on a kuchen crust and topped with crunchy poppy seeds and golden raisins, and, as a final touch, decorated with candied ginger pieces.

(SERVES 20)

Kuchen Crust

> 1 cup all-purpose flour
> 3 tablespoons granulated sugar
> 1/8 teaspoon salt
> 1/2 cup (1 stick) very cold butter, cut into pieces
> 1 egg yolk

Preheat oven to 350 degrees F.

If using a food processor, put all the dry ingredients into the bowl and turn on the motor once or twice to mix. Push the pieces of butter down into the mixture and process again for just a few seconds, turning the machine on and off until the butter is the size of small peas. Add the egg yolk and process once or twice again to just mix. Do not overwork the dough.

If you are not using a food processor, cut the butter into the dry ingredients with a pastry cutter or 2 knives, then gently stir in the egg yolk. Press into the bottom of a

9-inch springform pan. Bake for 25 minutes. Remove from the oven and set on a wire rack to cool in the pan.

Ginger Cheesecake

> *1 pound pot cheese, at room temperature*
> *2 8-ounce packages cream cheese, at room temperature*
> *5 eggs*
> *1 tablespoon lemon zest (grated outer yellow rind)*
> *1¼ cups granulated sugar*
> *2 tablespoons all-purpose flour*
> *1 cup sour cream*
> *½ cup finely chopped candied ginger*

Preheat oven to 350 degrees F.

In a food processor, blend the pot cheese and cream cheese for a few seconds. With the motor still running, add the eggs, 1 at a time, the lemon zest, sugar, and flour. (If using an electric mixer, push the pot cheese through a fine sieve into the large bowl of the mixer, along with the cream cheese, lemon zest, sugar, and flour.)

Stir in the sour cream and chopped ginger. Pour the batter over the Kuchen Crust. Bake for 1¼ hours. Allow the cake to remain in the hot oven for 1 hour after the heat has been turned off. Cool to room temperature and then chill.

Poppy Seed Topping

> *1 cup granulated sugar*
> *⅓ cup water*
> *1½ cups poppy seeds (whirled in a blender until they are crushed to a dark-gray powder)*
> *1 tablespoon freshly squeezed lemon juice*

In a small stainless-steel or enamel pan, boil the sugar and water without stirring, until it is syrupy and forms a thread when it drops from a spoon. Stir in the poppy seeds and continue to cook over medium heat until the mixture reaches 234 degrees F. on a candy thermometer or is stiff enough to form a soft ball when a bit is dropped into a cup of cold water. Stir in the lemon juice. Cool to room temperature.

Golden Raisin Topping

> *1 cup light-brown sugar*
> *½ cup milk*
> *3 tablespoons sweet butter*
> *2½ cups coarsely chopped golden seedless raisins*

Boil the sugar, milk, and butter together until they form a thick syrup. Stir in the raisins and continue to boil for a minute or two, stirring constantly, until the mixture is nice and sticky. Cool to room temperature.

To assemble the cake:

Remove the cake from the pan and place on an attractive serving plate. Beat a little lemon juice into the Poppy Seed Topping if it's too thick, and spread over the cake. Top with the Golden Raisin Topping and decorate with pieces of candied ginger.

Weekend Spring Breakfast

My recipe for entertaining guests at a seasonal breakfast begins with: "Find a field with spring leaping up in the unripe grasses and fringing every bush and tree with green, . . . add the grace of a few grazing horses, a table napped with heirloom linens, a vase dripping with lilacs." Serve with the menu here to welcome weekend guests or to send them off, with a meal that doubles as breakfast, brunch, and/or lunch.

Menu

Apricot and Pink Grapefruit Nectar

*Spring-Fresh White Asparagus
Wrapped in Black Forest Ham*

*Crisp Apple Tart with Blueberry
Crème Fraîche*

Apricot and Pink Grapefruit Nectar

(SERVES 4)

> 1   *quart fresh-squeezed pink grapefruit juice*
> 4   *ripe apricots, peeled and pitted*
> 2   *tablespoons each honey and lime juice (or more or less to taste)*

Whirl in a food processor or blender until thoroughly pureed. Chill well.

Spring-Fresh White Asparagus Wrapped in Black Forest Ham

If white asparagus aren't available, substitute three pencil-thin green ones per serving.

(SERVES 4)

> 8   *tender, plump, white asparagus, or 12 slim green asparagus*
> 3   *tablespoons sweet butter*
> 4   *large, thin slices Black Forest ham or regular baked ham*
> *Squeeze of lemon juice*
> 4   *soft-boiled brown eggs*

Trim and scrape the asparagus, if necessary, and sauté them in 2 tablespoons of the butter until they are barely tender. Heat the ham slices in the butter and wrap them around the asparagus. Melt the remaining butter, add the lemon juice, and spoon it over the ham. Serve with the boiled eggs.

Crisp Apple Tart with Blueberry Crème Fraîche

I love the tartness of apple as a follow-up to this breakfast, but feel free to substitute other fruits.

(SERVES 4 TO 6)

> 1 recipe Pastry for Tarts (page 259)
> 4 tart apples, peeled, seeded, and thinly sliced, with peels reserved
> ½ cup granulated sugar
> 2 tablespoons lime juice
> ¼ cup ginger marmalade
> ½ cup macaroon crumbs

Prepare the pastry, line the tart pan, and bake as directed on page 259.

Preheat oven to 375 degrees F.

Boil the peels from the apples with the sugar and lime juice until the jelly thickens. Spread the marmalade over the baked tart crust, cover with the crumbs, and arrange the apple slices attractively over all. Strain the apple-peel jelly over the apples and bake for 10 minutes.

Blueberry Crème Fraîche

(MAKES 1⅓ CUPS)

> ½ cup blueberries
> 2 tablespoons ginger marmalade
> 1 cup Crème Fraîche (page 253)

Puree the blueberries and marmalade in a food processor or blender. Stir the puree into the Crème Fraîche and chill well. Serve over (or pass with) the fruit tart.

Summer

A Dockside Lunch After Boating

The lazy pleasures of summer meals are all the more enjoyable when the menu can be prepared in its entirety a day, or even two, before a boating outing, and then quickly set up whenever and wherever it's most convenient. If you get off to a late start, you might prefer to lunch dockside first, then serve dessert and iced espresso on the boat. In any case, this lunch can easily accommodate your schedule.

Menu

Pernod Planter's Punch

Swirl Soup with Tequila

Tequila Swirls

**Stone Crab Claws with Chiffon
Mustard Sauce and Melted Butter**

**Mushroom-Potato-Leek Salad with
Walnuts and Fresh Curd Cheese**

Rye Loaf with Garlic-Herb Butter

**Upside-Down Praline Brownies with
Amaretto Cream**

Double Espresso on Ice

Pernod Planter's Punch

A float of Pernod on a Planter's Punch not only lends an intriguing flavor boost but adds an appealing glow of liquid sunshine to the top of the glass. Because the appearance of this festive drink enhances the enjoyment of it, grenadine is not only added to the drink itself, but slipped into the bottom of the glass so that the color goes from deep rose, to pink, to orange, to gold, to pale green. My version of the drink is not traditional . . . merely delicious.

(MAKES 1 DRINK)

½ cup freshly squeezed orange juice
   (honey bell oranges make the best juice)
1½ ounces Demerara or Jamaica rum
2 teaspoons grenadine
Squeeze of lime juice
Dash of curaçao
Splash of soda water (optional)
Crushed ice or mini-ice cubes
⅓ ounce Pernod (or more to taste)
1 orange slice
1 cherry

Mix the orange juice, rum, 1 teaspoon of the grenadine, lime juice, curaçao, and soda water. Half fill a large balloon- or tulip-shaped wineglass with crushed ice and pour the punch over. Add the other teaspoon of grenadine carefully along the side of the glass so that it settles in the bottom of the drink. Do not stir. Float the Pernod on top of the drink and garnish with the orange slice and cherry. Serve immediately.

Swirl Soup with Tequila

This soup has several layers, each with a different density, the heaviest of which is swirled into the lightest one just prior to serving, to produce an attractive pattern. I call this a "soupwork," the effect of which is even more striking when it is created in individual bowls.

Once, when I streamlined this meal into a basket lunch, Swirl Soup, with its generous splash of tequila, quite naturally evolved into a refreshing and restorative drink on the order of a Bloody Mary. Here, then, are the directions for preparing both the soup and the drink. Like the soup, the drink is most effective when you pour the liquids into the glasses in layers.

The soup can be prepared more than three hours in advance of serving, but in that case whirl the avocado into the yogurt mixture just prior to serving, to prevent it from darkening.

(SERVES 6)

> 2 buttery-ripe avocados, peeled and pitted
> 1/3 cup freshly squeezed lime juice
> 1/4 cup each chopped watercress and coriander leaves
> 1/2 Vidalia or Texas sweet onion, peeled and coarsely chopped
> 2 cups unflavored yogurt
> Salt and pepper
> Juice of 1/4 lime
> 2 cups cold tomato juice (not vegetable cocktail)
> 3/4 cup cold tequila
> 1 tablespoon Triple Sec
> 2 cups cold buttermilk
> Additional yogurt and chopped coriander

In a food processor fitted with the steel blade or a blender, whirl the avocado, lime juice, watercress, coriander, onion, and yogurt until they are almost, but not quite, pureed. The mixture should have a little "tooth" or texture. Season to taste with salt and pepper. Spoon the puree into an attractive bowl (glass is nice), squeeze the juice from 1/4 lime over it and press plastic wrap onto the surface to cover completely, and chill well, about 4 hours.

Mix the tomato juice, tequila, and Triple Sec, remove the plastic wrap, and pour over the puree. Ladle the buttermilk over the soup carefully, so as not to mix the layers. At table, stir once with a large spoon and ladle into bowls. Pass additional yogurt and coriander. Have on hand a bucket filled with ice cubes to add to the soup if the day is unusually hot or the soup a little too thick.

Tequila Swirls

These make a nice light lunch if the day is a scorcher or if you're on a diet . . . or both. Never stir this drink. Merely dip a spoon down one side of the glass, pull it neatly across the bottom, and up the other side. This will give a vertical streak of color across the horizontal ones. Very nice indeed.

(SERVES 6)

> 3 cups cold tomato juice
> 1½ cups tequila
> 2 tablespoons Triple Sec
> ¼ cup freshly squeezed lime juice
> Salt and Tabasco sauce to taste
> 2 cups cold buttermilk
> Freshly ground black pepper
> Sprigs of coriander or parsley

Mix the first 4 ingredients and season with salt and Tabasco. Pour equal amounts into 6 wineglasses and gently divide the buttermilk among them. Slide a spoon down along the inside of each glass, across the bottom, and up the other side to slightly mix each drink. Do not stir! Sprinkle with pepper and decorate with coriander or parsley.

Stone Crab Claws with Chiffon Mustard Sauce and Melted Butter

In Florida, the perfect midday meal centers around stone crab claws. Where these superb shellfish aren't available, well-chilled lobsters or shrimp (or even cold chicken) may be substituted. All are perfect with Chiffon Mustard Sauce.

Buy the claws cooked, cracked, and well chilled. Serve cold Chiffon Mustard Sauce and hot butter.

(SERVES 6)

> 2 dozen stone crab claws
> Enough well-washed, small whole lettuce heads to fill the bottom of a serving
>   plate or dish
> 2 cups Chiffon Mustard Sauce (page 254)
> 2 cups (4 sticks) sweet butter, melted, hot

Arrange the chilled claws attractively on the lettuce. Pass Chiffon Mustard Sauce and hot melted butter.

Mushroom-Potato-Leek Salad with Walnuts and Fresh Curd Cheese

Prepare this lusty salad at least twenty-four hours in advance of serving. The cheese takes that long to form, and the salad requires some time to marinate.

Whole mushrooms, tiny red potatoes, and thick slices of tender leeks are marinated in Walnut Vinaigrette, then topped with blanched walnuts and fresh cheese, a cold dish at once tart, chewy, crunchy, and mellow.

(SERVES 6)

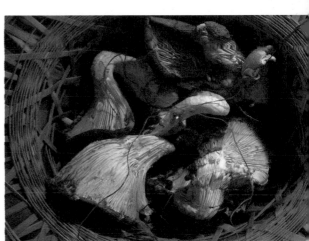

> *18–24 medium-size mushrooms, wiped clean and trimmed, or 2 cups sautéed sliced wild mushrooms*
>
> *12–18 tiny red potatoes, well washed, steamed until tender and, if they are larger than a 25-cent piece, cut in half*
>
> *4 medium-size leeks, trimmed of roots and all but 2 inches of green top; reserve several of the long green tops*
>
> *2 tablespoons white wine vinegar*
>
> *Chicken broth, brought to a boil*
>
> *Walnut Vinaigrette (page 255)*
>
> *½ cup walnut meats*
>
> *1 recipe Fresh Curd Cheese (see below)*

Place the mushrooms and the steamed halved potatoes in separate bowls. Split the leeks lengthwise and rinse them well without letting them fall apart. Cut the reserved tops into strips about ¼ inch wide and use these to tie the split leeks in several places. Cut the leeks into 2-inch-thick slices, cutting between the ties, and place in a skillet. Add 2 tablespoons of vinegar and enough boiling broth to barely cover. Simmer until the leek pieces are tender or easily pierced with a fork, but don't let them get limp and mushy. Remove the leeks with a slotted spoon and place them in a colander to drain.

Reduce the broth remaining in the skillet to ¾ cup, pour it over the mushrooms, stir for a few moments, and let stand for 30 minutes. Drain the mushrooms well.

Arrange the mushrooms in the bottom of a serving bowl, cover with the potatoes, then with the leek pieces. Pour the Walnut Vinaigrette over the salad, making sure not to miss any areas, but do not toss or stir. Cover tightly with plastic wrap and refrigerate for 24 hours. One hour prior to serving, remove the salad and toss it with the walnuts and crumbled curd cheese. If there seems to be too much cheese for the salad, reserve it for another use—it is lovely with fruit.

Fresh Curd Cheese

You will probably prepare this as frequently as I do once you see how simple it is. The tang is a bit on the acid side, which goes well with salads, but if you prefer more of a bland taste, mix in a bit of heavy cream. I've included fresh sage in this but substitute different herbs, garlic, and so forth, to complement any meal or other dish. The flavors marry and mellow as they stay together, becoming more integrated and interesting on the third day than they were on the first.

(YIELD: ABOUT 1½ CUPS)

> 1 quart freshest yogurt you can find (or make your own, page 257)
> 1 tablespoon minced sage or other herbs
> 1 tablespoon sour cream (optional)
> Salt to taste

Line a large strainer with several thicknesses of clean cheesecloth and arrange the strainer over a large bowl. Pour in the yogurt. Drape it with more cheesecloth and let it drip overnight, or until the cheese firms up. Mix in the herbs, sour cream, and salt if desired.

Rye Loaf with Garlic-Herb Butter

Unless you have an air-conditioned kitchen or a freezer full of breads baked in colder weather, you'll probably opt for just picking up a loaf at your bakery. If the bread is a good one, serve it as is; if not, dress it up a bit with this garlic-herb butter.

(YIELD: 1 LARGE LOAF)

> 3–4 cloves garlic, peeled and minced
> 3 tablespoons minced fresh mixed herbs (sage, thyme, rosemary, basil, and so
>   forth)
> ¾ cup (1½ sticks) butter, at room temperature
> 1 large loaf fresh rye bread, sliced

Mix together the garlic, herbs, and butter. To serve the bread hot, spread each piece with the butter, reassemble the loaf, wrap it loosely in foil without closing the top completely, and bake until the top is crisp and the butter is melted. Remove the foil, wrap the loaf in an attractive tea towel, and serve in a basket.

Upside-Down Praline Brownies with Amaretto Cream

I can hardly think of these outrageously delicious brownies without taking out my beater and whipping some up. Brown sugar and butter are lavishly spread on the bottom of a nonstick cake pan, pecan halves are neatly lined up on top, and moist, slightly bitter chocolate brownie batter is spread over all. When this is turned out, the pecans are set top-side up in a kind of praline crust. Of course, you can stop at this point and have a dessert no one is likely to soon forget, but if you pile a puff of unsweetened whipped cream laced with Amaretto next to each square, you're very likely to be designated a living national treasure.

(SERVES 6)

> 11 *tablespoons sweet butter*
> 1 *cup light-brown sugar*
> 2 *cups pecan halves*
> 2 *1-ounce squares top-quality unsweetened chocolate*
> ¾ *cup granulated sugar*
> 2 *eggs*
> ½ *cup all-purpose flour*
> 1 *teaspoon vanilla extract*
> 1 *tablespoon Amaretto*
> 1 *cup heavy whipping cream*

Preheat oven to 350 degrees F.

Allow 4 tablespoons of the butter to soften, then spread it in the bottom of an 8-inch-square nonstick baking pan. Sprinkle the brown sugar evenly over and arrange the nut halves, top- (round-) side down, in even rows beginning around the outside edge, each row nearly touching the one before it.

Melt the chocolate in a microwave oven or in the top of a double boiler over hot water. In another bowl, beat the remaining butter until light, and cream in the granulated sugar. Thoroughly stir in the eggs, flour, cooled chocolate, and the vanilla extract.

Use a spatula to very carefully spread the batter over the nuts without disturbing the pattern. Bake for 30 minutes (you will not be able to tell that the brownies are done by looking at them or touching the center). Remove the pan from the oven, cool on a rack for only 3–4 minutes, then slide a knife around the sides. Place a large serving plate over the pan and turn it over in one motion. The brownies should unmold in 1 piece with the pecan topping intact. If some of the pecans stick to the pan, it probably means you didn't work fast enough and the brown sugar hardened a bit. If this occurs, warm the dish by setting it in a little hot water, carefully loosen the pecans left behind in the pan and replace them neatly on the cake. Scrape out any misplaced sugary bits and save them to decorate the top of the cream. Wrap the uncut brownies with their plate in foil. Chill them only if you won't be serving them for 24 hours. Return to room temperature.

If necessary, neaten up the edges, and pile Amaretto-flavored whipped cream on top just before you carry the dessert to the table. It will still taste delicious especially with espresso.

Weekend Summer Lunch

Guests love a poolside, beach, or meadow picnic that reminds them how far away from home they really are. It's your job to make it memorable as well as free from worry for all concerned . . . including yourself.

For those who love the luxury of wine in the afternoon, perfection is a white zinfandel, chilled in the bottle to the exact temperature of the brook bubbling beside the picnic site. Also pack your favorite sparkling water, a thermos of iced ginger tea, and a few sprigs of mint for those who limit their imbibing to after five in the P.M.

Indulge in a set of splashy '30s ruby glassware or other unusual but inexpensive dishes you might keep just for picnicking. Some tag-sale sets are no more expensive and therefore just as worry-free as the spiffy new paper sets you find in specialty shops. To me, there's nothing like the sparkle of glass to heighten the drama of luncheon in the wild.

ℳenu
Carrot Vichyssoise
Pork Marinated in Lime, Mint, and Red Currants
Biryani with Eggplant and Mushroom Curry
Sweet Potato Halwa Pies

Carrot Vichyssoise

"Creamy! Simply creamy!" is how Marilyn Monroe would have characterized this frosty soup. Take the silkiness of vichyssoise and fortify with carrot, yellow summer squash, and the smallest pinch of saffron. Chill the soup, smooth it further with yogurt and heavy cream, and transport it by thermos to the picnic site, then add squares of golden plum tomato, yellow sweet pepper, circles of endive, and fiery slivers of hot cherry pepper (or sweet pepper, if that pleases you more).

For a less elaborate picnic, save this soup to sip just prior to dinner.

(SERVES 6)

> 4 *medium leeks, white part only, split lengthwise and well washed*
> 3 *tablespoons butter*
> 3 *medium-size potatoes, peeled and sliced*
> 3 *medium-size carrots, scraped and cut into 1-inch pieces*
> 2 *4-inch yellow squash, cut into 1-inch pieces*
> 4 *cups chicken broth or water*
> 1 *teaspoon salt*
> *White pepper to taste*
> *Pinch each of nutmeg, cardamom, and saffron*
> *Milk*
> 1 *cup cubed and seeded fresh plum tomatoes*
> 1 *cup Belgium endive, cut into ¼-inch-thick slices*
> *Yogurt and heavy cream*

93

Coarsely chop the leeks, place them in a heavy pot with the butter, and sauté until they wilt. Add the potatoes, the carrots, and the squash pieces, broth or water, salt, white pepper, and other seasonings. Cook over medium heat until the vegetables are soft. Cool them slightly and then puree them in their broth in several batches. Chill this soup base thoroughly and adjust the seasonings.

Just before you pour the soup into a good-sized thermos, thin it with a little milk if the consistency is thicker than you like soup to be. Pack the tomato cubes and endive each in a snap-closed plastic box. At the site, stir in a bit each of yogurt and heavy cream to make the soup nice and creamy.

Pork Marinated in Lime, Mint, and Red Currants

The lengthy marinating period allows you to stagger the cooking chores over a few days so that last-minute weekend preparations will be minimal.

(SERVES 6)

> 2 cups red currants, gooseberries, or pitted fresh sour cherries (if you use the
> cherries, add 2 tablespoons of wild flower {or other} honey)
> ⅓ cup freshly squeezed lime juice
> 1 cup consommé
> 1 cup finely chopped fresh mint
> 6 pork chops or a small loin of pork
> 2 cloves garlic, peeled and minced (optional)

Crush or chop the fruit, mix it with lime juice, consommé, and mint, and let the mixture stand overnight in a glass bowl. Arrange the meat in a glass ovenproof dish; if you're preparing the loin of pork, use the garlic by inserting it in cuts ¼-inch deep made in the top and bottom of the meat. Pour the marinade over all and marinate for 24–36 hours, turning several times.

Preheat oven to 300 degrees F.

To prepare the chops, bake in the marinade uncovered for 1 to 1½ hours or until the chops are very tender. Add a little consommé, if necessary, to prevent scorching.

To prepare the loin of pork, broil it just until the meat is opaque, not overdone, turning it several times and basting it with the marinade. Cool the meat, cut it into slices ⅓ inch thick, wrap them in foil, and chill well. Boil the marinade to the thickness of honey and spoon into a small jar.

Pack the sauce and the meat in a glass, enamel, or plastic box with a lid, and keep in the cooler box until 15 minutes prior to serving. Pass the sauce with the meat.

Biryani with Eggplant and Mushroom Curry

Rice is the central pillar upon which Indian and Pakistani cooking is built. One variation of that structure is a highly seasoned rice dish called a Biryani. Somewhat richer than a pilaf, colored and flavored with saffron or turmeric, layered in a dish with a rich meat curry or, as in this case, with a vegetable curry, it is baked and then topped with crisp-fried onions, hard-cooked eggs, nuts, and raisins. What is more, it's totally satisfying, a lovely meal on its own. If your guests are the sort who prefer dining on the light side, you might omit the pork altogether. Because of its superior keeping qualities I've chosen a light vegetable curry to pair off with the rice, but do try this dish with chicken or seafood added as well.

Seasoned Rice

Ever since a Malaysian friend introduced me to her country's version of Biryani, I've introduced coconut and cashews into my own authentic Indian recipe. This does, as she promised, make the rice layer much more flavorful. If you're not fond of coconut, not to worry. Only the flavor is included here; the grated meat is discarded. Of course, fresh coconut is best, but the grated, packaged kind, if it is unsweetened, is fine, too.

(SERVES 6)

> 8 *ounces fresh coconut, grated, or packaged shredded, unsweetened coconut*
>   *(reserve the coconut milk from the fresh coconut)*
> 3 *cups water*
> 3 *medium-size onions, peeled and coarsely chopped*
> 1½ *tablespoons each butter and cooking oil*
> 1 *large clove garlic, peeled and minced*
> 4 *whole cloves*
> 1 *1-inch stick of cinnamon*
> ¾ *cup halved cashew nuts*
> ¾ *cup seedless raisins*
> 1 *tablespoon peeled and minced ginger*
> 1 *teaspoon each paprika, chili powder, and salt*
> ½ *teaspoon ground cardamom*
> 2 *cups rice*

Steep the coconut in 1½ cups of the water for 10 minutes, then squeeze it out. Discard the coconut and reserve the coconut water.

In a large, heavy pot sauté the onions in the butter and oil until they are lightly browned. Stir in the garlic, cloves, and cinnamon, and cook for 1 minute. Add the nuts, raisins, and seasonings, and sauté for 2 minutes more. Pour in the coconut water, the remaining 1½ cups of water, and the milk from the fresh coconut if there is any. Add the rice, stir once, then cover and bring to a boil over medium-high heat. Turn heat to low and cook the rice for 10 minutes. Let stand, covered, while you prepare the curry.

Eggplant and Mushroom Curry

This curry is not only delicious but extremely nourishing as well, but let that remain our secret. While they're dining, guests should be spared discussions that emphasize anything other than the sheer pleasure of food. Nothing is more off-putting than diners detailing their latest diet, . . . calorie by weary calorie, or pushing seven lonely string beans about on their plates. A party is meant for pleasure, so give yourself to the moment . . . and enjoy.

(SERVES 6)

2 large eggplants
½ cup (1 stick) butter
2 medium onions, peeled and coarsely chopped
1 pound mushrooms, wiped or rinsed, dried, and sliced
1 teaspoon peeled and minced ginger
½ teaspoon each ground turmeric and chili powder
2 tablespoons each chopped fresh coriander and basil
Salt to taste
2 large tomatoes, peeled, seeded, and coarsely chopped
1 teaspoon Garam-Masala (recipe below) or curry powder
1 cup plain yogurt
2 onions, peeled, sliced, and separated into rings
Oil

Pierce the eggplants in several places with a fork, lay in an ovenproof baking dish and bake at 400 degrees F. until they are soft all the way through—this may take up to one hour. Split them, scrape out the pulp, and discard the skin. Melt the butter in a large, heavy skillet and sauté the chopped onions, mushrooms, and ginger until the onions are golden. Add the turmeric, chili powder, coriander, basil, and salt, and stir for 3 minutes. Add the tomatoes and eggplant pulp, cover, and cook for 15 minutes. Stir in the Garam-Masala and the yogurt. In a separate pan, fry the sliced onions in a little oil until they are lightly browned.

To assemble the dish:

½ cup coarsely chopped cashew nuts or almonds
½ cup seedless raisins
2–3 hard-cooked eggs, shelled and coarsely chopped
Butter

Preheat oven to 300 degrees F.

Butter an ovenproof baking dish (preferably a glass soufflé dish that allows the layers to show) and layer the Seasoned Rice and the Eggplant and Mushroom Curry, beginning with the rice and ending with the curry. Decorate the top with nuts, raisins, and hard-cooked eggs. Dot with butter, cover tightly with aluminum foil, and bake for 20 minutes. Remove the foil, raise the oven temperature to 400 degrees F., garnish with the fried onions, and bake 10 minutes more. Wrap in several layers of aluminum foil and a brightly colored kitchen towel, and transport to the picnic site.

Garam-Masala

This blend of spices is used frequently in Indian cooking. Buy it in a gourmet food outlet or prepare it yourself. The authentic powder is made from whole cardamoms, caraway and coriander seeds, peppercorns, and cloves, and is not powdered but finely ground. If you can find the whole ingredients, grind them yourself. If not, the following works well, too.

2 *tablespoons caraway seeds*
3 *tablespoons each ground coriander and cardamom*
2 *tablespoons freshly ground black pepper*
2 *teaspoons each ground cloves and cinnamon*

Place all the ingredients in a blender and cover tightly. Whirl until the caraway seeds are fine. Wait for the spices to settle, then store in an airtight container.

Sweet Potato Halwa Pies

A Halwa pie is akin to the mellow sweet potato pie of our own Southlands, but its Indian heritage is evident in the way its ingredients—carrots and almonds—are cooked in milk. The result is a sweeter, more candied filling, beautiful in color and fresh in taste. Plan on cooking this at the same time that you are preparing the Biryani, since the process is easy and requires only a watchful eye and a stir or two every few minutes. It's not at all tricky. The pie may be prepared with two crusts or open-face, or the Halwa may simply be spread on a buttered dish, sprinkled with the nutmeg and almonds, and served as a sweetmeat. At any rate, since it takes a little time to prepare and the finished product is unusually satisfying, this recipe yields two rather thin pies or one pie and a plate of sweets.

(SERVES 6)

1½ *cups milk*
4 *medium sweet potatoes, peeled and grated*
6 *medium carrots, scraped and grated*
1½ *cups granulated sugar*
⅓ *cup seedless raisins*
1½ *tablespoons Golden Syrup (available in gourmet food shops or substitute*
    light Karo syrup or honey)
6 *tablespoons butter*
Sprinkle of nutmeg
¾ *cup blanched, slivered almonds*
1 *recipe, Baked Pie Shell (page 258), or 1 recipe Double-Crust Pie Pastry (page*
    258)

In a large, heavy saucepan, bring the milk to a boil and sprinkle in the sweet potatoes and carrots. Cook over medium-low heat for about ½ hour, or until the mixture is very thick; stir frequently to keep it from sticking to the bottom of the pan. Stir in the sugar, raisins, syrup, and butter, then immediately transfer the mixture to a deep, heavy skillet (nonstick is best), and continue to cook at a low boil, stirring frequently, until the Halwa begins to solidify. Sprinkle with the nutmeg and nuts, and cool to room temperature. Use as filling for an open-face pie, a double-crust pie, or small pies or tarts, or serve as candy. This will keep for several days, or even longer if it is refrigerated.

A Tandem Beach and Garden Party

With the inspiration, expense, and work equally shared, traveling parties are a wonderful way to stage a very special evening with minimum effort, maximum effect, and some of the best food ever. Several hosts each invite guests to enjoy drinks at the beach or by the pool, followed by dinner in someone's garden, . . . and if yours is a particularly energetic group, dessert in a third setting. City weekenders, in particular, seem to relish this relaxed action.

Ideally, everyone meets on the beach for clams, freshly opened *in situ,* sprinkled with lime, and perked up with hot sauce. Serve these with pitchers of a smooth Bloody Mary variation I call Bloody Butterfly and a basket of hardtack flatbread, or puffy low-cal rice cakes, spread with Radish Butter. Relaxed conversation completes the first course.

An hour or so before the sun dips below the horizon, the party moves on to its garden location for the main course—Grilled Sesame-Marinated Halves of Duck and Grilled Sweet Onion, Sweet Potato, and Peach prepared over dried branches of thyme. To finish the meal, move to the patio, porch, or deck for Wild Berries Dolloped with Penuche Foam.

Menu

Bloody Butterflies

Clams In Situ

Hardtack Crackers with Radish Butter

Grilled Sesame-Marinated Halves of Duck

Grilled Sweet Onion, Sweet Potato, and Peach

Wild Berries Dolloped with Penuche Foam

Bloody Butterflies

Never tamper with success. Stop while you're ahead. Don't believe everything you hear! Admittedly, the Bloody Mary is an immensely popular drink, but it's just possible that this version, incorporating five Oriental ingredients in addition to most of the more familiar ones, may be slightly better. Here, soy sauce supplies the saltiness, hoisin sauce adds mystery and a touch of sweetness, hot oil floats on the surface where your taste buds get the full impact of the sizzle, freshly ground Szechwan peppercorns add to the impact, and sesame oil smooths any jagged edges. A nice touch is to slit a fresh snow pea pod in half lengthwise and slip it over the edge of the glass. Its cool green crunch is a refreshing counter to the spicy drink.

(MAKES ABOUT 12 6-OUNCE DRINKS)

3 quarts Sacramento tomato juice (not tomato juice cocktail)
3 tablespoons soy sauce
2 tablespoons hoisin sauce
3 tablespoons lemon juice
2 tablespoons sesame oil
2 tablespoons Worcestershire sauce
½ teaspoon Chinese hot oil
Salt and cayenne pepper to taste
1 shot glass vodka for each person (or more, or less)
Snow pea pods (optional)

In a blender or cocktail shaker, mix 1–2 cups of tomato juice with all the other ingredients except the vodka and snow pea pods. Combine this with the remaining tomato juice and the vodka, and chill the mixture well. Mix the drink thoroughly before serving in chilled glasses, decorated, if you wish, with slit snow pea pods.

Hardtack Crackers with Radish Butter

Sweet butter is the perfect foil for two varieties of radish—the little rosy ones and the pungent, horsey kind. Perfection with any tomato drink.

(MAKES ABOUT 1 CUP)

2 tablespoons freshly grated or minced horseradish, or bottled horseradish,
    drained
½ cup sliced red radishes
1 cup (2 sticks) sweet butter, at room temperature
Coarse salt

Whirl the horseradish and the radishes in a food processor, fitted with the steel blade, for a few seconds only, or until they are rather finely chopped. Change to the plastic blade, add the butter, and whirl until mixed. If you are not using a processor, mince the radishes with a sharp knife and mix in the butter and horseradish with a spatula. Spread on hardtack, rice crackers, toasted pita, or any bland, crisp cracker. Sprinkle with coarse salt.

Grilled Sesame-Marinated Halves of Duck

This sounds more complicated than it is. The marinating method adds flavor to the flesh and dries the skin of the duck a bit so that it crisps as it grills.

> ¾ *cup olive oil*
> ⅓ *cup each soy sauce, sesame oil, and hoisin sauce*
> 4 *tablespoons lemon juice*
> ¼ *teaspoon each ground cardamom, cumin, and dry mustard*
> 1 *large clove garlic, peeled and crushed*
> ½ *small, young duck for each person, halved*

In a blender or a food processor fitted with the steel cutting blade, whirl all the ingredients but the ducks until thoroughly incorporated.

Two days prior to your party, brush the duck halves with one-third the marinade, arrange them skin-side up in a glass baking dish, and refrigerate them uncovered over night. The morning prior to your party rub half the remaining marinade into the skin of the ducks and refrigerate them skin-side up until the morning of your party.

Preheat oven to 500 degrees F. and bake the ducks for 15 minutes, skin-side up, to eliminate excess fat. Remove the ducks from the oven and let them cool to room temperature. Rub them with the marinade once more and refrigerate skin-side up until 1 hour prior to grilling.

Just prior to serving, grill the bird halves for 5–10 minutes over medium coals, turning them once and removing them when the meat next to the bone is slightly pink and the skin is beautifully browned. During the last few minutes of grilling, push a few dried branches of thyme or rosemary into the flames directly under the bird halves so that the smoke will infuse the skin with flavor. Larger birds may need longer grilling time.

Serve at once with grilled halves of sweet potatoes, sweet onions, and fresh peaches.

Grilled Sweet Onion, Sweet Potato, and Peach

Since the potatoes take much longer to cook than the onions, I halve them lengthwise, wrap them in foil, and arrange them along the back of the grill as soon as the coals are lighted. Keep the top of the grill down and turn the potatoes often. The foil keeps the potatoes from burning and speeds up cooking time. When it is time to put the onions and peaches on the grill, unwrap the potatoes, brush the cut sides with butter, and arrange them alongside the other vegetables to finish cooking. This shortcut ensures an entrée that is ready to eat as soon as the salad course is finished and frees the host or hostess to relax with the guests, far from the heat of the grill.

> 1 *medium-size sweet potato for each guest*
> 1 *large sweet onion for each guest*
> 1–2 *fresh peaches for each guest*
> 1 *recipe Sesame Marinade (see above)*

Prepare the sweet potatoes as directed above. Peel the onions and cut them in half crosswise.

Dip the peaches in and out of scalding water and pull off the skins. Cut them in half and discard the pits. Brush the onions and peach halves with marinade, then arrange them, cut-side up, to marinate while the potatoes are on the grill.

As the salad is served, arrange the ducks on the grill with the potatoes. Put the onions in a hinged wire basket if you have one, rounded sides down. When it's time to turn the ducks, brush them, the vegetables, and the peaches generously with the marinade. Turn the vegetables. Grill the peaches, also in a hinged wire basket if available. If you do not use the wire baskets, take extra care in turning the peaches and onions. The potatoes should be served fork-tender, the onions and peaches with a bit of a crunch.

Wild Berries Dolloped with Penuche Foam

To my mind, wild berries surpass their cultivated cousins, but like all wild things, they are elusive. I do know of a scratchy patch where blackberries ramble, mysteriously dark against the lemony morning light, and these I shamelessly pillage. A friend has tame blueberry bushes that grow very nearly wild in a field moistened by salt-sweet breezes off the bay. Since I'm up before the birds and don't care for worms, I make a point of catching the blueberries my feathery foes would normally devour shortly after dawn if I didn't beat them to it. Of course, I do divvy up with the owner when she isn't in some far corner of the world. In addition, my very own strawberries are a bit on the wild side. This combination of berries eventually finds its way into a cobbler, a fool, or as here, into a pretty glass dish where they are dolloped with this sauce that is an offspring of old-fashioned penuche fudge. Almost any combination of fruits is lovely served this way.

> *1 cup mixed wild (or tame) berries per person*
> *1 tablespoon eau-de-vie or other liqueur per person*
> *1 recipe Penuche Foam (see below)*

Slice the strawberries if they are large. Toss all of the berries with the liqueur. Refrigerate for not less than 1 hour and not more than 24 hours. Spoon into pretty glasses and, just prior to serving, top with Penuche Foam.

Penuche Foam

A froth of this brown-sugary sauce can transform almost any fruit into a very special dessert.

> *1 cup light-brown sugar*
> *1 cup light cream*
> *⅓ cup butter*
> *⅛ teaspoon salt*
> *½ teaspoon vanilla extract*
> *1 cup heavy cream, whipped*

Thoroughly mix together the sugar, light cream, butter, and salt, and bring to a boil in the top of a double boiler, stirring frequently. Let cool to room temperature, then stir in the vanilla extract. Just before serving, gently stir in one-third of the whipped cream. Finally, fold in the remainder of the whipped cream and serve with the berries.

Fruit and Salad Bar Supper

More than any other area of gastronomy, the salad interlude has been transformed from a jaw-jarring chomp on a forkful of roughage to an elegant nibble of multihued and multiflavored edible treasures. America's unrivaled farm machine guarantees year-round availability of a stunning profusion of what used to be referred to as salad "greens."

Now, iceberg is nearly a distant memory; instead, we have more refined offerings: ruby radicchio, red oakleaf, bronze-leaved mignonette, buttercrunch, arugula, watercress, endive, and spinach. Rural gardens erupt with verdant rows of leafage, purposely overplanted to yield infant kale, collard, chard, and the like when the rows are thinned. Herbs and edible flowers spring up: mint and coriander, lemon balm and borage, hyssop and

sweet cicely, candytuft, nasturtium, and squash blossoms. Following the European tradition, many of us now seed our salad gardens with a bed of "mesclun," the Provençal mixture of baby lettuce, dandelion, and arugula, or with "misticanza," the Roman version, containing upwards of seven wild greens. I get a head start every year by deliberately allowing one area of my lettuce garden to go to seed and then spring up at its own discretion when the weather warms. As a result, a bouquet of red and green and bronze leaves (plus a few surprise varieties that revert back to their ancestors) decorates my table early on, when neighbors' gardens are still in an embryo state.

Even this exuberant explosion is eclipsed in the wild. Country fields are spongy underfoot with an assortment of fern, dandelion, wild onion, carrot and ginger shoots, ours for the finding.

To a selection of the greenery mentioned above, immature squash, snow peas, cucumbers, carrots, turnips, mushrooms, red and gold cherry tomatoes, asparagus, scallions, and string beans—are added for this fete. For the Fruit Bar, set out fresh strawberries, cherries, raspberries, grapes, spring plums, and apricots. Out-of-season melons are wonderful here, too, if they are nice and sweet, as are miniature bananas.

To sustain more hearty appetites, feature bowls of tiny shrimp and crayfish, cubes of smoked chicken breast, and slices of marinated and broiled butterflied leg of lamb. If you like, include some pickled or preserved treasures such as hearts of palm, quail eggs, ears of miniature corn, and smoked oysters. Alongside, arrange an assortment of fresh goat cheeses and creamy blue varieties to crumble over salads or eat with fresh-baked breads.

Improvise a flower cart: Use plastic-lined clean wheelbarrows (antique wooden ones are most attractive) or arrange tables to hold greens and other makings. Then, let guests create their dream salads with a difference, light, healthful, and beautiful, moistened with any from a quartet of dressings: Extra-Virgin Olive Oil and Pear Vinaigrette, Sesame Mayonnaise, Pear-Tomato and Strawberry Dressing, Creamy Yogurt-Blue. End the party on a sweet note with light and moist Sugar-Crusted Round Cakes from Grandmother's book of "receipts." Cold and hot teas and coffees will add the finishing touch.

Menu

Ruby Radicchio, Red Oakleaf, Bronze
Mignonette, and Buttercrunch Lettuce

Arugula, Watercress, Endive,
Spinach, Infant Kale, Collard, and
Chard

Hyssop, Sweet Cicely, and Candytuft

Nasturtium and Squash Blossoms

Miniature Squash, Snow Peas,
Cucumbers, Carrots, Turnips,
Mushrooms, Red and Gold Cherry
Tomatoes, Asparagus, and
String Beans

Strawberries, Raspberries, Grapes,
Plums and Apricots, Tiny Melons and
Bananas

Shrimp and Crayfish

Cubes of Chicken and Lamb

Hearts of Palm, Quail Eggs,
Miniature Corn

Smoked Oysters

Fresh Goat Cheese, Cottage Cheese,
and Creamy Blue

Extra-Virgin Olive Oil and Pear
Vinaigrette

Sesame Mayonnaise

Pear-Tomato and Strawberry Dressing

An Assortment of Cheeses

Grandmother's Sugar-Crusted
Round Cake

Fruit and Salad Bar

Quantities will depend not only on the number of guests but also on the variety of ingredients you decide to include; the larger the assortment, the smaller the quantity you will need of each. Buy or pick ingredients as close to serving time as possible. Dip each variety separately in tubs of cold water to inflict the least damage, particularly to the more delicate, colorful varieties. Spin or drain each for a few seconds, then, if they are not to be used at once, loosely wrap in paper towels, pack separately in plastic bags, and refrigerate until needed.

The easiest procedure is to approximate the amount of salad makings needed for two guests, then multiply and make adjustments from there. These are generous proportions, but remember . . . in this case salad is appetizer *and* entrée.

(SERVES 2)

½ *small head limestone or Boston or Buttercrunch lettuce*
½ *small head radicchio*
½ *head each red oakleaf and bronze-leaf lettuce*
½ *small bunch arugula*
½ *bunch watercress with the coarsest stems discarded*
½ *bunch dandelions*
1 *cucumber, finger length*
1 *yellow summer squash or zucchini*
3 *each chopstick-thin asparagus, scallions, and string beans*
½ *cup young lettuce leaves pulled from your garden when thinning the rows (optional)*
4 *each fiddleheads and snow pea pods*
1 *each small stem mint, coriander, lemon balm, basil, borage, hyssop, sage, oregano, dill, sweet cicely, and candytuft, or an equivalent amount of whichever of these are available*
2 *each nasturtium and squash blossoms*
A *few each strawberries, cherries, and grapes*
1 *each plum, apricot, and miniature banana*
1 *small, thin slice 2 different melons*
3–4 *small cubes smoked chicken breast*
3–4 *small cubes broiled leg of lamb*
1–2 *each smoked oysters, quail eggs, and miniature picked corn*
½ *ounce each 2 favorite creamy blue cheeses*
½ *ounce each 2 favorite fresh goat cheeses*
½ *cup cottage cheese*

For this party I set out attractive combinations of ingredients in a collection of ice-filled antique white-enamelware trays of various sizes and depths. I push the root ends of the lettuces directly down into the ice to form a green, leafy canvas on which to create with the other ingredients a kind of vegetable still-life. Similar small, shallow trays function as individual serving platters.

The cucumbers, squash, carrots, asparagus, and scallions show off to advantage tucked in among the lettuce heads, but smaller ingredients—string beans, snow peas, mushrooms, cherry tomatoes, fruits, shellfish, meats, hearts of palm, oysters, quail eggs, and such—require individual trays or bowls (glass or clear plastic are nice too, because they recede into the background). All vegetable ingredients should be served cold and crisp . . . preferably in a beautifully shaded outdoor area. Arrange plates, flatware and napkins, and so forth, near one end of the display, and cheeses and dressings at the other. Desserts and drinks are most effective presented on their own table.

Extra-Virgin Olive Oil and Pear Vinaigrette

When I can find the time, I prepare my own vinegars from fruit wines I've fermented, to be sure of combinations that please me most. My all-time favorite was born of a very dry pear wine, into which I placed a twig of wild mustard rubbed between my palms to warm and bruise it to help release the flavor. That vinegar, alas, is long since gone, and none is in the making. To try to re-create these past pleasures, I concocted this dressing which begins with my favorite store-bought white wine vinegar enhanced with a modest libation of pear brandy. Which last, despite its sizable cost, should be a staple in any really civilized household.

First, prepare the vinegar.

> 2 cups good white wine vinegar
> 2 tablespoons fine pear brandy

Rinse a wide-mouthed jar with baking soda to sweeten it, then rinse it again thoroughly with tap water. Pour in and mix the vinegar and brandy, and let the mixture stand uncovered in a warm place for 8 to 48 hours.

Now, prepare the dressing.

(MAKES 4 TO 5 CUPS)

> 1/4 cup Pear Vinegar (see above)
> 1 tablespoon Dijon mustard
> 4 egg yolks
> 1/2 teaspoon salt
> Freshly ground black pepper to taste
> 3 1/2 cups extra-virgin olive oil, or 1 1/4 cups each extra-virgin olive oil and
>   safflower oil

Wire-whisk together all the ingredients except the oil. While still whisking, add the oil in a thin, steady stream.

Sesame Mayonnaise

2 *tablespoons sesame oil*
4 *cups Mayonnaise (page 252)*

When you prepare the mayonnaise, replace 2 tablespoons of the other oils with the sesame oil and continue as directed.

Pear-Tomato and Strawberry Dressing

Unlikely combination? Actually this fresh-tasting, tart fruit dressing is wonderful splashed over fruits and cottage cheese. It will keep, refrigerated, for weeks

(MAKES 4 CUPS)

2 *dozen yellow pear-tomatoes*
2 *cups hulled and coarsely chopped strawberries*
2 *cups granulated sugar*
4 *lemons*
3 *limes*
3 *slices peeled fresh ginger, minced*

Plunge the tomatoes into scalding water, and slip off and discard the skins. Cut the tomatoes into quarters lengthwise, discard the seeds, and coarsely chop the fruit. Combine the tomatoes and strawberries in a bowl, then sprinkle the sugar over them and let them stand overnight.

Into a 3-quart stainless-steel or enamel pan, drain the syrup that the fruit has formed and cook it until it's nice and thick, skimming off and discarding any foam that forms. Be careful not to let the mixture scorch.

Cut the zest, or thin outer skin, from the lemons and limes without including any of the bitter white underskin (a swivel-type vegetable peeler does this best). Slice the zest into julienne strips $1/16$ inch thick and 1 inch long. Squeeze the lemons and limes to produce $1/3$ cup of juice.

Add the tomatoes, strawberries, lemon and lime zest, citrus juice, and ginger to the syrup in the pot and stir over medium heat until the tomatoes are translucent and the syrup is about the consistency of warm honey. Somewhere along the way you should sample the dressing and add more sugar or citrus juice to suit your taste. Serve at room temperature.

Grandmother's Sugar-Crusted Round Cake

(SERVES 8)

Butter
1 ½ cups light brown sugar
A sprinkle each of ground nutmeg and cinnamon
¾ cup blanched almonds, finely chopped
8 ounces cream cheese, at room temperature
3 extra-large eggs, plus 1 egg white
1 cup sour cream
1 cup granulated sugar
3 tablespoons melted butter
3 tablespoons all-purpose flour
2 tablespoons bourbon

Preheat oven to 350 degrees F.

Generously butter the bottom and sides of a 9-inch nonstick cake pan and sprinkle the bottom first with the brown sugar, and then with the spices.

Use a food processor fitted with a steel blade to thoroughly mix the remaining ingredients. Pour the batter carefully over the sugar. Bake 30 to 40 minutes, or until the center of the cake no longer quivers when tapped lightly with your finger. Loosen the sides of the cake with a knife. Cover the pan with a large plate and flip it over to unmold it. If the cake does not become loose, rest the pan in ¼-inch hot water for 5 minutes, then try again.

Serve the cake at room temperature.

Variation: End-of-Summer Bounty Cocktail Party

This cocktail version of the Salad Bar Supper came about late last August, just prior to the departure of my summer friends. When we began ticking off all the "can't do withouts," the guest list, like Topsy, just grew and before the frenzy ended, the total topped two hundred and fifty Very Special Persons whose faces, burnished by the fading sun, we longed to behold once more, before the summer (was it really over?) ended.

We decided to kiss the season goodbye with a party that would utilize that dazzle of fresh Hampton harvest blooming at farm stands along the winding backways on this tip of rural Long Island (long called the "breadbasket" of New York City).

Why not offer guests the opportunity to satiate the longing for perfect fruits and vegetables of every kind . . . gorgeous green and gold and red and orange sweet peppers, plump heads of lettuce, bunches of scarlet and white radishes, red and yellow and cherry and plum and Big Boy and beefsteak tomatoes, pots of growing herbs, boxes of ripe green and purple figs, bunches of grapes, and just for good measure, a bin of homebaked breads, rounds of cheese, and a seafood-filled paella salad?

Two days before the party I scouted nearby farms, picked up whatever produce was near the peak of perfection, ordered the rest to be specially picked Friday morning, purchased the seafood, cooked two enormous bowls of Paella Salad, chose dozens of baskets from my tag-sale collection, and fell into bed. By 6:00 A.M. on party day I was hurtling from farm to farm in my station wagon, frantically gathering baskets of perfect plants and fruits and vegetables. By noon I was at work in my kitchen.

The vegetables were all washed in tubs of cold water and carefully wrapped in paper towels to absorb some of the water and prevent damage. At mid-afternoon I set up two long tables in a narrow gallery in my husband's studio barn. I edged one of them with metal window boxes from the garden department of our local 5-and-10, filled these nearly to the top with crushed ice and began arranging whole lettuces and other greens root ends first in the ice. Each variety of pepper, tomato, and so forth, was lovingly set out in its own basket; potted herbs were arranged in among these, and knives and children's scissors were tied to ribbons long enough for guests to cut the salad makings they preferred.

This is a particularly difficult party for which to give quantities. My primary concern was to achieve a visual effect. The freshness of the produce was enhanced by the freshness of the idea—to provide a bountiful indoor farm stand from which guests could create their own favorite salad combinations. The result turned out to be quite a theatrical production in which both the food and the guests participated in a unique way to produce an entertaining experience greater than the sum of its parts.

The abundance that lent so much to the *feel* of the party was made possible by my opportunity to purchase produce directly from the farmer at what amounted to wholesale prices. It was important that the display not be diminished in beauty while more than two hundred guests picked their fill and moved on. To make sure, I purchased half again what I thought might be consumed, heaped the baskets to overflowing, and refilled them as needed.

It is important to include a small mountain of excellent breads, home, or bakery-made, as a part of the extravaganza, and to match these to your own cheeses or top-notch store-bought ones. It is pleasant, but not necessary, to include a cold main-course for those guests who missed lunch or had a long drive or are short of patience when it comes to less hearty party food. I've sketched out a party for fifty, including the recipes for Paella Salad and Easy No-Cook Pickled Peppers. You *will* have leftovers if you do this party justice. But this is worth a week of eating rabbit food.

Menu

Various Lettuce Heads

Bunches of Arugula, Watercress, Parsley, and Dandelion

Baskets of Red, Green, and Yellow Mild and Hot Peppers

Miniature Cucumbers, Yellow Summer and Zucchini Squash

Cherry, Plum, and Beefsteak Tomatoes, Both Red and Yellow

Slender Asparagus and Scallions

Mint, Coriander, Lemon Balm, Basil, Sage, Oregano, Dill, and Thyme Plants Growing in Pots

Fresh Figs, Plums and Peaches, Pears and Grapes, Sliced Melons of All Kinds

Assortment of Cheeses

Caviar Sauce

Garlic Butter

Paella Salad

Easy, No-Cook Pickled Peppers

Dozens of Freshly Baked Loaves

Bounty Salad

(SERVES 50)

> 10 small heads leaf lettuce (Buttercrunch or other), including roots
> 4 large bunches each parsley, watercress, and arugula
> Crushed ice
> 10 each red, green, yellow, orange, and brown sweet peppers
> 3 bunches each white and scarlet radishes
> 3 bunches baby carrots, tops intact, peeled while still in the bunch
> 10 each yellow and red plum tomatoes
> 5 each medium-size red and yellow tomatoes
> 2 boxes each red and yellow cherry tomatoes or cherry tomato plants
>   dripping with fruit
> 4–5 pots of herbs (chives, mint, thyme, oregano, dill, or other)
> 1 hot pepper plant with peppers on it
> 4 large bunches grapes of assorted varieties
> 2 boxes ripe figs (about 24 in a box)
> 10 assorted plums
> 10 ripe apricots
> 10 ripe peaches

Set up two tables side-by-side against a wall, each about 7 feet by 4 feet, so that they meet in the center.

Carefully wash lettuce heads and bunches of parsley and watercress in tubs of cold water, changing the water often. Drain well and wrap each in paper towels so that they are well protected. Refrigerate until several hours prior to party time. Arrange long, narrow, waterproof window-box liners (or other suitable containers) around the sides and back of one of the tables. Fill the window boxes with crushed ice, and to form an attractive border, push in well the roots of the lettuce and the stem ends of the bunches of parsley, watercress, and arugula. Cover with damp paper towels.

Clean all the other vegetables and fruits as necessary. Leave the radishes and carrots in bunches. Arrange each variety of vegetable in its own basket to produce an attractive display. Set the pots of herbs among the baskets. Place the fruit in bowls and baskets, and arrange attractively at the opposite end of the table from the vegetables. Mound the breads in flat baskets next to the fruit and display the cheeses in front of these. Place the Paella Salad in the center where the 2 tables meet, with the salad dressings on either side. Tie children's scissors and small knives with long ribbons to the wall or back edges of the tables for guests to use to cut their selection of greens, herbs, radishes, and other produce. Serve with Extra-Virgin Olive Oil and Pear Vinaigrette (page 109) and Deep, Dark Caviar Sauce (page 46).

Paella Salad

Chicken? Yes. Lobster? Yes. Shrimp? Yes. Mussels, clams, chorizo? Yes, yes, yes! This saffron rice salad has everything, including avocado, Niçoise olives, and coriander.

(SERVES 50)

2 3½-pound chickens, skinned and cut into eighths
8 tablespoons vegetable oil
3 medium-size onions, peeled and coarsely chopped
5 cloves garlic, peeled
2 2-pound lobsters, uncooked, cut into 2-inch pieces
24 shrimp, shelled, deveined, and cut in half lengthwise
4 quarts water
8 cups long-grain rice
1 teaspoon saffron
2 teaspoons salt
24 oysters in their shells, well-scrubbed
24 clams, shucked and chopped (with their liquid)
1 chorizo, sliced
24 mussels in their shells, well scrubbed
6 tablespoons lemon juice
4 tablespoons light, fruity olive oil
2 avocados, peeled and pitted
1 cup coarsely chopped coriander
Salt and freshly ground black pepper to taste
Sesame oil
50 Niçoise olives

In a large, heavy pot (nonstick is best), sauté the chicken pieces in 2 tablespoons of the vegetable oil until they are golden on all sides, then set them aside in a bowl to cool. Pick the meat from the bones, cut it into ¾-inch dice, and reserve it. Reserve the bones.

Sauté the onions and garlic in another 2 tablespoons of vegetable oil until the onions are transparent. Place these in a blender or food processor. Add 2 more tablespoons of vegetable oil to the skillet and sauté the lobster and shrimp until the shells turn red. Pick out the lobster meat, liver, and roe. Add it with the shrimp to the reserved chicken. Place the chicken bones and lobster shells in 4 quarts of water and bring to just under a boil. Cook for 10 minutes, skimming off any froth that may form. Lower the heat and simmer for 1 hour. Strain the broth.

Heat the remaining 2 tablespoons of oil in the skillet. Add the rice, saffron, and 2 teaspoons salt and sauté until the rice is golden. Pour in 2½ quarts of the broth and simmer until the liquid is absorbed. Oil the sides and bottom of a large (10-quart) ovenproof serving dish. Spoon in one-third of the rice and cover with a layer of chicken, lobster, shrimp, oysters, clams, and chorizo. Cover with another layer of rice, another layer of chicken, lobster, and so forth, and a final layer of rice. (Reserve the lobster claws.) Pour about half the remaining broth over the rice and push the mussels, blunt end down,

1 inch deep in the rice. Cover lightly with aluminum foil and bake in an oven preheated to 350 degrees F. for 25–35 minutes or until the rice is barely tender, adding a little broth from time to time. Remove from the oven and cool to room temperature. Carefully set aside the mussels and oysters in their shells and reserve them to garnish the salad.

Meanwhile, make a dressing by pureeing the onions, garlic, lemon juice, and olive oil. Cut the avocados into ½-inch cubes and toss them with the dressing. Toss the avocados, the onion dressing, and ¾ cup of coriander with the cooled paella. Season to taste with salt, pepper, sesame oil, and additional lemon juice and olive oil if necessary. Place the salad neatly in the serving dish, garnish the center with the lobster claws, and surround with the remaining coriander. Edge the bowl with the mussels in their shells and the olives. Serve at room temperature.

Easy No-Cook Pickled Peppers

These superior pickled peppers are for you if you're nervous about canning. The only cooking you'll have to do here is to boil water.

> 15 *large sweet red or yellow peppers*
> *Boiling water*
> 5–6 *large cloves garlic, unpeeled but slashed*
>   *in several places with a sharp knife*
> *Sprigs of herbs (thyme, sage, marjoram, and/or dill)*
> *Red chili pepper (optional)*
> *White vinegar*
> *Granulated sugar (optional)*
> *Salt*
> *Olive oil*

Cut peppers into quarters lengthwise and discard stems, seeds, and white pith. Arrange the peppers in a bowl and add boiling water to cover. Let stand for 15 minutes. Drain, reserving the liquid. In a large, wide-mouthed quart jar, layer the pepper pieces with the garlic and herbs. Tuck in a small chili pepper. Add 3–4 ounces of white vinegar and 2 teaspoons of sugar to every quart of peppers. Heat the water the peppers soaked in. To 1 cup of this hot water stir in 1 teaspoon of salt until it is dissolved, and pour the salt water into the jar. Repeat this procedure until the jar is three-quarters full of liquid. Pour in enough olive oil to completely cover the peppers. Cover tightly with plastic wrap and let stand at room temperature for 3 days. Press your hand tightly against the top of the jar and turn it upside-down from time to time to coat the peppers with oil. Refrigerate for 3 days. Taste one of the peppers. If it seems bland, add a little more sugar and/or vinegar. Always push the peppers down under the oil before refrigerating them.

Swell Flicks and Swell Spaghetti

Gee! Watching a thirties movie on the VCR is a swell event around which to stage a party. Start with a swank selection of those vintage mixed drinks that are suddenly new again—Manhattans or martinis. Indulge in hors d'oeuvres that are passed around so no one has to raise a pinky, or pause for a stroll to the pool and a whimsical presentation of more substantial appetizers *al fresco*. You can even start dinner at this point and serve one of my favorite chilled soups, Saffron Consommé with Five Jewels. Leave out the "jewels" and you can serve it in wine glasses. Very glamorous.

As the sun goes down and the pool lights come

up, move the party inside to the screening room for a sip of pink champagne and a choice of a VCR Cleopatra, Colbert, Leigh, or Taylor. Several hours on, with Cleo and the asp committed to memory, gather in a room ablaze with flickering rose-colored candles. The table is draped with gold lamé, set with frosty rose glass collectibles, and decorated with African daisies and red ginger blossoms.

The entrée? A tangle of green angel's hair pasta with just about everything, escargots sizzling in garlic oil, cubes of succulent poached chicken and salmon, Greek olives, fresh mushrooms, and a tangy sauce flavored with green peppercorn mustard. Swell? You bet!

120

Menu

Chilled Saffron Consommé with Five Jewels

Swell Spaghetti with Escargots, Chicken, Salmon, Olives, Mushrooms, and Green Peppercorn Mustard Sauce

Arugula and Blood Orange Salad

Milk Chocolate Mousse with Fresh Raspberries and Aquavit

Chilled Saffron Consommé with Five Jewels

The golden gleam of this cool, saffron-infused chicken consommé is enhanced by a scattering of five edible jewels. I've chosen radicchio slivers, a thin slice of endive, half an asparagus tip, a slice of morel, and a rose petal. You might substitute a violet or halved squash blossom, an exquisite, verticle cross section of leek, a wafer of radish, or half of a medium-sized shrimp. The idea is to compose an edible collage onto the liquid saffron canvas.

(SERVES 6)

> 2 quarts rich chicken broth
> ½ teaspoon saffron
> 2 egg whites (uncooked) with their shells
> Tabasco sauce and salt to taste
> Garnishes (see above)

Boil the broth and saffron over medium heat until reduced by one-fourth (about 1 hour). To clarify the broth, add the egg whites and shells and cook over low flame for 10 minutes. Remove from the heat and let stand. Use a slotted spoon to remove the egg-white crust. Ladle off the clear soup without disturbing the cloudy particles in the bottom of the pan. Strain the remainder of the soup through several layers of dampened cheesecloth. Season the consommé with Tabasco and salt. Chill well and garnish as discussed above.

Swell Spaghetti

When is spaghetti not just spaghetti? When you spiff it up with nifty tidbits and serve it to a few swell friends. I set out to create my own dream pasta, with very pleasing results. You can, too, by adding to, or omitting from, the ingredients here. But try my version first.

(SERVES 6)

> 3 tablespoons each olive oil and safflower oil, mixed
> 2 cups ½-inch cubes center-cut skinless salmon filets
> 2 cups ½-inch cubes boneless and skinless chicken breasts
> 12 very compact small fresh mushrooms, stems cut off even
>   with the crowns and the crowns thinly sliced
> 2 large cloves garlic, peeled
> 1 7-ounce can escargots, drained, rinsed, and the larger ones
>   cut in half lengthwise
> 12 large Greek olives, pitted and quartered
> 1½ pounds fresh green angel's hair pasta

For the Green Peppercorn Mustard Sauce:

> 3 tablespoons first-press olive oil
> ½ cup peeled and coarsely chopped shallots
> Reserved garlic
> 2 tablespoons minced chives
> 2 tablespoons green peppercorn mustard
> 2 tablespoons freshly squeezed orange juice

For Garnish:

> 2 ounces salmon roe or caviar (whatever variety pleases
>   your fancy and your wallet; optional)

Put a large pot of slightly salted water to boil. In a large, heavy, nonstick skillet, heat 2 tablespoons of the combined oils and, over low heat, sauté first the salmon and then the chicken until they are opaque, adding a little more oil if necessary. (Stir the salmon with care so the cubes don't fall apart.) Use a slotted spoon to transfer the chicken and salmon to a bowl. Add 2 more tablespoons of oil to the pan and sauté the mushrooms until they barely wilt, then add them to the ingredients in the bowl. In an additional tablespoon of oil, sauté the garlic and the escargots for 2 minutes. Place the escargot and the olives in the bowl with the mushrooms, salmon, and chicken. Remove and reserve the garlic cloves for the sauce.

Keep all the cooked ingredients warm while you cook the pasta and make the sauce. Drop the pasta into the boiling water, immediately remove the pan from the heat, and allow the pasta to stand in the water for 2 minutes. Drain well.

While the pasta is cooking, make the sauce. Heat the olive oil in a small saucepan over low heat. Do not allow it to boil. Whirl all the remaining ingredients together in a food processor or blender. Add the heated hot olive oil and whirl again.

Toss the pasta with the sauce and, gently, with the chicken, salmon, mushrooms, olives, and escargots. Sprinkle the salmon roe or caviar over the dish and serve immediately.

Arugula and Blood Orange Salad

I like to link a meal together by overlapping the flavors from course to course like small stepping stones set in between larger ones. The orange juice in the mustard sauce above adds an undercurrent of freshness. Probably no one could ever identify it, combined as it is with the zesty taste of green peppercorns, but the link to this salad is there, and it's echoed back again in the peppery mustard flavor of the arugula. If you're lucky, you'll find blood oranges in spring and early summer; if not, use the ordinary navel variety.

(SERVES 6)

> 3 *bunches of young arugula, well rinsed and dried*
> 3 *blood oranges, peeled and sliced*
> 6 *scallions, trimmed and cut into ¼-inch-thick slices*
> *Orange Vinaigrette (page 255)*

Toss all the ingredients together, reserving a few slices of orange and a handful of sliced scallions to decorate the top.

Milk Chocolate Mousse with Fresh Raspberries and Aquavit

Milk chocolate and raspberries are made for each other. Both the red and golden varieties harmonize beautifully with this especially creamy chocolate mousse.

(SERVES 6)

> 4 *1-ounce squares high-quality milk chocolate*
> ½ *cup granulated sugar*
> ⅓ *cup water*
> 4 *egg yolks*
> 2 *tablespoons espresso*
> 1 *cup heavy cream*
> 1 *pint red (or golden) raspberries*
> 4 *tablespoons aquavit*

Melt the chocolate over hot, not boiling, water in the top of a double boiler. Boil the sugar and water together until the mixture is clear and syrupy. Pour the chocolate and the syrup into the bowl of a food processor and whirl together until blended. With the motor running, drop in the egg yolks, one at a time. Whirl in the espresso and pour into a large mixing bowl. Allow the mixture to cool to room temperature.

Whip the cream until it is thick, then fold it into the chocolate. Drop 4 or 5 raspberries into each of 6 pretty individual glasses. Top each with 2 teaspoons aquavit. Spoon mousse over all and arrange berries attractively on the top. Chill at least 4 hours.

A Firecracker Fourth of July!

Hooray for that good old razz-a-ma-tazz, red-white-and-blue holiday Fourth of July! We celebrate every year with a picnic supper at the Hampton home of Anthony Biddle Duke to benefit his Boy's Harbor Foundation. Who could resist the magnificent firework display organized by George Plimpton and executed by the Grucci family, who lit up the skies for the Statue of Liberty extravaganza? Or the explosion of flavors and colors in a far-from-traditional-but-truly-all-American menu like this one? At center stage: the New England Boiled Lobster with sweet herb butter, accompanied by Wisconsin blue cheese spread on California sourdough bread, and Hot Pennsylvania-German Potato Salad (page 211) garnished with ripe olives. For dessert: angel's food cake with blueberries, strawberries, and melty, just-churned vanilla ice cream.

Boiled Lobster

Herewith my rendition of a crustacean so scrumptious it threatens to replace turkey as the great American national dish. (I also adore steamed lobster but cringe at the slow death this method demands.)

Plunge two 3-pound lobsters, head first (to kill them quickly), each into its own pot, in enough boiling sea water to cover (or add 1 tablespoon salt to each quart of tap water). Counting from the time the water returns to a boil, cook the lobsters 14 minutes. (Or cook one-pounders for 8 minutes; two-pounders for 11 minutes.) Remove the lobsters from the water immediately. To serve, turn the lobster on its back, and use a sharp, heavy knife to split it from the head all the way down to the end of the tail. Discard the small, gritty sac at the base of the head and the long black vein that runs from the head to the tail. Pass around clarified sweet butter warmed with minced fresh chives, dill, and tarragon and small dishes of coarse salt.

Sculptor's Studio Supper

On special occasions we entertain in my husband Bill's studio-barn, with his carved sculptures standing among us almost like a second group of guests. Their surfaces reflect the movement of the candle flames, creating a setting that is at once inviting, stimulating . . . and a little intimidating. Something like taking tea at Stonehenge.

It's a good idea, every now and again, to create an atmosphere that makes guests feel a bit off balance. While "cosy and ever so comfortable" is the atmosphere we aspire to in most entertainments, an occasional offbeat background sharpens our senses, causes us to take notice, makes us aware of new surroundings, new people, new foods. Other sorts of unexpected oversize spaces can have this effect: palatial kitchens or intriguing wine cellars, gardeners' potting sheds, cutting rooms or gazebos, hobbyists' machine shops, athletes' gyms, scholars' libraries. The point is this: If you just glance about objectively, you might be surprised to find some fascinating corner under (or nearly under) your own roof that could spark a really special celebration. Elevator party, anyone?

Everything that needs doing to prepare this very pleasant little dinner can be done in advance, with the exception of heating the broth for the soup. The remainder of the meal is served at room temperature. For ultimate simplicity, serve rich, ripe Casaba Melon spiked with Sambuca for dessert.

Menu

Deep-Fried Eggplant Soup with Mint and Dill and Your Own Mascarpone

Turkey Scallopini in Balsamic Vinegar with Arugula and Orange Slices

Casaba Melon with Sambuca

Deep-Fried Eggplant Soup with Mint and Dill

The garnishes for this unusual soup are prepared in advance, then slipped into each bowl of hot soup as you serve. If you have lacquered Chinese bowls on hand, this is the time to use them. The soup may be sipped right from the bowl, with the garnishes captured with chopsticks. Otherwise, any small bowl that is not too deep will do.

(SERVES 8)

1 turkey carcass
14 cups water
4 cloves garlic, peeled
1 large onion, peeled and halved
1 medium-size carrot, scraped and quartered
2 medium-size eggplants, peeled
Salt
4 tablespoons cornstarch
Cooking oil
2 cups minced turkey, thigh meat with no skin or fat included
5 water chestnuts (fresh are best but canned will do), minced
2 cloves garlic, peeled and minced
1 recipe Your Own Mascarpone (see below)
½ cup each minced mint leaves and dill
8 scallions, each with 3 inches of green top, chopped
¼ cup Sesame Seed Powder (see below)
Pepper to taste

Preheat oven to 450 degrees F.

Brown the turkey carcass in the oven for about 45 minutes. Break it into manageable pieces, place in a large pot, and add the water. Bring to just under a boil, and hold at this temperature for 10 minutes, skim, lower the heat, and simmer for 1 hour, skimming as necessary. Add the whole garlic cloves, onion, and carrot, and simmer until reduced to about 10 cups (about 1 hour). Strain the broth.

Meanwhile, cut the eggplants into sticks about 2 inches by ½ inch, sprinkle them with salt, and arrange them between several thicknesses of paper towels to drain for 15 minutes. Toss the eggplant sticks with 2 tablespoons of sifted cornstarch and fry in hot oil 1 inch deep until they are golden on all sides. Place on paper towels to drain.

Mix the minced turkey with the water chestnuts and minced garlic, roll into 1-inch balls, and dust with the remaining cornstarch. Fry in hot oil until lightly browned on all sides. Remove with a slotted spoon and set aside on paper towels to drain.

Roll the mascarpone cheese into 1-inch balls. Sprinkle the mint and dill on waxed paper or plastic wrap, and roll the balls in this mixture to cover them.

To serve, arrange bowls of chopped scallion, turkey balls, fried eggplant, cheese nuggets, and Sesame Seed Powder in a semicircle in front of you. Ladle the hot broth into the soup bowls, and add some of each garnish, sprinkle with Sesame Seed Powder and pepper to taste.

127

Sesame Seed Powder

(YIELD: ABOUT ¾ CUP)

>   1½ *cups white sesame seeds*
>   2 *teaspoons salt*

Rinse the seeds under running water and place them in a heavy skillet. Stir over low heat for 3–4 minutes or until plumped and lightly browned. Toss the seeds with the salt and pulverize to a fine powder in a blender, or use a mortar and pestle.

Your Own Mascarpone

A little sweet, a little sour, very creamy. You'll most likely use only half of this wonderful cheese for the Deep-Fried Eggplant Soup above, but it is so special you'll be happy to have extra on hand. If you like, serve it with drinks, along with a bowl of nice oily black olives and a rich dark bread.

(YIELD: 1¼ POUNDS)

>   1 *pound cream cheese*
>   ½ *cup ricotta cheese*
>   2 *tablespoons sour cream*
>   2 *tablespoons heavy cream*
>   1 *tablespoon each sugar and fresh-squeezed lemon juice*

Whirl all the ingredients in a food processor or blender until they are thoroughly mixed and very smooth. Place the cheese in a plastic container with a cover or wrap in several thicknesses of plastic wrap. Refrigerate. The cheese will keep for 6–7 days.

Turkey Scallopini in Balsamic Vinegar with Arugula and Orange Slices

On a trip to Maryland a friend presented us with two small, breasty turkeys, one of which became the star of an informal but far from ordinary dinner. The white meat was boned and skinned, cut into thin slices across the grain, and pounded lightly to flatten and thin it. Finally, the turkey slices were marinated in wine and robust balsamic vinegar to tenderize and flavor them, dipped in egg and then in fine bread crumbs, and lastly, sautéed in olive oil. The scallopini were delicious served at room temperature over a tangle of arugula leaves dressed with olive oil and topped with orange slices and raisins macerated in Cointreau.

No other vinegar is really an adequate substitute for the sweet, musky flavor of balsamic vinegar. A high-quality light red wine vinegar seems to come closest. Similarly, for an arugula fanatic, there is no green that has half the sass or hint of mustard that this one has. Substitute watercress or fresh spinach only if arugula is nowhere to be found.

(SERVES 8)

8 slices turkey breast, boned, skinned, and ¼ inch thick (cut across the grain), placed between sheets of plastic wrap and lightly pounded with a rolling pin

½ cup each balsamic vinegar and white wine

4 navel oranges, peeled with a sharp knife to remove all pith and membranes

½ cup golden seedless raisins

3 tablespoons Cointreau or Grand Marnier

1 handful arugula leaves per guest

2 eggs

1 teaspoon salt

2 teaspoons water

2 cups fine, white, dry bread crumbs

Nice, fruity olive oil

Squeeze of fresh orange juice

Salt and coarsely ground black pepper to taste

Arrange the turkey slices, without overlapping them, in 1 or 2 flat glass dishes, and pour the vinegar and wine over them. Refrigerate overnight, turning once. Cut the oranges into slices ¼ inch thick, place them in a flat bowl with the raisins, pour the Cointreau or Grand Marnier over them, and refrigerate overnight.

Pick over the arugula, discard any tough stems, then wash and drain the leaves. Wrap in paper towels and refrigerate.

Beat the eggs with the 1 teaspoon of salt and then with the 2 teaspoons of water. Spread the bread crumbs on paper towels. Dip the turkey slices first in egg and then in crumbs. (The scallopini actually benefit from exposure to the air for a few hours at this point— covered lightly with paper towels and kept in a cool, dry place.) Anywhere from 3 hours to 30 minutes prior to serving, fry the scallopini in hot olive oil until nicely browned on both sides. Drain on paper towels.

Toss the arugula with 2 tablespoons of fruity olive oil and a squeeze of fresh orange juice, and divide evenly on 8 plates or a platter. Season to taste with salt and freshly ground black pepper. Top with the turkey scallopini. Drain the orange slices and raisins, and use to garnish. Serve at room temperature.

Casaba Melon with Sambuca

Peel the surface and underskin from a ripe casaba melon and discard its seeds. Cut the melon into lengthwise slices ½ inch thick and arrange these in a dish. Sprinkle Sambuca over all and refrigerate for about 2 hours. Serve cold in the shape of a rose.

Torchlight Picnic

This is an elegant dinner where tag-sale-variety Oriental rugs, plushy pillows, potted plants, torches, and baskets of wonderful food transform an outdoor dinner into a kind of Arabian Nights extravaganza centered around a beach fire, patio fireplace, or grill.

A first course of Curry-Marinated Mussels in the Shell and/or Corn-off-the-Cob and Crab Chowder fills the gap while the fire crackles along on its way to becoming glowing embers, the necessary state for pan-frying or grilling individual small whole fish stuffed with wild rice, bulgur, and pistachios.

Guests are provided with splashy china, silver, and glassware, plus plenty of napkins for tidying up if they resort to finger-pickin' the fish down to the bones. Also on hand are individual baskets or see-through hampers filled with additional accompaniments for each guest: crunchy Endives with Sun-Dried Tomato Chutney Dressing, Gooseberry-Pecan Tarts, fruit, cheese, and thermos bottles of Iced Almond Coffee.

Menu

Curry-Marinated Mussels in the Shell

Corn-off-the-Cob and Crab Chowder

Pan-Fried or Grilled Butterfish

Wild Rice, Bulgur, and Pistachio Stuffing

Endives with Sun-Dried Tomato Chutney Dressing

Gooseberry-Pecan Tarts

Iced Almond Coffee

Apricots and Almonds in Rosewater-Flavored Nectar

Curry-Marinated Mussels in the Shell

Once steamed, mussels open their sleek, steel-blue wings like armor-clad butterflies. It's this beauty that adds another dimension to their tender texture and pleasant taste. How much more appetizing, then, to serve the marinated mussels in their lovely violet-lined, purple-black shells! Figure six per person if you are offering chowder in addition to mussels (a nice touch if the evening is on the damp or cool side); otherwise, prepare ten to twelve, or one pound, for each guest. If you can't locate plump, three inchers, don't bother. Go with the chowder alone.

Purchase or gather your mussels a day in advance and let them stand overnight in fresh, cool, salted water to avoid any sand and to freshen their flavor. Change the water several times. Use a stiff brush to scrub the mussels in cold water, discarding any that do not close tightly when you press them between your thumb and forefinger or any that feel abnormally heavy (these may be filled with mud or sand). Pull off the little beards that dribble from the hinge end.

(SERVES 10 TO 12)

> *3 cups each dry white wine and water*
> *10 small white whole onions, peeled*
> *1–3 sprigs of parsley and thyme*
> *Small bay leaf*
> *10 pounds large, plump mussels, well scrubbed and debearded*
> *1 cup each wine vinegar and light olive oil*
> *1 teaspoon light, mild curry powder*

Place the wine, water, onions, parsley, thyme, and bay leaf in a large kettle, and bring to a boil over high heat. Add the mussels, cover, and boil until the shells open, adding a little more wine and/or water, if necessary. Discard any mussels that do not open after 7 or 8 minutes. When they are cool enough to handle, transfer the onions and mussels to a large, flat dish. Take care not to dislodge the meats from the shells—if any have fallen out, slip them back into an empty shell. Let the broth settle, then strain it off without including any of the sand, and reserve for use in the following recipe.

Whirl the vinegar, oil, and curry in a food processor (or shake them together in a jar) until well mixed. Spoon this vinaigrette sauce over the mussels and onions, and refrigerate. When you pack for your picnic, cover the dish and take it as is, or transfer ingredients to a see-through box or dish with a top, without separating the mussels from their shells. Serve with drinks.

Corn-off-the-Cob and Crab Chowder

Silver Queen Corn, with its rows of seed-pearl kernels, pairs perfectly with the fragile tenderness of crab. The broth from the marinated mussels reduces to a winey base that is further enhanced by the corn-milk scraped into it from the cut cobs. When it's available (not often enough), goat's milk, with a little of its cream, is absolute perfection stirred into this, but store-bought half-and-half smooths the soup nicely, too.

(SERVES 12)

3 tablespoons sweet butter

1 large Vidalia or Texas sweet onion (or other sweet, white onion), coarsely chopped

2 ribs celery, minced

3 cups mussel cooking broth (see recipe above); if you have more, substitute it for an equal amount of the clam broth listed below (if you have not included the mussels use 7 cups clam juice and omit the water)

2 cups each water and clam juice (bottled will do)

½ cup minced parsley

10 ears Silver Queen corn, husked, de-silked, the kernels cut from the cobs, and the milk scraped into a small bowl

2 cups milk

2 cups half-and-half or goat's milk, if available

4 cups crabmeat, picked over

¼ cup each small, tender leaves of basil and thyme

Cayenne and freshly ground black pepper to taste

Melt the butter in a large pot and sauté the onion and celery until the onion is transparent. Add the mussel cooking broth, water, clam juice, and parsley, and bring to a boil. Turn the heat to low and cook for 15 minutes. Add the corn and corn milk, and simmer for 5 minutes. Add the milk, half-and-half or goat's milk, and crabmeat. Pour the hot soup into a large thermos or plan to reheat it over the campfire or grill. Serve in bowls or mugs garnished with the herbs, seasonings, and extra pats of butter.

Pan-Fried or Grilled Butterfish (or other small whole fish)

As wonderful as small whole fish taste when they're cooked indoors, they are even more irresistible sizzled over a live fire in the open air. The combined aromas of wood fire and sizzling butterfish are nearly enough to drive hungry picnickers mad. Put your guests to work arranging pillows and plants for your picnic environment, while you choose an upwind fire site that won't envelop your party in smoke. It's important to prepare the fire just as soon as you arrive, especially if you will be warming the chowder over the flames while you're waiting for the coals to burn down and glow intensely enough to provide the steady heat needed for the fish. In the meanwhile, pass the mussels and a white wine sturdy enough to hold its own with the curry vinaigrette, yet pliant enough not to overwhelm the delicacy of the crab chowder.

(SERVES 12)

> 12 *butterfish, snappers, or other whole small fish, cleaned and scaled*
> *Salt and freshly ground szechwan pepper*
> *1 recipe Wild Rice, Bulgur, and Pistachio Stuffing (see below)*
> *1 cup all-purpose flour*
> *3 eggs, beaten*
> *Crackers, coarsely crushed*
> *Equal parts of butter and oil for frying*

If you catch the fish yourself, be sure to clean and scale them immediately and put them on ice. If you buy your fish, have them scaled and cleaned (this includes removing the gills). Before you leave home, rinse the fish inside and out, dry them well, then rub them inside and out with salt and pepper, fill them with the rice stuffing, and chill them well. I've learned not to overstuff these fish and to handle them with care, so I don't usually sew or skewer them shut; if you're unsure, however, use either of these procedures to keep the filling from falling out during cooking. The less you have to do at the picnic site, the greater the likelihood that you'll enjoy yourself, so I suggest that in the convenience of your own kitchen you dust each fish with flour and dip it in the beaten egg and then in the cracker crumbs. Arrange the fish on trays covered with plastic wrap and leave them for about 15 minutes while the coating sets. Carefully turn them over without breaking the crusts, and refrigerate them, uncovered.

When it's time to pack for the picnic, cover the fish with additional plastic wrap and transport them to the site without stacking anything on top of them or jouncing them in any way. A large, clear plastic box with a lid makes this easy. As soon as the coals are ready, heat the butter and oil to sizzling in 2 skillets large enough to hold the fish without overlapping. Fry them for 8–10 minutes per inch of thickness (measured at the thickest part of the fish) or until golden brown on both sides, turning them once about halfway through the cooking time. Handle the fish gently at all times so as not to break the crispy crusts, and serve on plates. Let the guests unwrap the filled endive (recipe below) and serve themselves this and the remainder of the meal from their individual hampers.

Note: If you wish to grill the fish, you need only to dust them with flour and brush them with melted butter. Place them in well-greased, hinged wire baskets and broil them about 4 inches from the coals for 8–10 minutes per inch of thickness or until they are golden brown on both sides. Baste the fish frequently with additional melted butter.

Wild Rice, Bulgur, and Pistachio Stuffing

Fish crunch inside and out when they're filled with this splendid, textured stuffing.

(MAKES ABOUT 5 CUPS)

4 *tablespoons butter*
1 *large onion, peeled and minced*
1 *cup coarsely chopped mushrooms*
1 *cup wild rice*
3½ *cups light fish stock*
1 *cup bulgur*
1 *cup sour cream*
½ *cup heavy cream*
½ *cup pistachio nuts, shelled*
½ *cup coarsely chopped pistachio nuts*
¼ *cup minced parsley*

Melt half the butter in a large, heavy saucepan. Add the onion and mushrooms and sauté, stirring frequently, until the onion is transparent. Stir in the wild rice and 2 cups of the stock, and bring to a boil. Cover and simmer, without stirring, for about 50 minutes or until it is just tender and the stock has been absorbed. Do not overcook.

Meanwhile, melt the remaining butter in a large skillet. Stir in the bulgur and the remaining 1½ cups of stock, and bring the mixture to a boil over medium heat. Cover and cook over low heat for 10 minutes. Remove from the heat and let stand for 15 minutes more.

Mix the sour cream with the heavy cream, then mix all the ingredients together. Let the stuffing cool to room temperature, then cover and refrigerate until needed.

Endives with Sun-Dried Tomato Chutney Dressing

If the hard-to-find, finger-length endives are available at your local supermarket or green-grocer, these are the ones to snap up. If not, the more familiar longer and thicker variety will do.

(SERVES 12)

12 *finger-size endives or 6 larger endives*
½ *cup Sun-Dried Tomato Chutney (page 258), finely chopped*
¼ *cup each walnut oil and safflower oil*
2 *tablespoons red wine vinegar*

Rinse the endives and drain them upside-down in a dish rack for a few minutes. Pat them dry with paper towels and refrigerate them. Shake the chutney, the oils, and the vinegar together in a jar to mix them. If you're using small endives, spread open the leaves of each slightly and drizzle a little of the chutney dressing down into each. If you're using larger endives, split them lengthwise, remove 1 or 2 of the center leaves, and spoon a little dressing into the base of the leaves and also into the centers. Put the 2 halves back together and wrap the endives (large or small) in plastic wrap. Refrigerate for a day, or even two, until the last minute before you pack the picnic.

Gooseberry-Pecan Tarts

When a friend's gooseberry bushes are overly bountiful, I inherit part of that lovely excess. First I whip up a Gooseberry Fool and immediately thereafter bake Gooseberry-Pecan Tarts. These two dishes may seem an odd couple, but they coexist beautifully in this updated version of an English housewife's recipe strongly influenced, obviously, by her move to the colonies.

(MAKES 12 TARTS)

> 1 *recipe Double-Crust Pie Pastry (page 258)*
> 4 *tablespoons granulated sugar*
> 3 *cups corn syrup*
> 6 *tablespoons all-purpose flour*
> 7 *eggs, beaten*
> 1 *teaspoon salt*
> 2½ *teaspoons vanilla extract*
> 3 *tablespoons butter, melted*
> 1 *cup roughly chopped pecans*
> 2 *cups gooseberries, stems removed, or ripe peaches, peeled and sliced*
> 12 *heaping teaspoons light-brown sugar*

Prepare the pastry and roll it out into circles 1 inch larger than your small tart pans. Press into 12 (3-inch) tart pans. Crimp the edges of the pastry shells and refrigerate.

Preheat oven to 375 degrees F.

Mix the granulated sugar, corn syrup, and flour in a food processor or by hand. Add the eggs, salt, vanilla, and melted butter, and mix well again. Divide the filling among the tart shells. Sprinkle equal amounts of the chopped nuts and gooseberries over the top of the filling. Top each tart with a teaspoon of brown sugar. Arrange the tart shells on a baking sheet and place in the preheated oven. Immediately turn the heat to 350 degrees F. and bake the tarts for 20–30 minutes or until the centers are set but not firm. Cool the tarts to room temperature and then chill them well so the centers do not become too soft if the day is hot. By the time you devour them the texture should be just right.

Iced Almond Coffee

Begin with a really potent brew of good black coffee, then flavor it with ground almonds and a cinnamon stick. You can use Amaretto—it's easier, to be sure—but the effect here is more subtle. This drink is extremely refreshing. Bring crushed ice or cubes in a wide-mouthed cooler jar. Crushed is by far the best.

(SERVES 12)

> 12 *cups good strong hot coffee*
> ¾ *cup ground almonds*
> 1 *generous-size cinnamon stick*
> *Crushed ice*

138

Steep the coffee, almonds, and cinnamon stick until the coffee reaches room temperature. Pour the coffee through a strainer lined with 3 or 4 thicknesses of cheesecloth. Remove the cloth from the strainer and squeeze it over the coffee, without letting any almonds fall into it. Chill well. Serve over crushed ice.

Apricots and Almonds in Rosewater-Flavored Nectar

Make an effort to find rosewater in your gourmet food outlet. It lends intriguing aroma and flavor, the very essence of the East. If you can't locate it, however, you may want to extend the influence of the almonds by substituting Amaretto.

(SERVES 8)

> 2 *pounds fancy dried apricots; those from the Near East are best*
> 1 *quart apricot nectar*
> 1 *cup freshly squeezed orange juice, strained*
> 2 *teaspoons rosewater, or 2 tablespoons Amaretto*
> ¾ *cup whole blanched almonds*

Rinse the apricots, drain them well, and place them in a glass serving bowl. Stir in the remaining ingredients and refrigerate for 2–3 days. Serve very cold.

Japanese Poolside Party

Raw fish is the ultimate diet dish, low in calories and cholesterol, cool, clean, and classy. At the shore or wherever *really* fresh saltwater fish or shellfish are available, it's easy enough to prepare your own. Just be sure you buy the best boneless, skinless filets that are exquisitely fresh and deeply chilled but not frozen. There are dozens of complicated shapes and sizes into which these may be cut, but the general rule is to use a razor-sharp knife to cut firm fish, such as tuna or salmon, into 1½-inch-wide pieces, then cut across at a slight slant to form bite-size pieces. Cut moist, tender fish, such as flounder, into nearly transparent flat slices about 2 inches by 1 inch.

Sushi and sashimi are to me the ne plus ultra of poolside hors d'oeuvres. Most Japanese restaurants that have sushi bars will neatly package a variety of their creations for you to quickly transport to the coldest corner of your refrigerator, there to await your guests.

An Unusual Sashimi Dipping Sauce

(MAKES 1 CUP)

> 1 *teaspoon wasabi (horseradish) powder (available in oriental groceries and specialty-food shops)*
> *Water*
> 1 *cup soy sauce*
> 1 *teaspoon grated fresh ginger*
> 1 *teaspoon sesame oil*

Mix wasabi with water to make a thick paste. Work in all the remaining ingredients.

Autumn

Scallops on Sunday

The brilliant Autumn air masses that sweep down from Canada through the bristling Pennsylvania pine forests rake, comb, strain, and crisp each breath we breathe here on the chill salt flats of Long Island. The stiffening breezes hone our appetites "right smart," too, and inspire us to reach for our stew pans and call a friend or two to celebrate.

Scallops can be plain or fancy, grace a fisherman's chowder or lend their opaque opulence to the dressiest Sunday sit-down. Whether paired with lusty potato, leek, and fish fumet and set forth in a chipped ironstone soup plate, or swathed in saffron, cradled in tender Buttercrunch lettuce baskets, and displayed in Tiffany's finest, scallops are sublime.

It's hard to imagine a less troublesome, more cushy meal than this one. True, the scallops in their baskets must be prepared immediately before serving, and true, thereafter someone must assist you in carrying these to the table posthaste, but the remainder of the feast practically prepares itself days in advance of your party.

No salad course is necessary with this meal since the entrée includes whole heads of lettuce. The dessert acknowledges early autumn's lingering backward glance—a parfait of late summer blueberries and peaches. It is elegant and almost embarrassingly easy. Forgotten Cookies are meringue-based pecan nibbles for which I am indebted to my friend, Louisiana-born Ernestine Lassaw. To make sure you have enough, you have to make hundreds. For best results, prepare them on a dry day and keep them in an airtight container.

144

TABLEWARE, TIFFANY AND CO., NY, NY

Menu
Baked Red, Green, and Yellow Tomato Soup with Blue Cheese Nuggets
Scallops in Saffron Butter Wrapped in Buttercrunch Baskets
Blueberry Peach Parfait
Forgotten Cookies

Baked Red, Green, and Yellow Tomato Soup

The fortuitous coinciding of tomato and scallop seasons proves once again that Mother Nature may not be daft after all. A more fitting union can scarcely be imagined than scallops preceded by a naturally thickened soup of just-picked red and green tomatoes, baked first to concentrate their natural sweetness. A minute or two prior to serving, heat the soup to steaming and finish it with ripe golden tomatoes cut in cubes. Slip a melty fried blue cheese nugget into each bowl, or serve them as a side dish to be eaten with the soup.

(SERVES 8)

> 5 *each medium-size red and green tomatoes, seeded and cut in eighths*
> 1 *large leek, white part only, split, thoroughly washed, and cut into*
>   *1-inch slices*
> 4–6 *large cloves garlic (depending upon your lust)*
> 2 *tablespoons light olive oil*
> 1 *tablespoon confectioners' sugar*
> *Leaves of fresh rosemary, thyme, and parsley*
> *Rich Fish Stock (page 256)*
> *Salt and white pepper to taste*
> 4 *cups seeded, coarsely chopped golden tomatoes*
> 1 *recipe Blue Cheese Nuggets (see below)*

Preheat oven to 375 degrees F.

Arrange the red and green tomatoes, leek slices, and unpeeled garlic cloves in an oiled large, flat baking dish with 2-inch-high sides. The vegetables should not overlap. Sprinkle the tomatoes with the sugar.

Bake in the preheated oven for 20 minutes or until the tops of the red tomato wedges look slightly dry and dark red.

Use your fingers to squeeze the garlic pulp from the skins and into a food processor or blender. Discard the skins. Add the herbs and baked vegetables with their juices and coarsely puree them. Do not overprocess—it's nice to have a bit of "tooth" to the soup base.

Measure the tomato mixture into an enamel or stainless-steel soup kettle, and add enough stock to make a total of 10 cups. Add the seasonings and set aside until ready to serve. The soup can be made in advance and kept for a day or two in the refrigerator.

To serve the soup, heat to steaming, adjust the seasonings, and ladle into bowls. At table, add the golden tomatoes and the cheese nuggets.

Blue Cheese Nuggets

The reason that those creamy blue cheeses are sparking passion among food aficionados becomes clear with the first bite of these melty, golden fritters. If anything, heating heightens their distinctive, nutty, slightly tart silkiness. These nuggets are at their finest prepared directly before serving.

(SERVES 8)

12 ounces Blue Costello cheese, cut in 2½-inch-thick slices
2 small eggs
1 sprinkle each of nutmeg and cayenne
1–2 blades fresh mace, or a sprinkle of dried
1 cup each fine dry bread crumbs made from crustless white bread and minced
 pecans
Oil for deep frying

Chill the cheese and cut it into squares 2 inches by 2 inches by ½ inch thick. Beat the eggs with the seasonings. Dip the cheese squares in the egg mixture and press them into the mixed bread crumbs and pecans and refrigerate. Fry the squares until golden in hot oil to cover. Serve immediately.

Scallops in Saffron Butter Wrapped in Buttercrunch Baskets

Lettuce is only occasionally presented as a warm vegetable, and even then it's often limp and lacking in the tender crispness and flavor the fresh green possesses in such abundance. Here, whole young heads of Buttercrunch are washed, thinned of their curly centers, filled with scallops, and then slipped under the broiler, not to sizzle them but merely to slightly relax their leaves. The hot saffron sauce cooks the bottoms just enough to mellow them but not to diminish their crunch.

I generally figure on ½ pint of scallops per person, though this is not an overly generous portion to satisfy a hearty appetite.

And yes, I do know saffron is more pricey than platinum, but it is also one of the seven wonders of the culinary world. Use it even if you have to sell the Rolls to pay for it. If you've already sold the Rolls, you could substitute a really pungent white curry powder for the saffron, but the dish won't be the same. Besides, a relatively tiny amount is used.

> *8 compact young heads Buttercrunch or Boston lettuce. Choose firm heads with*
> *leaves that are fat right down to the root; thin, leggy leaves with skinny,*
> *attenuated stems will not work here—beware of the hydroponically grown*
> *kind for this reason*
> *½ cup peeled and minced shallots*
> *4 tablespoons sweet butter*
> *Very generous pinch each of saffron threads and cayenne pepper*
> *1 cup dry white wine*
> *4 cups Rich Fish Stock (page 256)*
> *2 teaspoons arrowroot*
> *Salt and white pepper to taste*
> *2 cups heavy cream*
> *2 quarts bay scallops, lightly rinsed, picked over, and drained*
> *4 cups cooked rice (optional)*

147

Rinse the lettuce heads gently to remove soil and pinch out the small center leaves so that the heads form baskets large enough to hold about 1 cup of scallops and sauce. Don't get carried away and remove too many leaves—you can always take out more, but it's difficult to attach them again. Trim the thick bottom stems so that the heads stand evenly. Wrap each lettuce carefully in paper towels to maintain its basket shape. Refrigerate.

In a large, heavy skillet, sauté the shallots in 2 tablespoons of the butter until golden —do not let them brown. Stir in the saffron and cayenne, and sauté 1 minute. Add the wine and fish stock, and cook over medium heat until the liquid is reduced to 2 cups. If you wish, the recipe can be prepared in advance to this point and refrigerated until needed.

Just prior to your guests' arrival, mix the arrowroot and salt and pepper to taste into the cream, add it to the reduced stock, and cook over medium heat, stirring occasionally, until the sauce is nicely thickened—a little thicker than you ultimately want it to be; the scallops will ooze some additional liquid as they cook. Cover and let stand in a cool place until just before you serve the soup.

In another skillet, sauté the scallops in the remaining 2 tablespoons of butter for 1–2 minutes. Pour in the sauce, heat to steaming, and adjust the seasonings.

Preheat the broiler.

Arrange the lettuce baskets in individual broiler-proof dishes just large enough to hold the heads. If the dishes are too large, the heads will fall over and the sauce won't be deep enough to partially cook the stems. If your dishes are a little small but don't crush the lettuce too much, they will probably do.

If you wish, place several spoonfuls of hot rice in the bottom of each lettuce basket, top with equal portions of scallops and sauce, and put the dishes on a baking sheet (with sides). Slide under the preheated broiler for a few seconds or only until the lettuce leaves warm a little bit and relax ever so slightly. Serve immediately.

Blueberry Peach Parfait

4 large, ripe peaches, peeled, pitted, and thinly sliced
2 tablespoons each light brown sugar and rum
A pinch of ground nutmeg
2 cups blueberries with stems removed
3 tablespoons each granulated sugar and orange juice
1 quart vanilla ice cream
Whipped cream (optional)

Bring the peaches, brown sugar, and rum to a boil in a small, heavy saucepan; then lower the heat and cook at a low boil, stirring constantly, until the juices are syrupy. Add the nutmeg. In another small, heavy saucepan, cook the blueberries, granulated sugar, and orange juice at a low boil, stirring constantly, until the juices cook away. Chill the two pots of cooked fruit.

Beginning with the peaches, layer the fruits alternately with the ice cream in parfait glasses (as shown) and top with dollops of whipped cream if desired. Serve immediately or freeze the parfaits until time to serve.

Forgotten Cookies

To make sure these little beauties are crisp rather than moist, bake them on a dry day, remove them from the oven as directed, and store them immediately.

(MAKES ABOUT 50)

2 egg whites
2/3 cup granulated sugar
1 teaspoon vanilla
1 cup broken pecans
1 6-ounce package sweet chocolate bits

Preheat oven to 350 degrees F.

Whip the egg whites until they begin to stiffen, then beat in the sugar a little at a time until the meringue is stiff and glossy. Fold in the vanilla, pecans, and chocolate bits.

Line a baking sheet with aluminum foil, shiny side up. Drop the meringue onto the sheet a teaspoonful at a time, leaving about 2 inches in between each cookie. Place in the oven, turn off the heat, and forget about them for 4 hours or overnight. Remove from the foil and store in an airtight container.

The Joy of Afternoon Tea

Tea time. How I love it! From the weak, milky brew I sloshed into dolly's tea cups eons ago, to the molten dynamite I poured from a precious 1770's silver tea service beside the pool at our Caribbean hideaway, nothing takes the place of tea for me. Just the thought of this civilized ritual unfrazzles my nerves and sets even the most frantic day in order. For some time I felt alone with my tea mania while the rest of the country guzzled coffee, but recently the rage for tea has influenced many American hotels to offer a revitalizing afternoon cuppa. Even business executives now occasionally offer a nice little tea with bread and butter, croissants, and cookies, rather than the usual coffee break. Bridal showers and children's birthday parties have become the newest candidates for the niceties of afternoon tea. Something about tea time seems to inspire the most exquisite attention to detail. Gifts and little girls arrive wrapped in the finest.

The rules for a really fine tea are quite simple. A silver pot is most impressive, but unless you're serving a crowd, I think small china pots brew the best-flavored tea that gets used up quickly. Tea that is steeped too long will become bitter— bitter and strong are not at all the same thing. Most appropriate are loose teas that complement sweets, such as Darjeeling, Oolong, Earl Grey, Irish Breakfast, English Breakfast, and my favorite, Indian Breakfast. For a nice change of pace serve an unusual herb tea in a tea set from the twenties as shown here. Spoon in one heaping teaspoon of loose tea per cup, add steaming hot water, and steep for five minutes. Pour the tea through a pierced strainer into each cup. For those who like pallid tea, allow enough room so that near-boiling water from a water jug or second pot can be added. Offer milk or slim, seedless wedges of lemon.

Aïoli
Monstre

On one of those shimmering August afternoons in Provence, with the sun burnishing every cobble-stone, every church cross, every leaf, we happened upon the final day of an annual fête that honored a village's patron saint. The central square was choked with celebrants—children and parents, priests and widows, friends and strangers—all jostling amia-bly, drinking glasses of blush-rose wine, joyously devouring Aïoli Monstre.

The feast, already in progress, centered around huge mortars of aïoli, creamy, golden mayonnaise redolent of garlic, served surrounded by platters of salt cod, snails, hard-cooked eggs, fresh and steamed vegetables ready for dipping, and crusty, fresh-baked French bread. Later on there was dancing and echoing laughter as villagers and their guests called their good nights across the moonlit streets.

An aïoli monstre is perfect in late summer or very early fall. To treat your friends to a relaxed cocktail or buffet party featuring this traditional dish of Provence, you might want to include a few innovations that work very well for me. Rather than the raw power of traditional aïoli, I use garlic baked in its papery skins. The marvelous flavor is still there, but the brassiness of uncooked garlic is somewhat muted. Directions are given for both versions.

Here, Five-Herb Peasant Bread, baked as one monstrous loaf, then partially cut into forty or more small slices, is much more serviceable than many smaller loaves. The texture is pleasantly coarse and the crust crisp.

For small aïoli parties I like to serve a light red Bellet. It possesses, to my taste, the perfect color and character to stand up to this show-off of a sauce. At larger parties—thirty or more—served in the heat of day, I substitute a nice reasonably priced dry rosé with buckets and buckets of ice to help diminish the effects of sun and alcohol. At parties like this one the wine should flow generously.

It's practical and pleasant to include plenty of hard-cooked eggs and a wheel or two of mellow cheese with this if you intend for your party to go on and on.

In any case, Aïoli Monstre expands with great ease to accommodate large numbers of guests.

Putting the Party Together

This is a great party for a warm autumn afternoon. It's strictly a dip-and-drip entertainment best served on the patio or terrace rather than on your prized Oriental floor-covering. The Aïoli, in its large mortar, stands in the star spot and should be highlighted accordingly. Create a dramatic backdrop of autumn leaves in combination with your favorite collectibles, or literally place it on a pedestal (I've used a low, black-marble sculpture base for this with stunning effect).

To serve an overflow crowd, surround the Aïoli with platters of vegetables arranged in attractive combinations—perhaps have the whole broccoli and cauliflower heads in the centers with the miniature or flash-cooked vegetables around them.

Arrange the cod on one platter, the remaining seafood on a second, and the meat on a third. Place these on either side of the vegetables with a bowl of peeled hard-boiled eggs and a sliced loaf of bread on either end of the table. The cheese, with additional bread, should have its own table, preferably near where the wine is served.

For a relatively small group, all the food will probably fit on one table. It might be a good idea to get the party off to a fast start by arranging a few individual plates ahead of time so that the guests will know how to proceed.

Menu

Aïoli

Miniature Vegetables: Uncooked Turnips, Zucchini, Celery, Carrots, Scallions, Endives, and Cherry Tomatoes

Flash-Cooked Vegetables: Slender Blue Lake Beans, Green Beans, Asparagus, and Tiny Ears of Corn

Steamed Vegetables: Broccoli, Cauliflower, and Miniature Red Potatoes

Seafood

Chicken and Sliced Lamb

Hard-Cooked Eggs

Five-Herb Peasant Bread

Aïoli

Traditionally, the most difficult aspect of a party featuring this monster aïoli was—you guessed it—preparing the title dish, the distinctive garlic-laced mayonnaise. For the contemporary home cook without a food processor it would be nearly unthinkable. *With* a processor it is not only thinkable, it is easily do-able. Authentic, mortar-and-pestle-made aïoli is slightly lighter, fluffier than its processor counterpart, but in the flush of party madness, drinking up the wine of human contact, the lack of this subtlety won't be noticed.

It is important to have all the ingredients for your aïoli at room temperature and not attempt to produce a large amount of sauce at one whirl. For a really big bash, prepare four or five batches in the days prior to your party. As you make each batch, stabilize it with a bit of boiling water to keep for nearly a week. I prefer this sauce prepared with prebaked garlic, but you might like raw. Try both ways and decide for yourself.

The recipes below are calculated to serve ten (the minimum number to do this feast justice), and so may be easily multiplied by five or ten, to entertain fifty, one hundred, two hundred, or any number in between.

(SERVES 10)

1 large whole egg
3 egg yolks
Olive oil
4 large cloves baked garlic or 3 large cloves raw (see note)
½ teaspoon salt
Salt to taste
Freshly ground white pepper
Lemon juice

Use the steel cutting blade of a food processor to beat the whole egg until it is pale yellow. With the blade still whirling, drop in the egg yolks 1 at a time. Process until smooth and creamy, then begin to whirl in the olive oil, a few drops at a time, until the mixture resembles a thin mayonnaise.

If you are using raw garlic, crush the cloves with the flat side of a knife, discard the skins, and drop into the feed tube while the motor is still running. If using baked garlic cloves, squeeze them with your fingers (as you would a tube of toothpaste) so that the pulp emerges from the skin and falls into the processor bowl. Discard the skins.

Add the salt and continue to add the oil in a thin, steady stream until the mayonnaise thickens enough to hold a spoon upright. Whirl in more salt, pepper, and lemon juice to taste and, if the sauce is not to be used within a few hours, add a teaspoon of boiling water. Cover tightly and refrigerate.

Note: To bake a whole head of garlic, wrap it in several layers of aluminum foil, without peeling or separating its cloves, and bake at 325 degrees F. for 45–60 minutes or until the cloves feel very soft when you pinch them between your fingers. If the weather is too sizzling hot to light the oven, separate the cloves and sauté them, unpeeled, in a little olive oil until they are very soft.

Miniature Vegetables

This party is the ideal setting for an exquisite collection of miniature vegetables. With their tender flesh and convenient size, these are perfect cocktail fare. Whenever possible, merely wipe these with a damp cloth and present them in their virgin state, with stems, leaves, and even roots intact. Vegetables that require cooking should be flash-cooked or steamed to preserve their beauty and nutrition. Set these out whole, beautifully arranged in groups on platters, or on individual plates, with knives placed close by so that guests may cut their own portions.

154

(SERVES 10)

> 10 *each tiny whole turnips, zucchini, celery, carrots, scallions, endives, and*
> *cherry tomatoes, rinsed, dried, scraped and/or trimmed where necessary*

Any of the above, with the exception of the tomatoes, may also be flash-cooked or steamed. Arrange as part of Aïoli Monstre.

Flash-Cooked Vegetables

(SERVES 10)

> 15 *each young, slender Blue Lake beans, green beans, and asparagus*
> 10 *miniature ears corn, husked*
> *Salted water*

Rinse the vegetables and trim appropriately. Bring a large pot of salted water to a boil. Arrange the vegetables in a wire basket, 1 variety at a time, then plunge them into the boiling water, cover the pot, and allow the water to return to a boil over high heat. Cook until slightly underdone—the vegetables should retain a bit of crunch but should not be hard and chewy. Drain, run under cold water, and drain again. Arrange as part of Aïoli Monstre.

Steamed Vegetables

(SERVES 10)

> 1 *head broccoli, thick bottom stems evenly trimmed just below point where florets*
> *come together*
> 1 *head cauliflower, leaves removed and thick bottom stem evenly trimmed*
> 10 *tiny red potatoes*
> 10 *each red and golden beets, if possible*

Rinse and trim the vegetables. Arrange them in a vegetable steamer (or place in a colander over hot water), cover, and steam until the centers of the vegetables may be pierced with a fork. The potatoes and beets may be steamed together. Leave the skins on the potatoes but slip off the beet skins. Serve these vegetables whole. Cut the broccoli and cauliflower into bite-size florets. Arrange as part of Aïoli Monstre.

Seafood

(SERVES 10)

> 10 shrimp, unpeeled
> 2 3-pound lobsters
> 10 scallops
> Butter
> 10 escargots (canned)
> 2 pounds fresh center filet of cod

Plunge the shrimp into boiling salted water and cook only until they turn bright red-orange (2–3 minutes). Drain and cool. Serve in the shell.

Plunge the lobsters headfirst into a large pot of boiling water, cover, return to a boil, then lower the heat and simmer for 12–15 minutes. The lobster shells should be bright red. Drain and cool. Remove the tail and claw meat, chill it well, then cut the tails into slices ⅓ inch thick. (This would be a wonderful opportunity to prepare and refrigerate some Lobster Butter [page 252] for another meal utilizing the lobster shells and any coral or roe.)

Simmer the scallops in butter until opaque. Sauté the escargots in butter.

Steam the cod over boiling water until it feels firm to the touch and flakes reluctantly when prodded with a fork. Arrange as part of Aïoli Monstre.

Chicken and Sliced Lamb

(SERVES 10)

> 10 chicken wings, with tips and first joints removed
> Butter
> 10 thin slices cooked roast leg of lamb

Preheat oven to 350 degrees F.

Brush the small, drumstick-like pieces of chicken wings with butter and bake until tender, about 20–25 minutes.

Five-Herb Peasant Bread

Bake this pleasantly flavored herb bread as two medium loaves or as one very impressive large oval loaf.

(YIELD: 2 MEDIUM LOAVES OR ONE LARGE LOAF)

> 2 packages dry, active yeast
> 2 cups warm chicken broth (about 110 degrees F.)
> 1 tablespoon salt
> 1 tablespoon olive oil
> 2½ cups whole-wheat flour
> 5–6 cups all-purpose flour
> 2 tablespoons each: minced fresh thyme, sage, dill,
>   marjoram, and basil
> 4 tablespoons crushed black pepper
> Cornmeal
> 1 egg white
> 1 tablespoon cold water
> 3 tablespoons coarsely crushed black pepper

In the mixing bowl of an electric mixer, stir together the yeast, broth, salt, and oil at low speed. Let stand for 5 minutes. Beat in the whole-wheat flour at high speed until well blended (about 2 minutes), then add 1 cup of the white flour and beat at high speed until well incorporated. Stir and knead in enough of the remaining white flour, half a cup at a time, to produce a stiff dough firm enough to hold its own shape.

Knead the dough 2 minutes with a dough hook or 6 minutes by hand (page 260). Let the dough rise in a warm, draft-free place for 1 hour. Punch the dough down, and sprinkle the herbs and the 4 tablespoons of pepper, a tablespoon at a time, on the kneading surface and knead them in.

Cut the dough in half and roll each piece up into a loaf. Oil a large baking sheet, sprinkle with cornmeal, and arrange the loaves on this singly or shape both into semicircles and place one alongside the other to form one large oval loaf. Cover loosely with a towel, and allow to double in bulk about 1 to 1½ hours. Beat the egg white and water together. Score the surfaces by making several ¼-inch-deep slashes with a very large, sharp knife. Brush the breads with the egg wash and, while it's still wet, sprinkle the pepper evenly over the loaves. Preheat the oven to 400 degrees F. and bake until the breads are golden brown (about 55 minutes). Remove the breads from the oven and cool it on a wire rack.

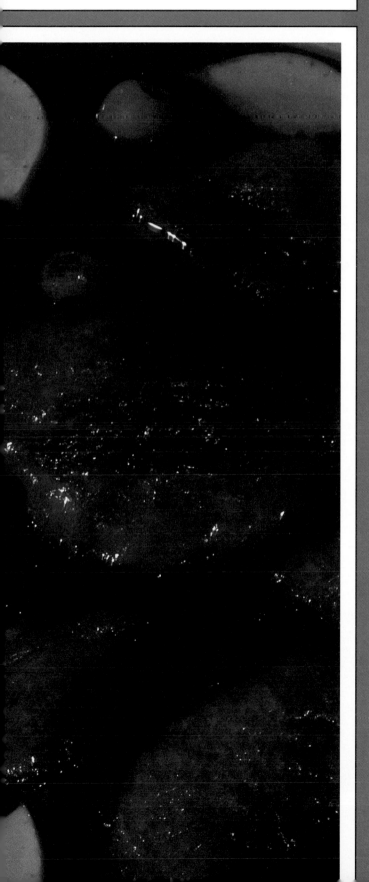

Weekend Harvest Dinner

When home gardens, farm stands, and greengrocer stalls overflow with a bounty of fruits and vegetables, it's time to take advantage of the freshness and reasonable prices of the autumn harvest to produce this nurturing dinner. Begin with Summer Squash, Wax Bean, and Golden Pear Tomato Bisque; follow with Ragoût of Duckling, Pumpkin, and Olives in a clear, dark sauce, accompanied by comforting Jalapeño Polenta and Saffron Shortbread Muffins. If you feel the need for a salad after all the vegetables in the soup, toss a mixture of greens with oil and lemon juice. End with Macaroon Cake with Apples and Blueberries.

Menu

Summer Squash, Wax Bean, and Golden Pear Tomato Bisque

Ragoût of Duckling, Pumpkin, and Olives

Jalapeño Polenta

Saffron Shortbread Biscuits

Macaroon Cake with Apples and Blueberries

Summer Squash, Wax Bean, and Golden Pear Tomato Bisque

This soup may look and taste as though it's calorie-laden, but it actually couldn't be lighter or less fattening. Lemon-yellow summer squash and wax beans are flash-cooked, drained, and pureed with sweet golden pear tomatoes and fresh lemon sage, then smoothed with yogurt and well chilled. Hardly a calorie in a carload.

(SERVES 6)

> 8 *ounces wax beans, with tips removed*
> 4 *6-inch yellow summer squash, quartered lengthwise and seeds removed if necessary*
> 10 *golden plum tomatoes, peeled and seeded*
> 2 *tablespoons minced chives*
> 1 *clove garlic, peeled and minced*
> 1–2 *leaves golden sage (or basil), minced*
> 2¾ *cups cold plain yogurt*
> *Salt and black pepper to taste*
> 6 *golden plum tomatoes, sliced*

Drop the beans in briskly boiling salted water. When the water returns to a boil, cook until barely tender. Remove with a slotted spoon, splash with cold water, and drain well. Drop the squash into the boiling water, cook for 3 minutes, drain, splash with cold water, and drain well. Cut the squash, beans, and 10 golden plum tomatoes into 1-inch pieces, and coarsely puree with the chives, garlic, and sage. Mix the puree and 2½ cups of the yogurt, and season to taste. Chill well. Garnish each bowl with slices of tomato and a spoonful of the remaining yogurt.

Ragoût of Duckling, Pumpkin, and Olives

Here on Long Island, ducklings are almost as plentiful as pumpkins, so these two ingredients are natural choices to enhance a harvest dinner. Luckily, duckling is also readily available in nearly every area of the country now, so every cook can have the pleasure of serving it. This recipe calls for the breast to be boned, with the bones used once again as the sauce is reduced, which provides a deeper, richer base. Most of the fat is also removed, resulting in a sauce as light as a duck sauce can be. The duck legs require more cooking than do the breasts and so are best roasted in a separate pan.

(SERVES 6)

3 5-pound ducklings, quartered
Salt and coarsely ground black pepper
1 recipe Sautéed Pumpkin and Olives (see below)
1 clove garlic, peeled and chopped
Pinch of thyme
Pinch of sage
½ cup each grated carrot, minced onion, and minced celery
¼ cup sherry
2 cups rich red wine
4 cups rich beef broth
1 teaspoon arrowroot
3 teaspoons butter

Preheat oven to 500 degrees F.

Remove any excess duck fat and rub the duck quarters on both sides with salt and pepper. Prick the skin all over with a fork. Using 2 roasting pans, arrange the breast quarters in 1 pan and the leg quarters in the other. Set the pans side by side in the preheated oven. Roast the breasts for 20 minutes, then remove them from their pan. Cut the breast meat from the bones, slice it with the grain, set aside, and keep warm. Reserve the bones.

Meanwhile, continue to cook the leg quarters for 10 minutes more or until the skin is crisp and the meat is pink. Prepare the pumpkin and olives. When the duckling legs are ready, remove them from their pan and, with a sharp knife or poultry shears, cut the thighs and drumsticks into serving pieces and keep them warm.

Pour off the fat from both roasting pans and discard any burned bits or residue. In 1 pan, place the garlic, herbs, and vegetables, and sauté over medium heat until very lightly browned. Add the sherry and 1 cup of the red wine. Add the remaining cup of wine to the other pan, and bring the liquid in both to a boil, scraping the golden brown bits from the pans' bottoms as their contents cook. When the wine in the second pan is reduced to half, strain this mixture into the pan with the vegetables. Add the reserved breast bones of the ducklings and 3½ cups of the beef broth, and cook over medium heat until the sauce thickens slightly. Discard the bones and puree the sauce in a food processor, or press it through a strainer and return it to a clean saucepan. Mix the arrowroot with the remaining broth, add it to the sauce, and bring to a boil over high heat, stirring constantly. Whisk in the butter 1 teaspoon at a time, adjust the seasonings, remove from the heat, and keep the sauce warm.

To assemble the dish, pour the warm sauce into an ovenproof serving dish. Arrange the duckling pieces, pumpkin, and olives over all and serve hot. The completed dish may be reheated briefly in an oven preheated to 300 degrees F.

Sautéed Pumpkin and Olives

> 1 *4-pound pumpkin or 3-pound butternut squash, cut into manageable*
> *slices ½-inch thick*
> *Salted water*
> *Butter and oil*
> 24 *large pimiento-stuffed olives*

Plunge the pumpkin slices into boiling salted water for a few minutes or until they are not quite tender. Cut away and discard the skin. Drain well and place between paper towels to dry out a bit more. In a nonstick skillet, heat 1 tablespoon each of butter and oil, and sauté the slices a few at a time until tender, without letting them take on any color. Add equal amounts of oil and butter as needed to prevent sticking. Blanch the olives in hot water for 1 minute, drain well, and dry on paper towels. Sauté in butter and oil for 1–2 minutes.

Jalapeño Polenta

Whether served soft and creamy, as it is here, or formed into a loaf and fried or baked, this nourishing dish is exceedingly satisfying. I prefer polenta made from finely ground cornmeal to accompany duckling, but to accompany heartier dishes substitute coarse meal. Chill it in a loaf pan, then slice it and fry or broil.

(SERVES 6)

> 4½ *cups salted water*
> ⅔ *pound finely ground cornmeal*
> 4 *tablespoons butter*
> 1 *Jalapeño pepper, seeded and finely minced*

Bring the water to a rolling boil in a large saucepan, sprinkle the cornmeal in very slowly, stirring constantly until it returns to a boil. Lower the heat and simmer for 20 minutes, stirring frequently and pressing out any lumps that may form. Stir in 3 tablespoons of the butter, a little at a time. Sauté the pepper in the remaining tablespoon of butter for 1 minute and stir this into the polenta. Serve very hot. If the polenta should stiffen, stir in boiling water, 1 tablespoon at a time, until it softens.

Saffron Shortbread Biscuits

A biscuit with a difference—the golden color and subtle flavor of saffron.

(YIELD: 1½ DOZEN)

> *Pinch of saffron*
> *⅓ cup hot milk*
> *3¼ cups all-purpose flour*
> *1 tablespoon granulated sugar*
> *2 tablespoons baking powder*
> *1 teaspoon salt*
> *7 tablespoons butter*
> *1 egg*

Preheat oven to 400 degrees F.

Steep the saffron in the milk until the liquid reaches room temperature. Sift together the flour, sugar, baking powder, and salt. Cut the butter into the dry ingredients until the mixture resembles coarse meal. Beat the egg lightly with the milk and stir into the dry ingredients to form a soft dough. On a lightly floured surface pat the dough out to a thickness of ½ inch and cut out biscuits with a 2½-inch cookie cutter or the edge of a glass. Re-form and cut leftover dough into additional biscuits. Arrange on a well-greased cookie sheet and bake for 15 minutes or until golden brown. Serve immediately.

Macaroon Cake with Apples and Blueberries

This is a moist, spicy cake topped with blueberries. An added advantage is the sliced-apple center that makes the tip of each wedge nice and chewy.

(SERVES 8)

> *⅓ cup sweet butter*
> *1 cup granulated sugar*
> *2 cups all-purpose flour*
> *2 teaspoons baking powder*
> *½ teaspoon baking soda*
> *¼ teaspoon salt*
> *1 cup applesauce*
>
> *¼ cup sour milk or buttermilk*
> *½ teaspoon each cinnamon and*
>   *ground nutmeg*
> *1 egg*
> *6 soft macaroons broken into ½-inch pieces*
> *¾ cup large blueberries*
> *1 large Granny Smith apple, peeled*

Preheat oven to 350 degrees F.

Cream the butter until it is pale yellow. Cream in the sugar a little at a time until the mixture is light and fluffy. Sift together the flour, baking powder, baking soda, and salt. Mix the applesauce, milk, spices, and egg and beat these into the creamed mixture alternately with the dry ingredients. Fold in the macaroon crumbs and pour the batter into a well-buttered 10-inch cake pan. Sprinkle the blueberries over the batter to the edges. Neatly core the apple and cut it in half. Slice each half neatly and arrange in the center of the cake as shown, without letting the slices become separated. Bake for 45 to 55 minutes or until the cake tests done. Remove the cake pan from the oven and cool 10 minutes. Carefully remove the cake from the pan and allow it to cool on a wire rack. Serve warm or at room temperature.

A.M. to P.M. Stew

On one of those velvet twilights of Indian summer, a carrot-colored moon glows across the sleeping bay to the rushes beyond my garden, newly turned and raked and harvested of its last remaining fall vegetables. Having shared the common bloodline of my rich garden soil, these ingredients are bound to be compatible on the plate.

And so I take inventory: seven vermillion beets, each sprouting a fringe of tender red-veined, second-growth leaves; boa of late-blooming dill; five slender, tangle-rooted leeks; two spaghetti squash, the color of fresh cream; two sweet bell peppers, each turned fiery on one cheek while waiting to be picked; five nearly overripe tomatoes; fragrant horseradish roots, earth-brown on the outside, as white on the inside as the snows that will soon blow across the marshy fields to blanket the garden.

Also on hand, a just-stuffed string of plump vegetable sausages, a pound of ground veal, two loaves of crusty, whole-grained bread, and a jar of satin-smooth crème fraîche. Missing only is the glow of close friends to share the bounty of a stew set simmering just after breakfast, stirred occasionally throughout the day, finally to be served as the sun slips beneath the horizon. Unless you'd like the challenge of creating your own sausages (I've given the recipe just in case), this meal does practically prepare itself.

Menu

A.M. to P.M. Stew with Vegetable Sausages and Veal Nuggets

Fresh Sweet Pepper/Tomato Salsa

Horseradish Crème Fraîche

Marinated Spaghetti Squash and Zucchini Salad

Boysenberry Sherbet with White Peaches Marinated in Peach Brandy

A.M. to P.M. *Stew with Vegetable Sausages and Veal Nuggets*

This stew is meant to be flash-seared over high heat on top of the stove, then simmered, and finally baked to fix the seasonings and marry the flavors. None of the procedures is complicated in the least, and only one pot is used. In fact, after you have performed the preliminary tasks, this could turn out to be the easiest dinner you've ever prepared. The process may be hurried up or slowed down to meet your entertaining schedule, or the stew may be prepared a day or two in advance. The flavor is actually more mellow the second day.

If possible, cook the stew in a beautiful enamel pot that can go directly to the table, or transfer it to an unusual serving dish just prior to seating your guests. Pass the Fresh Sweet Pepper/Tomato Salsa and Horseradish Crème Fraîche at table.

(SERVES 10 TO 12)

2½ pounds each bottom round beef and boned lamb neck with
all fat removed
⅓ cup cognac
3 cloves garlic, peeled and cut in half lengthwise
¼ teaspoon each cinnamon and nutmeg
5 whole cloves, bruised
3 tablespoons olive oil
20 small white onions, peeled
3½ tablespoons all-purpose flour
1 large sweet onion, peeled and coarsely chopped
3 tablespoons tomato paste
2 cups light red wine
3 tablespoons each minced parsley and thyme, or 1 teaspoon dried
Beef broth
2 pounds Potato-Fennel Sausage (see below) or sweet Italian
sausages
Veal Nuggets (see below)
20 fresh medium-size mushrooms, wiped clean
1 teaspoon cornstarch
1 recipe Sweet Pepper/Tomato Salsa (see below)
1 recipe Horseradish Crème Fraîche (see below)

Early in the morning, cut the beef and lamb into 1½-inch cubes and toss them with the cognac, garlic, cinnamon, nutmeg, and cloves. Let the meats stand at room temperature for 4 hours. (If it's more convenient, do this step the evening before and refrigerate the meats overnight. Allow the meats to come back to room temperature before continuing.)

Pour the olive oil into a heavy stew pot and lightly brown the small whole onions. Remove them with a slotted spoon and set them aside in their own bowl.

Drain the meat cubes, reserving their juices, lightly squeeze them, then dry with paper towels. Dust lightly with flour. Brown the meat on all sides in the same pot, adding more olive oil if necessary. Add the chopped onion and sauté until golden.

Mix the tomato paste with the red wine, reserved meat juices, parsley, and thyme, and pour this over the meat. Add enough beef broth to barely cover the meat. Bring the liquid to a boil, then lower the heat and simmer the stew over very low heat for 1 hour, stirring occasionally.

Preheat oven to 300 degrees F.

Add the sausage and bake the stew for 1½ hours, adding broth as needed to keep the meat covered. Adjust the seasonings and add the Veal Nuggets, reserved onions, and mushrooms. Continue to bake until the meats and vegetables are tender but not falling apart—about 20–30 minutes. The onions should still be a bit crunchy. If you like a thicker sauce, spoon the meats, onions, mushrooms, sausages, and Veal Nuggets into a serving dish and keep them warm. Mix the cornstarch with a little broth, add it to the sauce in the pan and boil, stirring constantly until it thickens nicely. Reserve a few of the most attractive ingredients. Spoon the sauce over the stew. Arrange the reserved ingredients on top, cover with foil, and keep warm in a very low oven, if necessary, until ready to serve.

Serve the stew at the table and pass the Fresh Sweet Pepper/Tomato Salsa and Horseradish Crème Fraîche separately.

Vegetable Sausages

Rather than add potato quarters, dumplings, pasta, or other, more traditional starches to your stew, you might want to experiment with preparing these lusty vegetable sausages, nicely flavored with meat. If not, you may substitute sweet Italian sausages to deepen the flavor and texture of the stew.

Believe it or not, sausage casings aren't difficult to locate. Fine butcher shops nearly always carry them, as do many specialty food shops, farmers, and others who do their own butchering or make their own sausages. Basic directions for dealing with all phases of sausage-making are given on pages 260–61. Once cooked, these vegetable sausages are good hot or cold.

(MAKES 4 POUNDS)

> 1 *pound each pork shoulder and ham*
> 3 *large potatoes, peeled, cut in 2-inch pieces, and parboiled for 5 minutes, then drained and cooled*
> 1½ *cups each peeled and very coarsely chopped fennel root, winter squash, and onions*
> ½ *teaspoon each white pepper and dried mustard*
> ⅛ *teaspoon each ground allspice and nutmeg*
> 1½ *teaspoon salt (or more or less, to taste)*
> *Ice water*
> *Pork casings*
> 1 *tablespoon whole allspice*

In a food processor or grinder, finely mince first the meats, then the potatoes, and finally, the fennel, squash, and onions. Do not overprocess. Keep them in separate bowls.

Squeeze out and discard any juices from the vegetables. Use a large wooden spoon or your hands to thoroughly mix together all the ingredients and seasonings except the whole allspice. Add a very little ice water if needed to soften the mixture so it can be easily handled. Fry a bit of the mixture, taste it, and add more seasonings if you like.

Stuff the mixture rather loosely into 24-inch natural casings that have been soaked and rinsed (pages 260-61). Do not stuff the sausages tightly or they will burst during cooking. If any air bubbles form, prick them with a needle. Tie off the sausages in 2-inch lengths and refrigerate until needed.

Bring a large kettle of water to a boil together with the whole allspice. Plunge in the sausages, lower the heat a little, and cook for 10–15 minutes. Cut a sausage open to see if the center is done. If not, cook 5 minutes more, then add the sausages to the stew just long enough to heat them through. Remember to cut them apart as directed before serving them.

If using store-bought Italian sausages, parboil them for 15–20 minutes, pricking them frequently here and there with a needle. Drain and add to the stew when it goes into the oven for its final heating. Just prior to serving, cut the sausages into 2-inch pieces and return them to the stew.

Veal Nuggets

(MAKES ABOUT 18)

> 2 slices home-baked white bread or a good grade commercial white bread
> 3 tablespoons milk
> 1 pound veal, ground
> Zest (thin yellow skin excluding bitter white underskin) from large lemon
> 1 tablespoon minced parsley
> 2 cloves garlic, peeled and minced
> ¼ cup minced onion
> 1 small egg
> Sprinkle of ground nutmeg
> Salt to taste
> Fine bread crumbs

Soak the bread in the milk and squeeze it dry. Lightly mix all the ingredients together except the bread crumbs. Do not overhandle the mixture or the meatballs will be hard and dense rather than light and fluffy. Gently and quickly roll the mixture into 1-inch balls, then roll in bread crumbs. Fry in olive oil until brown on all sides but still raw in the middle. Set aside in a cool spot or refrigerate until needed. Drop the balls into the stew during the last 10 minutes of cooking.

Fresh Sweet Pepper/Tomato Salsa

While other dishes cry out for the torrid nip of hot-pepper Salsa Picante, this one requires only the clean flavor and freshness of fresh sweet red peppers and tomatoes. To spice up this same sauce for use with meat, fish, and egg dishes, just add minced hot peppers to taste.

(MAKES ABOUT 3 CUPS)

> *4 tomatoes, peeled, seeded, and chopped*
> *2 very red sweet peppers, seeded and chopped*
> *2 cloves garlic, peeled and minced*
> *2 medium-size sweet Texas onions or other very sweet varieties, peeled and finely chopped*
> *Salt to taste*
> *3 tablespoons lemon juice*

170

Place tomatoes, peppers, garlic, and onions in a glass bowl. Sprinkle with salt and cover with lemon juice. Refrigerate for a few hours or overnight. Serve cold.

Horseradish Crème Fraîche

This is the garnish that adds the sting to the stew.

(MAKES 2 CUPS)

> *3 tablespoons freshly grated peeled horseradish, or more to taste*
> *2½–3 cups Crème Fraîche (page 253), or ⅔ cup commercial sour cream and 2 cups heavy cream*

Mix in the horseradish with the Crème Fraîche at least 2 hours prior to serving. For a homemade facsimile of crème fraîche, place the sour cream and heavy cream in a jar, cover, and shake well. Let the combined creams stand in a warm room overnight. Shake the cream mixture again and refrigerate—it should keep for about a week.

Marinated Spaghetti Squash and Zucchini Salad

(SERVES 10 TO 12)

> *2 large spaghetti squash*
> *2 7-inch zucchini, trimmed, seeded, and coarsely grated*
> *½ cup thinly sliced scallions (include some green tops)*
> *1 clove garlic, peeled and crushed*
> *½ cup safflower oil*
> *½ cup white wine vinegar*
> *¼ cup confectioners' sugar*
> *1 teaspoon each dry mustard and salt*
> *1½ tablespoons sesame oil*

Puncture the spaghetti squash in 5 or 6 places and steam or bake it at 350 degrees F. until it can be easily pierced with a knife. The length of time will depend on the size of the squash. Do not overcook or the strands will be mushy. Cool the squash, cut in half, and discard the seeds. Use a fork to separate, scrape, and lift out the strands. Toss in a glass bowl together with the grated zucchini.

Place the scallions, garlic, safflower oil, vinegar, sugar, dry mustard, and salt in a jar with a cover and shake well to mix. Pour the marinade over the vegetables and refrigerate for about 3 hours. Toss the salad, then refrigerate again for at least 2 hours or up to 24 hours. Just before serving, drain well and toss with sesame oil.

Boysenberry Sherbet with White Peaches Marinated in Peach Brandy

I've chosen white peaches because they are grown here on Long Island and have a creamy color and texture that is hard to resist. Any peaches, preferably local produce, will do. If you are pressed for time and the peaches are nice and sweet, don't bother marinating them in the brandy. Also, if you can't find boysenberry, buy the tastiest high-quality fruit sherbet available. Should you have an ice-cream machine and a little leisure, the possibilities are limitless. Fresh peaches and good fruit sherbet in any combination are practically unbeatable.

> *1 large fresh ripe peach per person, or 2 small peaches per person*
> *1 tablespoon lemon juice*
> *Peach brandy (about 1 tablespoon per serving)*
> *1 large scoop boysenberry (or other flavor) sherbet per person*
> *   (about 3–4 scoops per pint)*
> *Mint leaves*

Just before your guests arrive, dip the peaches in scalding water for an instant and pull off the skins. Slice the peaches and toss them with the lemon juice and then the brandy. To serve, arrange the tepid fruit slices around the sherbet and top with 1–2 mint leaves or a flower.

TABLEWARE, TIFFANY AND CO., NY, NY

Main-Course Cheesecake

When you consider it, there's no reason to be surprised by unsweetened, warm cheesecake layered with smoked salmon and scallops and flavored with horseradish, curry, and tomato. Cheese is, after all, a protein as suitable to the entrée as to the dessert course. A little dinner party built around this unique dish is perfect preceded by a simple, clear soup, and followed by salad and fruit for dessert.

This savory cake is made in three layers, each with a flavor that is distinctive yet designed to complement one another. Each layer must be baked separately, which is rather a nuisance, but the first two may be prepared a day in advance. The cheesecake is accompanied by Hot Fresh Tomato Sauce.

(SERVES 8 TO 20 AS AN ENTRÉE, OR 16 TO 20 AS AN HORS D'OEUVRE)

Bottom Crust

> 1 *cup all-purpose flour*
> ½ *cup fine, dry bread crumbs*
> ½ *teaspoon garlic salt*
> ¼ *teaspoon salt*
> *Sprinkle of white pepper*
> 6 *tablespoons salt butter*
> 1 *large egg yolk*

Preheat oven to 350 degrees F.

Place all the ingredients except the butter and the egg yolk in the bowl of your food processor. Cut the butter into 6 pieces and bury them in the flour mixture. Use the steel blade to just cut in the butter until the mixture has the consistency of coarse meal. Add the egg yolk and turn the processor on and off two or three times to thoroughly incorporate it. Or, cut the butter into the flour using two knives or a pastry cutter, then mix in the egg yolk with a fork. Press the dough evenly into the bottom of an assembled springform pan, and bake 15 minutes. Cool the crust in the pan.

Horseradish Cheese Layer

> 8 *ounces cream cheese, at room temperature*
> 4 *ounces fresh goat cheese*
> 1 *egg*
> 1 *tablespoon each sour cream and well-drained horseradish*
> ⅛ *teaspoon salt*

Preheat oven to 350 degrees F.

Using your food processor or blender, mix all the ingredients thoroughly. Spread mixture over the cooled crust and bake for 25 minutes. Remove from the oven and cool in the pan set on a wire rack.

Smoked Salmon, Scallops, and Green Pea Filling

> *2 cups shelled, fresh green peas*
> *16 ounces cream cheese, at room temperature*
> *1 teaspoon curry powder*
> *¼ teaspoon salt*
> *2 large eggs, separated*
> *¾ pound smoked salmon (or other mild smoked fish), thinly sliced*
> *1 cup well-drained bay scallops (or sea scallops cut into quarters)*
> *1½ pounds large Greek olives, with meat cut from the pits in narrow strips*

Preheat oven to 350 degrees F.

Drop the peas into boiling water, lower the heat, and simmer a few minutes, or until barely tender. Drain the peas in a colander, splash with cold water, and drain very well.

Whirl the cream cheese, curry, and salt in your food processor or blender until well blended. With the motor running, add the egg yolks and blend well. Remove to a bowl. Beat the egg whites until stiff but not dry, and use a spatula to fold them into the curry-cheese mixture.

Layer the salmon slices and scallops over the horseradish cheese layer and cover with the olive strips. Spread the curry cheese over the salmon and olives, cover with the peas, and press down gently with the spatula. Bake for 35 to 45 minutes, or until the center no longer quivers when you tap the pan sharply. Remove from the oven and cool to room temperature on a wire rack. The cake may be chilled at this point and continued an hour or so before serving.

Ham and Sun-Dried Tomato Filling

> *½ pound boiled or baked ham, thinly sliced*
> *⅓ pound sun-dried tomatoes, drained if necessary, and finely chopped*
> *12 ounces cream cheese, at room temperature*
> *1 large egg*
> *1 tablespoon tomato puree*
> *½ teaspoon mild paprika*
> *⅛ teaspoon each salt and white pepper*
> *Cream cheese*
> *Hot Fresh Tomato Sauce (page 254)*

Preheat oven to 350 degrees F.

Arrange the ham and tomatoes over the cooled curry-cheese layer. Whirl the remaining ingredients in your food processor or blender until well mixed. Spread the mixture over the ham and tomatoes. Bake for 25 to 35 minutes, or until the center feels fairly firm. Cool for 5–10 minutes.

Just before carrying the cake to the table, frost it with cool cream cheese. Cut cheesecake into wedges and pass the tomato sauce at the table. If it's more convenient, show the finished cake to your guests while they are finishing the soup, then cut it in the kitchen, surround it with sauce, decorate with smoked salmon or tomato roses, and serve at once. The sauce should be hot, the cheesecake merely warm.

Winter

Winter White Dinner

In the winter, let the landscape set the scene as well as the menu, and you could come up with this elegant dinner party. While snow frosts the great outdoors, let candlelight shimmer indoors against your finest bone china, your best stemware, your purest linens. A bouquet of white lilies promises spring. To complement this, create a palette of ethereal dishes, each pale, each perfection. A rich, monochromatic understatement, with food and setting keyed to the season.

I serve chilled, paper-thin "natural growth" oysters, just pulled from swirling bay waters, with an innocent-looking sauce, that in fact is fired by a grated knuckle of horseradish root dug from my winter garden. The white theme continues with a feather-light Veal Blanquette with Sliced Raw Mushrooms and Cucumbers; White **Cheddar Rice** Ring; Hearts of Palm and White Asparagus in Lemon Vinaigrette, **and shivery** White Chocolate Mousse with Blanched Walnut Sauce.

Menu

Wild Oysters with Horseradish Crème Fraîche

Veal Blanquette with Sliced Raw Mushrooms and Cucumbers

White Cheddar Rice Ring

Hearts of Palm and White Asparagus in Lemon Vinaigrette

White Chocolate Mousse with Blanched Walnut Sauce

Wild Oysters with Horseradish Crème Fraîche

This is a simple, elegant way to begin, providing that wild oysters, or even cultivated ones, are available. The same goes for fresh horseradish. Actually, I can never understand how any garden could be considered complete without at least one of these pungent roots. If your garden soil is sandy, as ours is, mulching will make it possible for you to dig up a fresh knob of root in all but the most frigid weather.

Note: If oysters aren't available, substitute clams. The horseradish sauce is also an excellent accompaniment to a first course of nearly any smoked fish.

(SERVES 6)

> *36 oysters on the half shell, well chilled (see Note)*
> *2 cups Crème Fraîche (page 253)*
> *2 tablespoons finely grated fresh horseradish root, or 2 tablespoons newly opened, well-drained prepared white horseradish*

Arrange the oysters in their shells on oyster plates or dinner plates. Mix the Crème Fraîche and horseradish. Serve the oysters with the sauce.

Veal Blanquette with Sliced Raw Mushrooms and Cucumbers

Tender cubes of veal in a platinum sauce provide an excellent contrast in texture with **slices of fresh white mushroom and** blanched cucumber. For its initial cooking, the veal is **blanched rather than sautéed** to retain its snowy color.

(SERVES 6)

> *4 pounds veal shoulder, cut into neat 1½-inch cubes*
> *18 tiny whole white onions, peeled*
> *2 medium-size carrots, scraped and quartered*
> *2 ribs celery without leaves, cut in half*
> *¾ teaspoon salt*
> *5 whole black peppercorns*
> *1 bay leaf*
> *Pinch each of dried thyme and marjoram*
> *20 medium-size mushrooms, wiped clean and trimmed*
> *1 tablespoon lemon juice*
> *3 medium-size cucumbers, peeled, split lengthwise, and seeded*
> *½ cup Crème Fraîche (page 253)*

Place the veal in a large, heavy stainless-steel or enamel pot, add water to cover, and cook over medium heat for 5 minutes. Drain the veal and discard the water. Rinse the meat with a little cold water, and drain again.

Add the meat, onions, carrots, celery, salt, peppercorns, and herbs to the pot, and just enough water to cover. Bring to a simmer, then cover the pot and cook over very low heat until the meat is tender, 1½–2 hours. Discard the carrots and celery. Remove the veal and remaining vegetables with a slotted spoon and reserve them. Cook the stock over medium-high heat until it is reduced to 2 cups. If you like, you may combine the stock, meat, and vegetables, refrigerate them, and continue later.

An hour or so prior to dinner, begin to heat the stew in a 200-degree-F. oven. Meanwhile, cut the mushrooms into very thin slices and toss them with the lemon juice.

Cut the cucumber halves crosswise into slices ¼ inch thick, and cook for 1 minute in scalding water. Arrange the cucumber slices on a plate, weight down with another plate, and let stand for 15 minutes. Pour off any accumulated liquid and blot the slices with paper towels.

Raise the oven temperature to 250 degrees F. and cook the stew for 15 minutes. Remove the stew from the oven, mix in the Crème Fraîche, then gently stir in half the mushroom and cucumber slices to wilt them somewhat. As the vegetables mix with the hot stew they will cook ever so slightly. Transfer the stew to a glass or white ceramic serving dish, and arrange the remaining mushroom and cucumber slices on top. Serve immediately.

White Cheddar Rice Ring

If it is necessary to keep the ring warm for a few minutes while you finish other preparations, place the covered, unmolded ring in 1–2 inches of hot water.

(SERVES 6)

1¼ cups long-grain rice
2 cups boiling water
1 teaspoon salt
3 tablespoons butter
½ cup grated white cheddar cheese

Add the rice to the boiling water, stir once with a fork, and add the salt. When the water returns to a boil, stir it again with the fork, then cover and cook for 12 minutes. Remove the lid and test a grain to see if it is almost tender. If it isn't, cook for 2 minutes more, uncovered, then remove from the heat, cover, and let stand for 3–4 minutes or until tender. Mix in the butter with a fork and add the cheese 1 tablespoon at a time, stirring constantly. Press the rice into a well-buttered ring mold, cover with a serving plate, and in one motion turn both over and tap or shake the mold once sharply. The ring should unmold easily.

Hearts of Palm and White Asparagus in Lemon Vinaigrette

Rarely can canned items be considered treats. These gems are the exception. As you sample first one and then the other, the changes in texture and flavor are riveting. Of course, either the hearts of palm or the asparagus can go it alone, too.

(SERVES 6)

1 15-ounce can hearts of palm
1 15-ounce can white asparagus
12 leaves Buttercrunch lettuce, rinsed and dried
1 recipe Lemon Vinaigrette (page 255)

Chill the hearts of palm and asparagus well, and carefully remove them from their cans so as not to damage them. Arrange nicely on lettuce and serve with lemon vinaigrette.

White Chocolate Mousse with Blanched Walnut Sauce

The trembling whiteness and delicate flavor of this chilled mousse can hardly be imagined.

(SERVES 6)

> 5 *ounces white chocolate*
> *¹⁄₃ cup granulated sugar*
> 3 *tablespoons water*
> 4 *egg yolks*
> 2 *tablespoons Cointreau*
> 1 *cup heavy cream, whipped until stiff*

Melt the chocolate over hot water in the top of a small double boiler. In a smaller pan, boil the sugar and water together until the mixture turns clear and syrupy. Use a spatula to scrape the syrup and the chocolate into a food processor container. Whirl together until well mixed, then add the egg yolks 1 at a time, with the motor still running. Mix in the Cointreau, turn off the machine, and cool to room temperature. Use a flexible spatula to scrape all the chocolate mixture from the processor into a large mixing bowl. Gently fold in the whipped cream. Scrape into a 2-quart soufflé dish and chill for at least 4 hours.

Blanched Walnut Sauce

Blanching the nuts removes the slightly acrid aftertaste of the skins and also softens the meats so that they are more perfectly mated to the sumptuous white chocolate.

> 1 *cup walnut meats*
> *Scalding water*
> *²⁄₃ cup light-brown sugar*
> *²⁄₃ cup light cream*

Place the nuts in an ovenproof or stainless-steel bowl and pour the water over. Let stand until cool enough to handle. Meanwhile, boil the brown sugar and the cream together until the mixture thickens.

Drain the nuts and use a kitchen towel to rub the skins from them. Coarsely chop the nuts, then add them to the sauce. Cool to room temperature. Serve with the mousse.

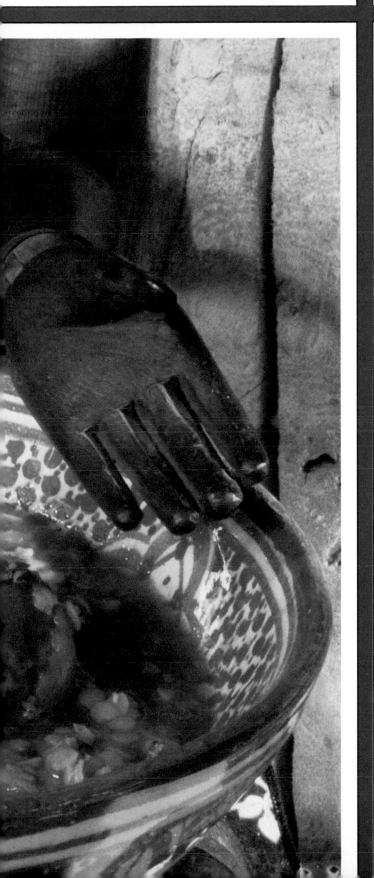

Soup for Supper... with a Difference

And in this case the difference is . . . supper's *in* the soup. Tender, meaty, osso buco is simmered in the same pot with red lentils, leeks, and fennel. At table, garnish with Coriander Gremolata, an updated version of the flavorful, typically Italian herb mixture. Here coriander substitutes for fresh minced parsley to partner perfectly with the garlic and lemon zest. Lusty red wine and crusty Salad-Herb Pull-Apart Bread, spread with sweet butter and sprinkled with coarse salt, are the only entrée accompaniments. For finishers, serve luscious Pear and Ginger Fool.

Menu
Red Lentil-Leek Soup with Osso Buco
Coriander Gremolata
Salad-Herb Pull-Apart Bread
Pear and Ginger Fool

Red Lentil-Leek Soup with Osso Buco

(SERVES 8)

> 3 *tablespoons olive oil*
>
> 2 *medium-size leeks, split, well washed, and cut into ½-inch slices (use the whites and 3–4 inches of the green tops)*
>
> 7 *cups water*
>
> 2 *cups dry white wine*
>
> 2 *cups red lentils, or other, rinsed and picked over*
>
> 2 *large cloves garlic, peeled and minced*
>
> ¼ *teaspoon each ground turmeric and cumin*
>
> ½ *teaspoon dried thyme leaves*
>
> 1½ *teaspoons salt*
>
> 2 *tablespoons butter*
>
> 8 *3-inch-thick veal marrowbones for osso buco (pieces of meaty shanks of young veal with marrow intact), rinsed and dried*
>
> 2 *medium-size carrots, scraped and grated*
>
> 2 *onions, peeled and coarsely chopped*
>
> 4 *ribs celery, coarsely chopped*
>
> ¼ *teaspoon each dried rosemary and sage*
>
> 2 *tablespoons tomato paste*
>
> *Light beef, veal, or chicken broth*
>
> 1 *recipe Coriander Gremolata (see below)*

Begin with 2 large, heavy stew pots.

In the first pot, heat 1 tablespoon of the oil and sauté the leeks until they are wilted, then transfer them to a bowl and set them aside. Put the water and 1 cup of the wine in the same pot and add the lentils, garlic, turmeric, cumin, thyme, and salt. Cover and cook over medium-low heat for 1 hour.

Meanwhile, in the second pot, heat the butter and the remaining 2 tablespoons of olive oil. Brown the marrowbones on all sides and then turn them upright so the marrow won't spill out. Sprinkle with the carrots, onions, celery, rosemary, and sage. Cover and simmer for 15 minutes. Mix the remaining cup of wine with the tomato paste and pour it over the marrowbones. Add enough water or broth (or both) to not quite cover. Cover the pot and simmer for 1½ hours, adding a little additional liquid, if necessary, to keep the level about halfway up the sides of the meat pieces. The recipe can be brought to this point and successfully continued hours or even a day later.

Pour the lentils and the reserved leeks into the largest of the 2 pots. Carefully arrange the marrowbones in an upright position on a platter and stir the sauce in which they were cooked into the lentils. This mixture, which is now the base for your soup, should be quite liquid. If it isn't, add enough broth so that the mixture has the consistency of thin soup. Arrange the marrowbones, again in an upright position, over the mixture, cover, and simmer for about 30 minutes or until the lentils are barely tender.

If you have cooked the lentils over too-high heat, they may have broken down into a puree at this point. Not to worry. Their flavor will still be there, even if their chewy texture has been somewhat diminished. The meat around the marrowbones should be very tender—almost, but not quite, ready to fall apart. If the meat is still chewy, set aside half the soup in a large pan or bowl, add enough broth to the pot to prevent scorching, then cover and simmer until the meat is tender.

To serve, place 1 of the meaty marrowbones upright in each of 8 good-size soup plates. If the soup is too thick, add a little hot broth. If it is too thin, quickly puree a cup or so of the lentils and stir them back in. Ladle the hot soup around the osso buco and pass Coriander Gremolata as a garnish.

185

Coriander Gremolata

I'm not one of those cooks who sprinkles garlic on everything but ice cream, but even I cannot resist the blaze of fresh garlic, lemon zest, and coriander partnered with veal and lentils. Gremolata is usually added to Osso Buco at table, as it is here, to allow guests the option of merely tasting or really indulging.

(MAKES ABOUT 1⅓ CUPS)

> 6 *large lemons*
> 1½ *cups finely chopped coriander*
> 10 to 12 *medium-size cloves garlic, peeled and minced*

Use a grater or swivel-type vegetable peeler to remove the thin yellow skins or zest from the lemons. Mince the zest and mix it with the remaining ingredients. Cover and refrigerate for up to 1 hour prior to serving.

Herb Pull-Apart Bread

This tender bread pulls apart to reveal hidden sprinklings of salad herbs and minced garlic.

(YIELD: 2 LOAVES)

> *6 to 7 cups unbleached white flour*
> *2 tablespoons sugar*
> *2 teaspoons salt*
> *1 package dry active yeast*
> *½ cup warm milk (about 110 degrees F.)*
> *1½ cups warm water (about 110 degrees F.)*
> *6 tablespoons butter*
> *3 large cloves garlic, peeled and minced*
> *2 tablespoons each minced coriander, thyme, and marjoram*

186

Place 2 cups of the flour, sugar, salt, and yeast in the bowl of an electric mixer and gradually stir in a mixture of the milk, water, and 3 tablespoons of the butter (the butter does not need to be melted). Beat 2 minutes, then add 1 cup of the flour and beat again for 2 minutes, scraping down the bowl from time to time. Stir in enough of the remaining flour to make a stiff dough. Knead the dough until it is smooth and elastic. Place the dough in an oiled bowl, cover and let it rise in a warm, draft-free place for 1 hour, or until it doubles in bulk.

Punch the dough down, divide it into 2 equal parts, place each on a floured surface, and let the dough rise for 15 minutes. Roll each piece into a 12-inch by 8-inch rectangle. Brush one rectangle with melted butter, sprinkle with half the herbs and garlic, and cut it into four 8-inch-long strips. Stack these strips and cut them into four 2-inch pieces. Stand the slices on end down the center of a 1-pound loaf pan. Repeat the process with the remaining dough. Cover the loaves and let them rise in a warm, draft-free place for about an hour or until they double in bulk.

Preheat oven to 400 degrees F.

Bake for 30 minutes or until golden brown. Remove the loaves from the pans and cool on wire racks.

Pear and Ginger Fool

Of all the treasured aftermaths that contain Crème à l'Anglaise, the most perfect seems to me to be that theme of cool, ivory custard, drifts of whipped cream, and fresh and cooked fruits—the Fool, or any of its variations. The wintery recipe below depends on pears and ginger marmalade for exquisite flavor, but most summer fruits are wonderful served this way.

(SERVES 8)

Custard Cream (Crème à l'Anglaise)

1 1/4 cups each milk and heavy cream
1 2-inch piece vanilla bean, split lengthwise, or 1 1/2 teaspoons vanilla extract
6 egg yolks
1 cup granulated sugar
2 tablespoons rum or sherry

Bring the milk and cream to just under a boil with the vanilla bean. (If you use extract, add it after the custard is cooked.)

Beat the egg yolks and sugar in the top of a double boiler until they are light and creamy. Gradually beat in the hot milk and cream, and cook the mixture over barely boiling water, stirring constantly, until the custard thickens enough to coat a spoon. This process takes a while, but don't get impatient and raise the heat or you will curdle the cream and end up with sweet scrambled eggs. Overcooking even a little will make the custard slightly grainy, but if this happens whirl the cream in a food processor fitted with the steel cutting blade until it is smooth or pass it through a fine strainer. Stir in the rum or sherry. Cover the top of the custard with plastic wrap and chill it well.

Fresh Pears

(MAKES ABOUT 3 CUPS)

3 cups juicy, ripe pears, peeled and thinkly sliced
1/3 cup granulated sugar
1 tablespoon lemon juice

Toss the pear slices with the sugar and lemon juice, cover and refrigerate.

Whipped Cream

2 cups heavy cream
1/4 cup granulated sugar

Whip the cream until it thickens slightly and continue whipping while you sprinkle in the sugar a little at a time. When the sugar is no longer gritty and the cream holds a peak, chill it well.

(continued)

To assemble the Fool:

> 1 8-ounce jar ginger marmalade *or more*

Line the sides of an attractive glass dish with ladyfingers. Spread a layer of cream on the bottom. Spread the sweetened pear slices over the cream, and then a layer of Crème à l'Anglaise. Repeat this layering process once again, this time with dollops of ginger marmalade for the sweetened pears. Top with the remaining whipped cream.

If there is any Crème à l'Anglaise left over, you may serve it in a sauceboat along with the dessert. Or eat it with a dessert spoon before your guests arrive, as I do.

Pick a Peck of Peppers

Peppers—sweet, hot, or pungent; pickled, fresh, or otherwise—can enliven almost any menu. Whether a chili, chilitepine, jalapeño, serrano, poblano, cayenne, pimento, yellow, purple, or red hot cherry, these spicy beauties are setting palates ablaze with a wide variety of ethnic favorites. Szechuan, Thai, Vietnamese, Indian, Arab, Spanish, and Mexican dishes all owe a good deal of their pungency to the lusty pepper.

For a walk on the milder side, choose the small, thin, green Italian pepper or the bell pepper in yellow, orange, red, purple, brown, or light or dark green. Whether you roast them, bake them, toss them in salads, fry them or dry them, they are high in vitamin C, vitamin A, and fiber and in all ways delightful.

Greek Restaurant Buffet

This is a particularly pleasant way to entertain . . . warm, friendly, low-key. Stack colorful plates, mugs, and bowls beside handsome pots of food kept conveniently warm on your kitchen stove. Although I also cook with both electric and gas heat, I find a ceramic cook top ideal for entertaining. It is attractive, very nearly invisible, and has a setting that is low enough to keep foods warm without scorching them. The enamel pots are extremely stylish, too, with a "come to the party" attractiveness that belies their Cinderella serviceability. The implements are an eclectic mix: Persian bowls, glasses and flatware from the thirties, kitchen-towel napkins, and the plastic baskets that hold the bread and wine are right off my local department store shelves.

And, incidentally, a Greek Restaurant Buffet needn't necessarily include foods that are exclusively Greek. This menu is based on traditional Greek expanded to include other flavors of the Mediterranean and lightened to please the hostess (me). The soup and the shrimp may be omitted for fewer guests or a less elaborate menu.

Menu

Almond Soup with Cayenne Whipped Cream

Baked Lamb and Olive Stew

Layered Deep-Dish Spinach and Bulgur Pie

Garlicky Eggplant-Rice Pudding

Shrimp with Fresh Tomato and Feta Cheese

Fresh-Fruit Baklava with Ouzo Kadaif

Almond Soup with Cayenne Whipped Cream

If you have the time, prepare this soup with a plump whole chicken to add strength to the broth and tender cubes of meat to back up the exotic flavor of the almonds. For a hurry-up version, forget the chicken and substitute canned chicken broth. The results will still be outstanding.

(SERVES 15)

> 1 *4-pound chicken, brought to a boil, skimmed of broth, and then simmered*
>   *until tender in 3½ quarts of water, or 3 quarts of rich chicken broth*
> 1 *pound blanched almonds, dried for 5 minutes in an oven preheated to 300*
>   *degrees F.*
> 6 *bitter almonds (if available)*
> *Juice of 1 large lemon*
> 1 *teaspoon ground coriander*
> 10 *hard-cooked egg yolks*
> 2 *cups heavy cream*
> *Cayenne pepper to taste*
> 10 *hard-cooked egg whites, finely chopped*
> 2 *tablespoons each minced dill and minced chives*

Discard the skin and bones of the chicken and cut the meat into ½-inch cubes. Place the chicken broth and meat in a stock pot. Use the steel blade of a food processor or blender to reduce the almonds to a coarse powder. Add the lemon juice, coriander, and finally the egg yolks rapidly, 1 at a time, through the opening in the top. Pour in 2–3 cups of the chicken broth, whirl for a few seconds to mix, and then stir the mixture into the soup remaining in the pot. Press out any lumps with the back of a spoon as you stir. Just prior to serving, whip the cream with the cayenne pepper and fold it into the hot soup. Mix the egg whites, dill, and chives, and serve as a garnish.

Baked Lamb and Olive Stew

You may bake the stew for the entire time rather than finishing it on top of the stove if you wish to prepare it all in one day (or if you don't mind removing only a part of the fat).

(SERVES 15)

8 pounds boneless lamb shoulder, trimmed and cut into 1-inch cubes
Salt, pepper, and ground oregano to taste
5 tablespoons olive oil
2 cloves garlic, peeled and minced
2 cups each coarsely chopped onions and celery
30–40 small white onions, peeled
2 cups dry white wine
1 bay leaf
½ teaspoon dried leaf thyme
1 tablespoon arrowroot
½ cup water
30 each large green and black olives
2 tablespoons lemon zest, grated or cut into very fine julienne

Preheat oven to 350 degrees F.

Sprinkle the lamb with salt, pepper, and oregano. Sauté until lightly browned in 3 tablespoons of the oil in a large stew pot. Add the garlic, chopped onions, and celery, and stir over medium heat until the onions are transparent. Pour in enough water to just cover the meat and bake for 30 minutes. Meanwhile, sauté the small whole onions in the remaining oil until lightly browned on all sides.

Remove the pan from the oven and cool the meat to room temperature. If you plan to finish the stew the following day, refrigerate the meat until the fat rises to the top and solidifies, then remove and discard it. To finish the stew on the same day, place a dozen or so ice cubes on top, and when the fat partially solidifies, spoon it off and discard it. Don't worry if some of the herbs and vegetables are discarded with the fat—their goodness will have permeated the meat and infused it with flavor.

Add the wine, bay leaf, thyme, and small onions to the pot. Cover and simmer the stew over very low heat until the meat is tender. Mix the arrowroot with ½ cup of water, pressing out any lumps with the back of a spoon, and add it to the stew. Bring to a boil over high heat, stirring constantly, until the stew thickens slightly. Blanch the olives in hot water, drain and dry them, and add them to the stew along with the lemon zest. Serve hot.

Layered Deep-Dish Spinach and Bulgur Pie

Spinach pie is even more delicious when it includes a layer of bulgur delicately flavored with mint and scallion. Top this with feta cheese and Béchamel Sauce, bake, and serve hot or at room temperature as a vegetable or as an hors d'oeuvre, chilled and cut into thin wedges.

(YIELD: 2 PIES)

> 4 *pounds fresh spinach, well washed, or 8 10-ounce boxes*
>   *frozen spinach, thawed*
> 4 *tablespoons butter, melted*
> *Nutmeg to taste*
> *Salt to taste*
> 3 *cups bulgur, soaked in cold water for 30 minutes*
> 2 *tablespoons freshly squeezed lemon juice*
> ½ *cup finely chopped mint*
> 1 *cup finely chopped scallions, including some of the green tops*
> 2 *recipes Béchamel Sauce (page 256)*
> ⅓ *pound feta cheese*

Discard the tough stems from the fresh spinach. In a heavy pot, cook the spinach for 4–5 minutes in the water that clings to the leaves. Cool to room temperature and squeeze out the excess moisture. If the spinach is still very wet, return it to the pan and toss it for 1 minute over medium heat to dry it out. Then finely chop it. (For frozen spinach, cook according to package directions, squeeze out moisture and, if necessary, dry out as directed above.) Stir in 2 tablespoons of the melted butter, a generous sprinkle of nutmeg, and salt to taste.

Drain the bulgur well and toss with the remaining 2 tablespoons of butter, the lemon juice, mint, and scallions. Mix together the Béchamel Sauce and crumbled feta cheese.

Generously butter two 9-inch ovenproof, deep-dish pie plates or nonstick skillets with ovenproof handles and layer one-fourth of the spinach in the bottom of each. Press down lightly, then cover each with half the bulgur mixture. Press the bulgur down lightly and cover each with half of the remaining spinach. The pies may be refrigerated at this point for up to 48 hours.

Just prior to serving, top each pie with half the cheese sauce and bake in an oven preheated to 350 degrees F. until the pies are hot and the tops are puffed and golden brown. Serve hot or tepid if the pies accompany the meal, lightly chilled if served as an hors d'oeuvre.

Garlicky Eggplant-Rice Pudding

Rice pudding served as a savory rather than a sweet . . . a really mellow combination of rice, egg, lemon, garlic, and fried eggplant slices. Don't miss it!

(SERVES 15)

> *3 cups long-grain rice*
> *Chicken broth*
> *3 tablespoons freshly squeezed lemon juice*
> *1 teaspoon dried oregano*
> *3 medium-size eggplants*
> *Salt to taste*
> *4 cloves garlic, peeled and crushed*
> *Olive oil*
> *2 quarts milk*
> *4 eggs*
> *4 egg yolks*
> *4 egg whites, stiffly beaten*
> *Freshly ground black pepper to taste*

Cook the rice in the chicken broth according to package directions and toss it with a fork over low heat for a minute or two if necessary to rid it of excess moisture. Cool to room temperature and stir in the lemon juice and ½ teaspoon of the oregano.

While the rice is cooking and cooling cut the eggplants crosswise into ½-inch-thick slices, discarding the small end pieces. Cut the slices in half and sprinkle both sides of each lightly with salt. Arrange on paper towels, cover with additional layers of paper toweling, weight down with plates, and let drain for 10 minutes. Wipe away the salt and brush the slices with a mixture of the garlic and olive oil. Broil until lightly browned on both sides, turning once. Set aside.

Scald the milk. Beat the eggs and the egg yolks together, slowly stir in a cup of the hot milk, then stir this mixture back into the remaining milk. Cook over low heat, stirring constantly, until the mixture coats a spoon. Cool to room temperature and mix with the rice. Fold in the whipped egg whites and season with salt and pepper. Spread in an oiled baking dish 9 inches by 14 inches by 4 inches.

Arrange the slices of eggplant attractively on the rice, sprinkle with the remaining oregano, and bake in an oven preheated to 300 degrees F. until the pudding is hot and the top of the eggplant is nicely browned.

Shrimp with Fresh Tomato and Feta Cheese

I expanded the menu with this fresh-tasting dish when out-of-town guests called to say that they *would* be in our part of the world after all. It complements nicely the chilled spinach pie when served with drinks.

(SERVES 15)

30 *large shrimp in their shells*

2 *tablespoons each oil and butter*

1 *large clove garlic, peeled and crushed*

6 *medium-size fresh tomatoes, peeled, seeded, and coarsely chopped*

¼ *pound feta cheese, rinsed and crumbled*

Salt and freshly ground black pepper to taste

Use your kitchen shears to cut through the tops of the shrimp shells deeply enough to remove the black veins. Do not remove the shells. Heat the oil, butter, and garlic in a large skillet and sauté the shrimp until they turn bright pink, turning them once. Set the shrimp aside and add the tomatoes to the pan. Stir over medium-high heat until the juices just begin to thicken. The dish may be refrigerated at this point and continued just prior to serving. Add the shrimp and feta cheese to the tomato sauce, season to taste (careful, the feta is salty), and slip under the broiler just until the shrimp are hot and the feta slightly melted.

Fresh-Fruit Baklava with Ouzo Kadaif

This is not baklava in the usual sense. In fact, it isn't baklava at all. What it really happens to be is a Norwegian nut torte with thin layers soaked in honey syrup and layered with fresh fruit. Not to worry. When the layers are spread with Ouzo-flavored Kadaif, and the syrup is perfumed with rosewater, North meets East in a lighthearted ethnic illusion.

(SERVES 15)

2½ *cups finely chopped walnuts*

2 *cups zwieback crumbs*

2 *teaspoons each baking powder and cinnamon*

¼ *teaspoon each powdered anise and salt*

2 *teaspoons vanilla extract*

7 *eggs, separated*

1 *cup granulated sugar*

1 *recipe Honey-Rose Syrup (see below)*

1 *recipe Ouzo Kadaif (see below)*

4 *cups sliced, peeled, fresh plums, peaches, apricots, and so forth*

16 *walnut meats, halved*

Preheat oven to 325 degrees F.

Mix the chopped walnuts, zwieback crumbs, baking powder, cinnamon, anise, salt, and vanilla extract. Beat the egg yolks into this mixture. Beat the egg whites until foamy, then continue beating while you gradually beat in the sugar. When the egg whites are stiff and glossy, fold them into the nut mixture.

Smooth the batter into 3 buttered round 9-inch pans and bake for 30 minutes. Remove from the oven and cool until still warm but no longer hot. Carefully remove the layers from the pans and cool them on separate plates. Cover each with Honey-Rose Syrup (see below) and Ouzo Kadaif (see below). Stack the layers, covering the bottom 2 with sliced fruit. Top with walnut halves. Chill overnight. Serve cold.

Honey-Rose Syrup

> 3 *cups water*
> 1 *cup honey*
> 1 *cup granulated sugar*
> 2 *teaspoons rosewater*

In a heavy pot, boil all the ingredients over a medium flame for about 30 minutes, or until syrupy. Cool to room temperature. Pour equal amounts over each nut layer and let stand for 4 hours. Spread the layers with Ouzo Kadaif.

Ouzo Kadaif

This is not actually authentic, but the flavor is marvelous and the name so romantic it seems to add to the pleasure.

(MAKES ABOUT 2 CUPS)

> 1 *cup unsweetened condensed milk*
> ½ *cup honey*
> 1 *cup ground blanched almonds*
> *Ouzo*
> 8 *ounces sweet butter*
> 2 *cups confectioners' sugar*

Boil the milk, honey, almonds, and 1 tablespoon ouzo together until the mixture is thick and sticky and has reduced, to measure about 1¼ cups. Chill well. Beat the butter in an electric mixer until it is pale yellow in color. Gradually beat in 1 cup of the sugar and continue beating until the mixture is light and fluffy.

Work the almond mixture and an additional tablespoon ouzo into the butter cream along with the remaining cup of confectioners' sugar. If necessary, work in additional ouzo to bring the cream to a spreadable consistency. Chill well. Just prior to serving, use a broad, fluted nozzle to pipe a decorative border of the cream around the edges of the baklava.

White Lightning Chili

At our house, chili is standard fare for the care and feeding of artists. This pale but piquant chicken chili, tawny with golden tomatoes and laced with white kidney beans, is far more subtle than its beefy counter-part. Serve it with hot cooked rice and bowls of cubed avocado, tomatoes, sweet onion, chopped olives, minced fresh hot pep-pers, grated Monterey jack cheese, and sour cream mixed with chopped fresh chives.

(SERVES 16 TO 18)

> *¹/₂ head garlic (about 10 cloves)*
> *3 tablespoons cornstarch*
> *6 pounds chicken breasts, skinned, boned, and cut into ¹/₃-inch cubes*
> *3 tablespoons or more vegetable oil*
> *5 medium-size onions, peeled and coarsely chopped*
> *12 medium-size golden tomatoes, peeled, seeded, and coarsely chopped*
> *10 cups cooked white kidney beans, well drained*
> *6 tablespoons chili powder (or more to taste)*
> *4 teaspoons each salt, ground cumin, and oregano*
> *Chicken broth*
> *Hot cooked rice*

Preheat oven to 350 degrees F. Bake the garlic for 50 minutes (see page 154).

Press the cornstarch through a fine sieve to coat the chicken pieces lightly. In a large, heavy nonstick pot, sauté the chicken pieces in the oil until pale gold, stirring from time to time. Do not let the chicken brown. Remove the chicken and set it aside. Sauté the onions until they are transparent. Add the tomatoes, the beans, and the seasonings. Squeeze the garlic cloves from their skins into the pot. Add the chicken and enough broth to cover. Heat the chili to just under a boil, then lower the heat and simmer, covered, for one hour or until tender, stirring occasionally; add broth or water if necessary. Adjust the seasonings.

Danish Whole Fish Dinner

This Scandinavian import serves as the basis for entertaining a few fascinating friends very nicely indeed. Although the affair may be dressed up—for one of those spiffy little dinners that pop up between Christmas and New Year's, for instance—it is most enjoyable as an informal supper with much passing back and forth of garnishes and lively conversation.

Cod or haddock are the fish varieties preferred for this meal and the ones I prepare most frequently, but just prior to the party shown here—one I had set my heart on—an ocean storm was raging and our local fishermen stayed safe and snug on shore. Panic! No whole fish! A frantic search ultimately turned up one lone deep-sea trawler laden with outsize cod, each roughly the size of a Dallas Cowboy linebacker, along with several exceedingly homely blackfish of roughly the size I needed.

The fact is, any properly prepared whole fish will be superb served this friendly way. Offer beer or ice-cold schnapps and let guests help carry the brightly colored dishes of garnishes to the table while you wrestle the fish. I like to time the meal so that I remove the fish from the pan to the platter and then immediately to the table at the instant when its quiver is precisely right. If your timing is a little off, or if you're nervous about bouncing your pièce de résistance on the floor, rather than slipping it gracefully onto the serving dish, there is a method for dealing with the thing before your friends swarm around you in awe, rattling your natural cool. See the recipe instructions for details.

202

Let the size of your fish determine the number of guests, or vice versa, but remember, aside from the fish, the ingredients listed are for six. To serve ten to twelve, double the amounts of garnishes, sauces, and so forth.

Menu

Poached Whole Cod (or Other) Fish

Traditional Garnishes

Ladyfinger Potatoes or Red Potatoes

Melted Butter, Hollandaise Sauce, and Grainy Mustard and Dill Sauce

White Chocolate Fondue

Poached Whole Cod (or Other) Fish

(SERVES 6)

> 1–2 4-*pound cod or other whole fish, or* 1 6-*pounder*
> *Boiling water to cover*
> ½ *cup (1 stick) butter, melted*
> ¼ *teaspoon each freshly ground white pepper and grated allspice*
> ½ *cup each minced parsley and dill (reserve a few sprigs for decoration)*
> *Slices of lemon and lime*
> ½ *cup capers, drained*
> 1 *cup each coarsely chopped dill pickle and red onion*
> 2 *cups coarsely chopped pickled beets*
> 1 *cup peeled, coarsely grated apple*
> 2 *tablespoons lemon juice*
> 6 *hard-cooked eggs, peeled and coarsely chopped*
> 1 *cup melted butter*

Place the fish on a rack in a large poacher or deep roasting pan and pour in enough boiling water to cover. Over low heat, bring the water to a quiver (just under a simmer) and continue cooking, maintaining this temperature for 8–10 minutes for one 4-pound fish, 12–15 minutes for two 4-pound fish, 15–18 minutes for one 6-pound fish. Do not allow the water to boil.

Remove the pan or pans from the heat and test the fish for doneness; the flesh should be translucent, spring back slowly when pressed with your finger, and flake reluctantly when prodded (on the underside) with a fork. If the flesh does not respond as directed, let the fish remain in the hot water until it does.

As the water cools a little, gently loosen and then remove the skin that comes away easily. Do not remove the fish from the rack or turn it over. Don't worry if bits of the underside of the skin adhere to the flesh—by the time you're finished with the garnishing, they won't be seen. Remove the fish from the water by picking up the rack. Cover it lightly with aluminum foil and drain it well. Slip the fish onto its platter, drizzle it with hot butter flavored with pepper and allspice, and garnish it with bits of parsley and dill, and slices of lemon and lime.

Should you prefer to deal with your fish prior to your guests' arrival, cook it and remove it from the water as directed above but wrap several thicknesses of buttered foil more tightly over the fish and then wrap the fish on its rack in a clean terrycloth towel that has been dipped in hot water and wrung out. Wrap another hot towel around the fish in the other direction and place the whole package on a baking sheet, taking care not to damage the fish in any way. Place the baking sheet in an oven preheated to 300 degrees F. and immediately turn off the heat. This should hold your fish for nearly an hour. To serve, remove the package from the oven, tip it slightly to one side to make sure that the fish is well drained, then unwrap it and use the buttered foil as a ramp or sling to help in maneuvering the fish into position on the platter without breaking its tail. Garnish as directed above.

Arrange the capers, minced parsley and dill, dill pickle, red onion, pickled beets, (with lemon juice squeezed on it to keep it from browning) and hard-cooked eggs each in a separate dish. Serve with melted butter, Grainy Mustard and Dill Sauce, and Hollandaise Sauce (page 253), and the steamy hot potatoes.

Ladyfinger Potatoes or Red Potatoes

24 small ladyfingers or red potatoes

Steam or boil the potatoes until tender. Serve hot with the fish.

Grainy Mustard and Dill Sauce

Sweet and sour, sharp and deliciously dilly. A superb accompaniment for fish of every kind.

(MAKES ABOUT 1 CUP)

3 tablespoons lemon juice or mild white vinegar
3 tablespoons grainy Swedish (or German) mustard
1 teaspoon dry mustard
¼ cup sugar
1 teaspoon salt
Pinch of ground cardamom
Coarsely grated fresh black pepper to taste
½ cup olive oil
2 tablespoons minced fresh or frozen dill, or 1½ teaspoons dried

Whisk together the lemon juice or vinegar, the 2 mustards, sugar, and seasonings. Add the oil, several drops at a time at first, whisking constantly, then in a thin stream, still whisking, until the sauce is thick. Mix in the dill.

White Chocolate Fondue

This dessert is so festive and entertaining all by itself, it can also be served alone, and is welcome in all seasons. And it is participatory, nicely suited to convivial outings shared with good friends—walks along deserted beaches or through wind-stripped woods, or after early-evening ice skating or a drive through a snowstorm to catch a flick. This is change-of pace hot chocolate with a twist. Feel free to add to the list of dipping tidbits below.

(SERVES 6)

> 1 *pound fine-quality white milk chocolate*
> ¾ *cup light cream*
> 6 *tablespoons kirsch*
> *Combination of assorted tidbits for dipping: slices of peeled melon, papaya,*
> *pineapple, kiwi, and so forth; unpeeled slices of pear, peach, orange, apple,*
> *and others; bits of candied ginger; candied or dried fruits; berries; nuts;*
> *tangerine or Mandarin orange sections; marshmallows; cubes of angel (page*
> *236) or pound cake.*

Cut or break the chocolate into 1½-inch pieces and place in a fondue pot or chafing dish with the cream. Stir over a low flame until the chocolate melts. Stir the kirsch into the hot melted chocolate and continue stirring over low heat for a minute or so. Keep the fondue hot but do not allow it to scorch. Arrange the tidbits attractively on a platter or on small individual plates. Provide each person with a small plate on which to spoon some fondue over an assortment of tidbits. At a small, informal get-together, everyone may use fondue forks to spear tidbits and dip them into the hot chocolate. This can be messy but a great deal of fun. Use a table covering that won't be ruined by dribbles of chocolate.

A Down-Home Dutch New Year's Day Celebration

Last year, on my way back from a Christmas visit to my parents' home beyond the snow-frosted mountains that border the Pennsylvania-Dutch farmlands, I was lured from the highway by visions of sugar cookies, sausages, scrapple, dried apples, and other plums available at the Dutch Market at Bird in Hand, Pennsylvania. There, in the chill white-washed interior, amid the scrubbed glass cases, a familiar madness overtook me. I began filling my wooden shopping basket with densely smoked, fat-flecked sweet bolognas wrapped in hand-sewn cotton cases; nutty dried corn; dusky pear and plum and apple butters; jars of green pickled watermelon rind; hams and turkey legs smoked to a deep cherry amber; brilliant relishes of every variety; syrupy-at-the-bottom shoofly pies and chewy little pillows of molasses-and-sugar cookies. Only when I unpacked did I face up to the awful truth —an absolute feeding frenzy would be necessary to do away with these treasures ourselves. A party of the holiday variety was definitely in order. New Year's Day at noon seemed ideal.

Because my father's people are Pennsylvania Dutch and I find their foods and traditions particularly appealing, I decided to build the party around the Good Luck New Year's Sauerkraut Soup that Grandfather Nicholas often prepared, along with a cornucopia of old-fashioned loaves—pumpernickel prune bread, dinner roll twist, and soft sour cream rye—that he, a baker, created when he was still a young man. In addition I'd include several breads from my own recipe files and lengths of my favorite sausages. My guest list for that party reached close to one hundred before I called a halt, but the party presented here is for a far more manageable twenty to thirty guests—a number that works equally well as an open-house extravaganza that goes on and on, or as a cocktail-with-food two-to-three-hour afternoon's diversion. My New Year's Day entertainment included pie and cookies, tea and coffee, but you should design your party to please you.

In putting together your own version of the Pennsylvania-Dutch New Year's Day Celebration, buy country-market-variety smoked meats, relishes, and desserts, if you like, but the soup, potato salad, and breads are best if they are made by you, so I've included recipes. A little preparation time is involved, but none of these is tricky in the least and only the potato salad need be made on party day. Of course, if you feel particularly energetic and are looking for a challenge, you may want to indulge your guests—create your own sausages (see page 260).

```
╔═══════════════════════════════════╗
║            𝓜enu                  ║
╠═══════════════════════════════════╣
║  Good Luck New Year's Sauerkraut  ║
║              Soup                 ║
╠═══════════════════════════════════╣
║      Apple Cider-Glazed Ham       ║
╠═══════════════════════════════════╣
║  Hot Pennsylvania-German Potato   ║
║              Salad                ║
╠═══════════════════════════════════╣
║        Red Cabbage Slaw           ║
╠═══════════════════════════════════╣
║       A Variety of Sausages       ║
║        and Smoked Meats           ║
╠═══════════════════════════════════╣
║        Watermelon Pickles         ║
╠═══════════════════════════════════╣
║           Corn Relish             ║
╠═══════════════════════════════════╣
║    Molasses-Applesauce Cookies    ║
╠═══════════════════════════════════╣
║           Shoofly Pie             ║
╠═══════════════════════════════════╣
║       Bierhaus Pretzel Bread      ║
╠═══════════════════════════════════╣
║  Tangy Sour-Cream Poppy Seed Rye  ║
╠═══════════════════════════════════╣
║    Pumpernickel-Wheat Bread       ║
╚═══════════════════════════════════╝
```

Good Luck New Year's Sauerkraut Soup

Tradition has it that to start the year off right you must enjoy sauerkraut, preferably with sausage and preferably in this snappy version flavored with ginger, fennel, and caraway. A pleasant prescription.

(SERVES 25)

8 *slices slab bacon, thickly sliced*
4 *large onions, peeled and coarsely chopped*
4 *pounds sauerkraut, drained*
5 *medium potatoes, peeled and grated*
8 *frankfurters, sliced on the slant*
3 *quarts rich beef broth or consommé*
3 *tablespoons tomato paste*

1 *teaspoon each caraway and fennel seeds*
2 *teaspoons paprika*
1 *teaspoon salt*
2 *cups coarsely chopped cooked ham*
20 *gingersnaps, crushed*
Sour cream
Red wine

In a large soup kettle, fry the bacon until fairly crisp. Add the onions and sauté until they are transparent. Rinse the sauerkraut and potatoes, drain them well, and add to the pot along with the remaining ingredients except the ham and gingersnaps. Bring the soup to a boil, cover, and boil gently for 45 minutes.

Refrigerate until 1 hour before party time, then bring slowly to a low boil, add the ham and gingersnaps, and cook 10 minutes more. Serve very hot with bowls of cold sour cream and splashes of wine if desired.

Apple Cider-Glazed Ham

Hams have long been the mainstay of country dinners. Time was when most farmers raised, slaughtered, cured, and smoked their own hogs and took pride in the subtle flavors their hams achieved. Now most home-smoked hams are available only in specialty markets. The ham around which I centered my "down-home" dinner was apple-smoked, boned, fully cooked, and brought to market by the farmer. Unlike some more slippery-textured, shallow-flavored commercial hams the finished product here was firm-to-the-tooth but remarkably tender. And an incredible convenience! If your country ham is uncooked, follow the directions on the package; if none exist, soak the meat 24–48 hours, changing the water several times. Then scrub it well, remove the skin, and set the ham, fat-side down, in a roasting pan. Add enough cider or water (or a mixture of both) to the pan to bring the liquid level three-quarters of the way up the sides of the meat. Bake in an oven preheated to 325 degrees F. Figure 20 minutes per pound, until the small bone at the shank end pulls out easily (turn the ham once). Glaze the ham if you want additional flavor, color, and shine.

There are dozens of good glazes, but this is my favorite for country hams.

Apple Cider Glaze

Dry the ham, place in a roasting pan, and baste it frequently during the last hour of baking with a mixture of ½ cup each of cider, molasses, and cider vinegar.

Hot Pennsylvania-German Potato Salad

There are times when throwing caution to the winds seems prudent if the rewards are satisfying enough. A New Year's Day with close friends is one of those times. Hot potato salad is one of those rewards.

(SERVES 25 TO 30)

20 medium-size potatoes, or 35 small red new potatoes
24 slices lean bacon, cut into 1-inch pieces
4 small onions, peeled, sliced, and separated into rings
2½ cups beef consommé (undiluted)
2 cups mild vinegar (wine or tarragon)
½ cup lemon juice
1 tablespoon granulated sugar
1½ teaspoons salt
2 tablespoons cornstarch
6 egg yolks, well beaten
10 scallions with 3 inches of green top each, chopped
1 tablespoon chopped sage
Salt and pepper to taste

Boil the potatoes in their skins until they are tender when pierced with a fork, but do not let them become mushy. Drain, plunge them into cold water for 5 minutes, then drain again, peel them, and cut them into ¾-inch cubes. If you are using new potatoes, peel half and leave the skins on the other half for a nice contrast, then cut into ½-inch slices.

Fry the bacon until crisp in a large kettle, then remove it with a slotted spoon and set it aside. Add the onion rings to the pan and cook them, stirring, until they are tender but still have a little crunch. Set aside a dozen or so rings of a uniform size to use as a garnish.

Mix together the consommé, vinegar, lemon juice, sugar, salt, and cornstarch until smooth. Be sure to press out any lumps with the back of a spoon. Add the mixture to the kettle and bring to a boil, stirring constantly, until the sauce thickens. Remove the pan from the heat and beat 1 cup of this sauce into the egg yolks, then immediately stir this egg mixture back into the remaining hot sauce.

Toss the potatoes, scallions, and sage with the hot dressing. Season to taste with salt, pepper, and extra lemon juice, if desired. Serve immediately or at room temperature with the reserved onion rings and a generous grind of black pepper on top.

Red Cabbage Slaw

(SERVES 25)

>   3 medium-size or 4 small heads red cabbage
>   2 teaspoons each salt, poppy seeds, and dry mustard
>   2½ tablespoons all-purpose flour
>   ⅓ cup granulated sugar (optional)
>   1½ tablespoons butter, melted
>   4 egg yolks
>   ⅔ cup hot lemon juice
>   ⅔ cup white vinegar
>   2 cups half-and-half

Cut the cabbages in quarters and discard the tough outer leaves and hard cores. Cut the cabbage leaves into very fine shreds with a sharp knife (a food processor produces coarser shreds).

In the top of a double boiler, stir together the seasonings, flour, sugar, butter, egg yolks, lemon juice, and vinegar. Pour in the half-and-half and cook over hot water, stirring constantly, until the mixture thickens. Stir the hot dressing and cabbage together. Adjust the seasonings and thin the slaw with a little cream or yogurt if necessary.

Watermelon Pickles

Serving your own pickles and relishes is a nice, loving touch that enhances any dinner, particularly the down-home variety. But not to worry if you haven't the time or the inclination . . . the gourmet section of your favorite market usually stocks a variety. Cauliflower, broken into florets, works well here, too.

(MAKES 3 PINTS)

>   3 quarts watermelon rind (about ½ medium-size melon), peeled and cut into
>   1-inch squares
>   ⅓ cup plus 2 tablespoons non-iodized salt
>   7–8 cups water
>   1 quart (1 tray) ice cubes
>   1½ cups white vinegar
>   4½ cups granulated sugar
>   3 1-inch pieces cinnamon stick
>   2 teaspoons whole cloves
>   1 lemon, thinly sliced

Cover the watermelon with a brine made by mixing the salt with 5 cups of the water. Add the ice cubes and let stand overnight or about 6 hours. Drain, rinse in cold water, place in a stainless-steel or enamel saucepan, cover with cold water, and simmer until the watermelon is just tender, about 10 minutes. Then drain again and return the watermelon pieces to the saucepan.

Mix the vinegar, sugar, remaining water, cinnamon pieces, and cloves, and boil for 5 minutes. Immediately pour this mixture over the watermelon, add the lemon, cover, and let stand for 5 hours. Bring the contents of the pan to a boil and cook until the watermelon is translucent, about 10 minutes.

Pack the hot pickles into hot pint jars, cover with the boiling syrup to within ½ inch of the top and adjust the lids. No need to bother with the tedious canning process, just allow the jars to cool and then refrigerate them until needed. They keep beautifully.

Corn Relish

(MAKES 3 TO 4 PINTS)

10 ears husked corn, white, yellow, or mixed varieties
1 cup diced onion
1 cup each diced red and green peppers
2 cups coarsely chopped celery
1 cup granulated sugar
2 cups white vinegar
Salt to taste
1 teaspoon each celery seed and whole cloves
2 teaspoons dry mustard
½ teaspoon turmeric

Plunge the corn into boiling water, then turn off the heat. After 8 minutes, pour off the water and cover the corn with cold water. Drain the corn and cut the kernels from the cob. Don't scrape the cobs or the relish will look milky. (You may substitute frozen corn, defrosted in the refrigerator, but it won't taste as fresh and sweet.)

Bring the onion, peppers, celery, sugar, vinegar, salt, celery seed, and cloves to a boil in a stainless-steel or enamel saucepan, then boil for 5 minutes, stirring occasionally. Blend the dry mustard and turmeric with a little boiling liquid (press out any lumps with the back of a spoon), and add to the liquid along with the corn. After the liquid returns to a boil, cook 5 minutes, stirring occasionally.

Pack the hot vegetables with their liquid into hot jars to within ½ inch of the top and adjust the lids. Refrigerate until needed.

Molasses-Applesauce Cookies

(MAKES 3 DOZEN)

> 7 tablespoons sweet butter
> 1¼ cups plus 2 tablespoons granulated sugar
> 1 cup molasses
> ⅔ cup applesauce
> 1 jumbo egg, lightly beaten
> 4½ cups plus 3 tablespoons all-purpose flour, sifted
> 3 teaspoons baking soda
> ¾ teaspoon salt
> 1½ teaspoons each grated nutmeg, ground ginger, and cloves
> 1½ cups hot water

Preheat oven to 400 degrees F.

In the bowl of an electric mixer, beat the butter until it is light and fluffy, then cream in the sugar, a few tablespoons at a time, beating after each addition until well incorporated. Stir in the molasses, applesauce, and egg until well blended.

Sift together the flour, baking soda, salt, and spices. Add a little of these dry ingredients to the creamed mixture alternately with a little of the hot water, blending in well after each addition. Butter a baking sheet well and drop on the cookie batter by tablespoonful at 3-inch intervals. Bake for 10–12 minutes, then remove the cookies from the oven and let them stand a few minutes, before loosening and removing them to a wire rack to cool.

Shoofly Pie

This pie keeps really well and can be baked several days prior to your party. Let it cool thoroughly, wrap it in aluminum foil, and store it in a not-too-warm spot—a pantry shelf or a chilly windowsill are ideal. If there is room in the refrigerator, that's fine, too, but bring the pie to room temperature or warm it slightly in the oven before serving it. At a party like this, where food is rich and abundant, cut the slices extra thin. A taste is probably all any guest will want.

(SERVES 8)

> 2 cups all-purpose flour
> 1 cup light-brown sugar
> 1 teaspoon baking soda
> 12 tablespoons (1½ sticks) butter
> 1 recipe Pastry for a One-Crust Pie (page 259)
> 1 cup molasses
> 1 cup simmering water

Sift together the flour, sugar, and baking soda. Use a food processor or pastry cutter (or 2 knives) to cut in 10 tablespoons of the butter to form a coarse meal. Refrigerate.

Prepare and roll out the pastry dough, line a 9-inch pie plate with it, and crimp the edges. Refrigerate. Preheat oven to 375 degrees F.

Mix the molasses and water, and pour one-third of the mixture into the pie shell. Sprinkle with one-third of the flour-butter mixture and repeat this process, alternating layers and ending with the flour mixture. Dot the top with bits of the remaining butter. Bake for 50 minutes. Serve warm or at room temperature.

Bierhaus Pretzel Bread

Soft pretzel dough is the stuff that this centerpiece bread is made of. The firmly knit texture, tawny crust, and crunch of coarse salt harken back to those small rolls, but this huge pretzel is sliceable!

(YIELD: 1 LARGE BREAD)

2 packages dry active yeast
1 cup warm milk
2¼ cups warm water
⅓ cup granulated sugar
5 tablespoons butter, at room temperature
1 egg
2¼ teaspoons salt
7–7½ cups all-purpose flour
1 egg yolk
1 tablespoon water
Coarse or kosher salt

In the large bowl of an electric mixer, sprinkle the yeast over the milk and stir until dissolved. Mix in the water, sugar, butter, egg, salt, and 3 cups of the flour. Beat at medium speed until the mixture is smooth, then add as much of the remaining flour as necessary to make a stiff dough. Pat the dough into a ball, put it into a large, buttered bowl, cover tightly with buttered aluminum foil, and refrigerate for 4–6 hours.

Dust a pastry board lightly with flour and turn the cold dough out onto it. Roll the dough between your palms into a long rope 2 inches thick, stretching it by pulling gently at both ends until it is about 3 feet in length. Twist the dough into an oversize pretzel shape.

Preheat oven to 400 degrees F.

Set the pretzel on a lightly greased baking sheet. Beat together the egg yolk and water, and brush over the top of the pretzel bread. Sprinkle the top of the bread liberally with coarse salt, cover, and allow to rise in a warm, draft-free place for 30 minutes. Bake for 50–60 minutes or until golden brown. Remove from the oven and cool on a wire rack for a few minutes. Serve warm.

This bread freezes and reheats superbly, but in this case omit the egg glaze and coarse salt prior to the initial baking. Bake the bread as directed, cool on a wire rack, wrap it well in aluminum foil, and freeze it. Completely defrost the bread in the refrigerator, brush it with the egg mixture, sprinkle it with the salt, and reheat it in an oven preheated to 350 degrees F. until the bread is golden, the egg is set, and the bread is warmed through. If you do not follow this sequence, the salt will retain moisture and make the top of the bread soggy.

Tangy Sour-Cream Poppy Seed Rye Bread

There's the tang of low-alcohol beer in here, as well as the smoothness of sour cream and the crunch of poppy seeds. If a better bread exists for slathering with mustard and piling with sausages, I'd love to taste it.

(YIELD: 2 LOAVES)

> *1 cup low-alcohol beer*
> *½ cup hot water*
> *2 packages dry active yeast*
> *½ cup commercial sour cream*
> *1 tablespoon salt*
> *1 teaspoon dry mustard*
> *1½ cups rye flour*
> *4–6 cups all-purpose white flour*
> *2 tablespoons poppy seeds*
> *1 egg*
> *1 teaspoon water*

Pour the beer and hot water into a large bowl. When the mixture is tepid, sprinkle the yeast over it. After 10 minutes, thoroughly mix in the sour cream and then the salt, dry mustard, rye flour, and enough of the white flour to make a fairly stiff dough. Knead the dough until it is smooth and elastic, about 10 minutes by hand or 2 minutes using a machine equipped with a dough hook.

Put the dough in an oiled bowl, smooth-side down, then turn the dough over, cover it lightly with a dish towel, and let it rise in a warm, draft-free place until it doubles in bulk. To test for double in bulk, push 2 fingers into the center of the dough; if the holes do not immediately fill up, the dough is ready to punch down.

Divide the dough into 2 equal pieces and sprinkle about ½ tablespoon of poppy seeds on the counter in front of you. Place 1 piece of dough on the poppy seeds and knead them in until they are evenly distributed. Roll the dough out into a rectangle that measures about 9 inches on one side. Roll the dough up tightly, starting at the 9-inch end. Pinch the edges to seal them and place the loaf, seam-side down, on one end of a baking sheet. Repeat the process with the remaining dough and place at the other end of the baking sheet. Cover lightly and allow to double in bulk (about 1 hour)

Preheat oven to 350 degrees F.

Beat the egg with the teaspoon of water and brush the breads with this mixture. Sprinkle the tops of the breads with the remaining poppy seeds. Bake for 50–60 minutes or until golden brown. Cool on the baking sheet for 10 minutes, then remove the loaves to a wire rack and cool to room temperature.

Pumpernickel-Wheat Bread

If there seems to be an unusual creamy density to this darkest of dark breads, it's most likely due to the chocolate and espresso that are locked deep in its heart. If it is more textured than ordinary pumpernickels, that almost surely is due to the inclusion of 100 percent whole wheat flour and rolled oats.

(YIELD: 2 ROUND LOAVES)

> 1 cup tepid water
> 1/3 cup dark molasses
> 2 packages dry active yeast
> 1/4 cup cider vinegar
> 1 square unsweetened chocolate
> 1 cup hot espresso, or 2 teaspoons instant espresso mixed with 1 cup hot water
> 3 slices dark pumpernickel bread, broken into small pieces (optional)
> 2 tablespoons cooking oil
> 2½ teaspoons salt
> 1 tablespoon caraway seeds, slightly bruised
> 3 cups each rye and all-purpose white flour
> 1 cup 100 percent whole wheat flour
> 1 cup quick rolled oats (not sweetened instant oats)
> 1 egg yolk
> 2 teaspoons water
> 1 teaspoon instant coffee flakes

Mix the water and molasses in a large bowl, sprinkle the yeast over, and set aside in a warm place for 10 minutes. In a food processor or blender, whirl the vinegar, chocolate, hot espresso, bread pieces, oil, salt, and caraway seeds until thoroughly blended. Add this to the yeast mixture along with 1 cup each of rye and white flour; mix well. Work in the wheat flour, ½ cup of the oats, and equal amounts of rye and white flours to produce a semi-firm dough. Knead 10 minutes by hand or 2 minutes by machine with a dough hook.

Transfer to a large, well-oiled bowl, turn the dough over, and cover with a towel. Allow the dough to rise until doubled in bulk in a warm, draft-free place.

Punch the dough down and knead about 10 times, or until it is smooth. Cut the dough in half, roll each piece out to eliminate any bubbles, and then pat each into a ball.

Place each bread in a round 8-inch cake pan, cover, and set aside to rise again in a warm, draft-free place until almost double in bulk, about 50–60 minutes.

Preheat oven to 350 degrees F.

Beat the egg yolk with 2 teaspoons of water and 1 teaspoon of instant coffee flakes and brush the breads with the mixture. Immediately sprinkle the tops of the loaves with the remaining oats. Bake for 50–60 minutes or until the loaves are nicely browned and sound hollow when you tap them with your finger.

The Main-Course Salad

Start with a gorgeous assortment of the freshest salad ingredients you can find (of course, your own just-picked are best): radicchio, spinach, miniature plum tomatoes, basil, and tender, uncooked summer squash. Add protein in moderation as a garnish: bits of smoked, pickled, grilled, or otherwise cooked meats, fish or shellfish; sliced or chopped hard-cooked eggs; cubed or grated cheese. Decorate with out-of-the-or-

dinary bits and pieces: an international assortment of olives, garlic croutons, sea-salted capers, edible vegetable and herb blossoms, rose petals, herbed nuts, and the like. Toss with an impeccable vinaigrette dressing or one of its flavorful variations.

My Favorite Classic Vinaigrette

Since olive oil is so much richer than peanut oil, the classic proportions for Sauce Vinaigrette are usually 1 tablespoon wine vinegar for every 3 tablespoons olive oil or 4 tablespoons peanut oil. I prefer a slight variation on this traditional theme. It seems to me that 3 tablespoons olive oil *plus* 1 tablespoon peanut oil, combined with a full-to-overflowing tablespoon of vinegar, lightens the dressing somewhat without diminishing the richness of its flavor. Try it both ways and decide for yourself. For four servings, whisk together ¼ teaspoon salt, a generous grind of black pepper, and 1 generous tablespoon wine vinegar. Thoroughly whisk in 3 tablespoons olive oil and 1 tablespoon peanut oil. Adjust the seasonings and whisk briefly once more. For Herb Vinaigrette, add 2 tablespoons minced mixed herbs to the dressing just before tossing.

A Vodka and Coffee Tasting Party

Vodka. The ultimate drink. Mercury smooth. Intense as chewing on an icicle. Refreshing as ice skating in a blizzard . . . bonfires beside a frozen brook. The essence of heat and chill. Impeccable served unembellished. Intriguing when the drink is flavored in the Russian manner with crushed peppercorns, ribbons of citrus peel, black cherries with their cracked pits, saffron, black tea, coffee, caraway, anise, garlic, dill, coriander, rosemary, or thyme. Both plain and in these many variations, vodka provides an interesting focal point for an unusually imposing entertainment. Tossed down in icy nips with portions of Peppery Lamb Tartare,

Tart Fish Tartare, smoked and pickled seafood of several kinds, multiple varieties of caviar, capered crème fraîche, all tucked into Lacy Crêpe Cones or piled onto Silver-Dollar Blinis and triangles of thin black bread. Sum up this heady experience with a sampling of elegant world-class coffee brews designed to both cleanse the palate and clear the head.

Plain vodkas form the focal point of the festivities. These should include the expected favorites, plus those brands you might have been meaning to try: a liter each of Stolichnaya, Finlandia, and Absolut, perhaps, plus a fifth each of Burroughs' English, Fleishmann's, Taaka, Wyborowa, and one or two of the American varieties. Freeze each bottle as is or place in a clean two-quart milk carton, fill to three-quarters with water, and freeze solid (the vodka becomes slightly syrupy but does not freeze). A large, top-loading freezer is great for this, but a conventional one with adjustable shelves will work just fine. In addition, freeze bottles of aquavit and tequila to pleasure the rare vodka hater

Flavored vodkas, besides pleasing the palate, are also conversation ticklers. The more flavors you present, the more interesting your party is sure to be. For a large gathering, infuse a fifth each of your favorites. For a smaller party, flavor vodka miniatures and place each bottle in a clean, empty eight-ounce juice box, fill with water, and freeze as directed above. To keep bottle labels from soaking off or becoming unreadable, it's best to chill both the water and the vodka thoroughly before putting the two together for the actual freezing. You might freeze into each ice block a branch of the fresh herb, citrus peel, a sprig of pine, a frond of fern, or a variety of flowers. Minutes before your first guest is due, cut away the surrounding milk or ice-cream carton, wrap the bottoms of the larger bottles in white linen napkins, arrange them on deep-sided trays or platters (to catch the melt-off), and place in the center of a table or buffet. Set a saucer or dish under each miniature bottle and group them on either side of the trays of larger bottles.

When it comes to food for this party, there are multiple choices. A simple offering of a few heaping bowls of caviar set in ice and surrounded by warm toast points would not be out of place. That aside, I suggest a kind of "finger food" smorgasbord approach with guests helping themselves, first to a small swallow of the particular vodka they feel might complement the initial "nibble" (or four or five) they favor, then a nip of a second flavored vodka, another trip to the buffet, and so on, back and forth, until they've had their fill. The "nips" of vodka might also be followed by a few swallows of cold Scandinavian beer or a bit of sparkling water to satisfy thirst as the imbiber enjoys the more substantial hors d'oeuvre.

Plan the food for this party to suit your own desires, needs, restrictions, budget, and so forth. Purchase any of the following treats you haven't time to prepare, or omit them and double up on the recipes you do particularly fancy. In any case, this party really demands finger foods. *Do* include some fish-based hors d'oeuvre (I've even included some based on jars of supermarket staples). *Do* cut foods into small portions or paper-thin slices. *Do* skewer them with olives, tiny gherkins, or other pickled vegetables. *Do* mince them so that they may be wrapped in crêpes or blinis or spread on flat breads.

Arrange the food "buffet style" at both ends of the table. In addition to the hors d'oeuvre already mentioned, you might serve rolled bits of roast beef, tongue, ham, lamb, chicken or turkey, plus a few good aged cheeses. In any case, guests should sample the milder smoked fish first, progress through to the sharper, pickled varieties, and then on to the meats, stopping after every fourth or fifth "nibble" for a neat drop of their favorite spirit.

About an hour after your first guest arrives, set out a selection of coffees on a second table. The coffees must be strong-shouldered and aromatic enough to measure up to such bold food and drink. Don't hold off serving coffee (and little cakes, if it pleases you) early. It won't put a damper on your party. You'll want even the guests who must leave early to experience the complex depths of these carefully chosen and matched brews. *Do* encourage your guests to linger over coffee and conversation.

223

Menu

Flavored Vodkas *Anise, Black Cherry, Black Tea,* *Coriander, Dill and Garlic, Coffee,* *Herb, Citrus, and Saffron Vodkas*	*Meat Hors d'Oeuvre* *Peppery Lamb Tartare, Various Meat* *Miniature Cones, Rolled Bits of Roast* *Beef, Tongue, Ham, Lamb, Chicken,* *and Turkey with Olives, Gherkins,* *and Pickled Vegetables*
Plain Vodkas *Stolichnaya, Finlandia, Absolut,* *Burroughs' English, Fleishmann's,* *Taaka, Wyborowa Vodkas*	*Three-Flour Flat Bread*
	Silver-Dollar Blinis
Fish and Shellfish Hors d'Oeuvre *Tart Fish Tartare, Scallop Seviche,* *Gravlax, Shrimp Vinaigrette,* *Herring and Tuna Nuggets in* *Ribbons of Fresh Ginger, Caviar in* *Lacy Crêpe Cones*	*Aged Cheeses*
	An Assortment of Coffees
	Chocolate Squares

Flavored Vodkas

Flavored vodkas attempt to improve upon perfection . . . with fascinating results. You'll find that even vodka purists will soon get into the spirit of the occasion and knock back a tiny nip of each flavor.

Measurements given below are for fifths. To flavor miniatures, use only one-third the amount of flavoring.

Anise Vodka (Anisovaya)

> 2½ teaspoons crushed anise seed
> 1 fifth vodka

Add the seeds to the vodka and infuse at room temperature for 24 hours. Close and freeze.

Black Cherry Vodka (Vishnyouka)

> 40 black cherries
> 1 fifth vodka

Cut the cherries in half and remove the pits. Crack the pits and put them, along with 20 cherry halves, into the bottle. Infuse at room temperature for 24 hours. Strain. Discard the pits. Mix all the cherry meats together and serve them over Chocolate Squares.

Black Tea Vodka (Chainaya)

> 2 tablespoons fruit-and-spice black tea, or use 5 teaspoons black tea and ½
> teaspoon whole cloves
> 1 fifth vodka

Add the tea to the vodka and infuse for 24 hours at room temperature. Strain, return the vodka to the bottle, and freeze.

Coriander Vodka (Koriandrovaya)

> 2½ teaspoons lightly crushed whole coriander seeds
> 1 fifth vodka

Add the coriander seeds to the vodka and infuse at room temperature for 24 hours. Strain, return the vodka to the bottle, and freeze.

Dill and Garlic Vodka (Chesnochnaya)

> 1 large clove garlic, unpeeled
> 1 branch dill, rinsed and dried
> 5 pink peppercorns (my favorites, but white or black will do)
> 1 fifth vodka

Make several slashes in the garlic but do not unpeel it. Add the garlic, dill, and peppercorns to the vodka and infuse at room temperature for 24 hours. Strain. Return the vodka to the bottle along with a small sprig of dill and the peppercorns, and freeze.

Herbed Vodka (Travnik)

> 1 sprig each fresh rosemary and thyme (or your favorites), bruised to release the
> flavor
> 1 fifth vodka

Add the herbs to the vodka and infuse at room temperature for 24 hours. Strain and return the vodka to the bottle. Leave a little of each herb in the bottle. Freeze.

Citrus Vodka (Mimonovka)

> 1 orange or lemon
> 1 fifth vodka

Use a vegetable peeler to remove the orange or lemon rind in 1 strip without including any of the bitter white underskin. Add the peel to the vodka and infuse at room temperature for 24 hours. Remove the peel. Freeze the flavored vodka.

Saffron Vodka (Shafrannaya)

> Generous pinch of saffron
> 1 fifth vodka

Add the saffron to the vodka and infuse for 24 hours at room temperature. Turn the bottle from time to time to color the vodka evenly. If the color isn't intense enough, infuse it 4–5 hours more. Turn the bottle every 30 minutes. Strain, return the vodka to the bottle, and freeze.

Coffee Vodka

I've never encountered this variation anywhere but in my own home; however, it is extremely pleasant.

> 1 tablespoon coffee beans
> 1 fifth vodka

Crush the beans and add them to the vodka. Infuse for 24 hours at room temperature. Strain and freeze the vodka.

Tart Fish Tartare

This is an exceptionally light minced-fish dish that falls somewhere between tartare and seviche. The ingredients are tartare-like and the process almost classic seviche in that the fish "cooks" not through heat but acidic juices of limes and lemons. Shad, mackerel, salmon, even scallops can take the place of the flounder; or if you're really on a tight schedule, you can substitute pickled herring filets and completely omit the pickling process outlined in the recipe. In that case, replace the egg yolk with two tablespoons of sour cream.

(SERVES 10)

> 2½ pounds flounder or fluke filets
> ½ cup each fresh-squeezed lime and lemon juice
> 1½ teaspoons kosher salt
> 3 tablespoons minced scallion, including some green tops
> 3 tablespoons capers, well drained
> 2 tablespoons minced fresh dill
> 1 egg yolk (reserve egg shell)
> ¼ teaspoon dry mustard
> 5 slices thin rye bread, toasted, trimmed and cut into triangles
> Coarsely ground white pepper

Rinse the filets, blot them dry, discard any bone or skin, and use a sharp knife to cut the flesh into ¼-inch dice. (Your food processor or blender will overprocess the fish).

Mix the fish with the juices and salt. Cover and refrigerate overnight, stirring 3 or 4 times and adding additional lemon juice if the fish seems dry on top. Drain the fish well, place in a shallow bowl, and cover with a plate small enough to fit inside the bowl and press down against the fish. Weight the top with an unopened 10½-ounce can of soup and refrigerate for 1 hour. Pour off any accumulated liquid, place the plate and soup can back on the fish, and refrigerate it once again. After 1 hour, drain the fish, then repeat the weighting and draining process until the fish no longer oozes moisture (4–5 hours for most varieties). Cover the fish tightly with plastic wrap and refrigerate up to 24 hours.

Just prior to serving, discard any liquid that may have gathered and press the fish into an attractively shaped bowl or mold. Turn out onto a flat plate about 4 inches wider than the mold and surround it with concentric rings of scallion, capers, and dill. Refrigerate.

Just prior to placing the minced fish on the buffet, mix the egg yolk with the dry mustard, spoon this sauce into half the egg shell, and set it in the center of the fish. Circle all with toast points. After your guests have started to sample the vodka, mix the egg sauce with the fish, scallion, capers, and dill. Sprinkle with pepper.

Scallop Seviche

Very few morsels have the tender-yet-firm texture and sweet-salt flavor of bay scallops. They match vodka in pure perfection.

(SERVES 10)

> 2 *pints bay scallops, shelled, lightly rinsed, and well drained*
> ½ *cup each lime, lemon, and orange juice*
> 2 *teaspoons kosher salt*
> 1 *tablespoon fresh-squeezed onion juice*
> ¼ *teaspoon finely ground white pepper*
> 3 *drops Tabasco sauce*
> 1½ *tablespoons olive oil*

Mix the scallops, citrus juices, and salt. Cover and refrigerate overnight, stirring occasionally. Drain the scallops, weight them with a small plate, and refrigerate. Immediately prior to serving, pour off any liquid and blot lightly with paper towels. Toss the scallops with the onion juice, pepper, pepper sauce, and olive oil. Refrigerate. Serve cold and with small skewers.

Gravlax

Normally, I wouldn't couple sugar-cured fish with vodka, since the drink, when served unembellished, has its own haunting hidden sweetness. This Gravlax, however, fairly kicks off the top of your head, flaunting its white-hot mustard marinade and matching punch-for-punch the spirited old one-two packed by these vodka variations.

(SERVES 10)

> 2 *2-pound center-cut salmon filets, scaled but unskinned*
> ⅔ *cup each salt and sugar*
> 2 *tablespoons dry mustard*
> 12 *branches of dill*
> 2 *tablespoons white peppercorns, lightly crushed*

If the salmon is sandy or has loose scales clinging to it, give it a light rinsing; otherwise, merely wipe it with a damp cloth. Blot the fish dry with paper towels. Mix the salt, sugar, and dry mustard, and press this mixture into the filets on all sides. Place 1 fish filet in a glass dish, skin-side down, top it with the dill and peppercorns, and arrange the other filet over it, skin-side up, placing the thickest part of the top filet over the thinnest part of the bottom filet. Tie the filets loosely together with string, cover with 2 thicknesses of aluminum foil, top with another glass dish that fits right down on the filets, and weight down with several unopened 10½-ounce cans of soup. Refrigerate for 4 hours.

(continued)

Pour off all accumulated liquid, rub the filets with more salt, sugar, and mustard, cover with plastic wrap, weight the fish down again, and refrigerate it for 24 hours. Pour off the accumulated liquid, cover once again, weight down, and refrigerate for 48 hours. Just prior to serving, remove the fish from the refrigerator and discard the string. Cut each fish filet on the diagonal against the skin into thin slices and serve cold with English Mustard Sauce (page 254).

Note: Save the skin. Cut it into thin strips and fry until crisp in butter. Serve it coarsely chopped, sprinkled over tiny steamed potatoes with a little Grainy Mustard and Dill Sauce (page 204) on the side.

Shrimp Vinaigrette

Plump, pink shrimp are welcome at any party, particularly when they have been marinated in vinaigrette sauce and are served skewered with a bit of coriander.

(SERVES 10)

> 20 *large shrimp*
> *Salt*
> 1 *bouquet garni*
> 1 *recipe Mustard Vinaigrette (page 255)*
> *Fresh coriander*

All that is required here is that cooked shrimp marinate in vinaigrette overnight. If you have a reliable seafood market that you can trust not to overcook shrimp or waterlog them in melted ice, and it you don't mind paying a little extra, by all means buy these shellfish cooked and cleaned. Otherwise, bring a large pot of salted water to a boil with the bouquet garni, plunge in the shrimp, and boil until they just turn red (about 3 minutes). Drain them, run icy water over them to stop them from cooking, and drain well again. Discard the shells, remove any black lines along the backs, and marinate the shrimp in the Mustard Vinaigrette sauce overnight in the refrigerator. To serve, drain well and skewer each with a bit of fresh coriander.

Note: To double the quantity of tidbits, split the shrimp lengthwise when you remove the black lines.

Herring and Tuna Nuggets in Ribbons of Ginger

The bite of ginger enhances the winey tartness of the fish.

(YIELD: 15 TO 20 PIECES)

> 2 8-ounce filets matjes herring, or 1 16-ounce jar herring in wine (try to buy a
> brand that doesn't include too many onions since you won't need them in this
> recipe; if some are included, mince them and add them to the Tart Fish
> Tartare recipe on page 226)
> 1 8-ounce slab of tuna (without bones or membranes)
> 2 teaspoons fresh lemon juice
> 1 6-ounce jar pickled ginger slices, or 1 large knob fresh ginger root, about 4
> inches by 2 inches, peeled (choose one that is not too gnarled)

Drain the herring and reserve the juices. Cut the herring and tuna into ¾-inch pieces.
Mix the herring juices and the lemon juice. Pickled ginger slices are the preferred ingredient but fresh ginger will do in a pinch. Use a vegetable peeler to cut narrow paper-thin
ribbons of ginger about 3 inches long and at least 1 inch wide. As you cut them, drop
them into the herring juice mixture. Wrap each piece of fish in a ginger ribbon and fasten
with a skewer or toothpick. Refrigerate. Serve cold.

229

Caviar in Lacy Crêpe Cones

Crêpes, those thin, silky little blankets that so well enclose practically any food, whether
alone or in combination, whether savory, sweet, or creamy, now enter a new dimension of
deep-fried crispness. While in a frenzy of preparation for a small vodka tasting, whipping
up Silver Dollar Blinis and Scandinavian Flat Bread (pages 232–33), I suddenly realized
that the perfect vehicle for caviar should be neither of these but something rather akin to
a thumb-size ice-cream cone just big enough to hold a small blob of Crème Fraîche, a dip
of caviar, and perhaps another garnish—minced onion or grated egg yolk. Four hours and
some two hundred crêpes later, the lacy little darlings I desired were perfected. The
kitchen was in chaos. Bowls of crêpe batter dribbled in starchy pools on every counter.
Over every machine, every towel rack, crêpes were draped: thick ones, thin ones, dry ones,
slippery ones, lumpy ones, bumpy ones. Perched on my kitchen stool in the center of this
combat zone, a sparkling cut-glass plate of crisp, caviar-filled crêpe cones on my lap, I sat
contentedly munching. Ahhhhh. The end of a perfect day.

(YIELD: 16 CONES)

> 3 level tablespoons all-purpose flour
> Generous pinch of salt
> Grind of black pepper
> Sprinkle of cayenne pepper
> 1 egg
> 2 tablespoons butter, melted
> ¼ cup milk
> 2 tablespoons ice water
> Butter

Mix the flour and seasonings. Whisk the egg, melted butter, milk, and ice water together, and then gradually whisk this into the dry ingredients until the mixture is smooth. Cover and set aside for 30 minutes.

Rub lightly with butter an 8-inch nonstick crêpe or omelet pan (or two 4-inch ones; I have a couple that came with children's play sets). Pour in a few tablespoons of batter, quickly rotate the pan off the heat so the batter covers the bottom of the pan, then immediately pour any excess batter back into the bowl. Brown each crêpe ever so lightly, turning it over and cooking it only long enough to count to 10. It should be firm to the touch. Turn the crêpe out onto a plate and cover it with a paper towel. Wipe the pan, rub with a little butter, and make the rest of the crêpes. If the batter gets too thick, stir in a few drops of ice water. The crêpes should be thin and lacy.

Trim off any uneven edges and cut the 8-inch crêpes into quarters. Wrap each piece around your finger to form a cone and fasten securely with a toothpick. Drop the cones, 2 at a time, into hot, deep oil and fry for a few seconds until crisp. With a small sieve or slotted spoon, remove the cones carefully from the oil without damaging them. Drain on paper towels.

At serving time, place the cones on a baking sheet and reheat for 2–3 minutes in an oven preheated to 450 degrees F. Remove the toothpicks and arrange the cones around small bowls of caviar, Crème Fraîche (page 253), minced onion, and sieved egg yolk.

Peppery Lamb Tartare

A nice change of pace from beef tartare.

(SERVES 10)

1 6-*pound leg of lamb, boned and butterflied, with the thick fat removed (it's best to order the meat in advance and pick it up on the morning of your party; meats darken as they are stored); prepare this as close to party time as you can manage*
3 *tablespoons ice-cold, freshly squeezed lemon juice*
Cayenne pepper to taste
Freshly ground black pepper to taste
1/2 *cup minced flat anchovies, drained before chopping*
1 *cup finely chopped sweet onion*
1/2 *cup capers, well drained*
Sprigs of dill
1 *egg yolk (reserve shell)*
1 *tablespoon Dijon mustard*

Carefully remove all remaining bits of fat and gristle from the lamb, then mince it medium-fine; if you are using a food processor, first cut the meat into 1-inch cubes to keep from overprocessing it. Use your fingers to work the lemon juice into the meat. Line an attractively shaped bowl with plastic wrap and press the meat lightly into it. Refrigerate until party time.

Just prior to the arrival of your guests, unmold the meat onto a plate that is at least 6 inches larger than the shaped meat. Remove the plastic wrap and sprinkle the meat on all sides with cayenne and black pepper to taste. Be careful with the cayenne! Arrange the anchovies in a circle around the edges of the meat, and continue with concentric circles of chopped onion, capers, and dill. Mix the egg yolk and the mustard, and spoon it into half the egg shell. Make a depression in the center of the meat and place the shell in it.

After most of your guests have assembled, use a knife to press the anchovies, capers, onion, and dill into the sides of the meat. Pour the mustard-egg sauce over the top, work it into the meat, spread a little of the lamb tartare on a few bread triangles, then leave your guests to pick up where you left off.

Various Meat Cones

This presentation follows the theory that "cone shaped" also means "easier to eat with the fingers without mishap." Preparing them this way is time-consuming, of course, particularly if you're working alone. An alternative is to have the meats roasted by a caterer or a market that provides this service. Most will also slice the meats for you, and some will roll them as well. Of course these hors d'oeuvre made by others may be lacking in the combinations of flavors that add so much. To compensate, and to make the meat rolls more attractive, slip a sprig of dill, parsley, or coriander, or a few threads of freshly grated horseradish into each.

(YIELD: 12 OF EACH CONE)

Miniature Ham and Egg Cones

> 6 large thin slices cooked ham
> 1 teaspoon sweet butter
> 1 large egg, thoroughly beaten
> 12 paper-thin slices cucumber pickle (available in supermarkets)

If necessary, trim the meat with a very sharp knife to tidy the edges. Cut any overly large slices on the diagonal, and roll each piece around your finger to form a cone. Fasten each with a small skewer or toothpick. Heat the butter in a nonstick 8-inch omelet pan. Add the beaten egg and rotate the pan, above the heat, until the egg covers the bottom of the pan. Cook for a few seconds only, until the top of the egg feels dry to the touch. Trim off any dry edges and cut the egg into strips ½ inch wide. Make a cut in each pickle slice from the center to the outside edge and twist each slice around your finger to form a cone. Wrap a strip of egg (or part of a strip) around each pickle and tuck these little packages neatly into the ham cones. Cover with plastic wrap and refrigerate until you set up the buffet.

Miniature Lamb and Egg Cones

Make sure the lamb is professionally sliced—that is, thinly, evenly, and neatly. Beat ¼ teaspoon of curry powder into each egg before cooking it as in the recipe above.

Miniature Roast Beef Cones

Follow directions for Miniature Ham and Egg Cones but omit the egg and wrap each pickle slice around a few blades of chive and threads of fresh horseradish.

Three-Flour Flat Bread

This is more like a cracker than a bread, but it is excellent with fish, meats, or cheese.

(YIELD: 16 BREADS)

> 1 cup each all-purpose and rye flours
> 1¼ cups boiling water
> 2 tablespoons butter
> ½ teaspoon salt
> 1 cup whole wheat flour

Preheat oven to 450 degrees F.

Mix the all-purpose and rye flours. Mix the boiling water, butter, and salt, and beat this mixture into the 2 flours until well mixed. Stir in the whole wheat flour until the mixture is smooth. If the dough is too dry, thoroughly mix in 1–2 tablespoons more of hot water, or enough to make a dough similar to that of a biscuit dough.

Cut the dough into 4 equal portions, divide each piece in 4 equal pieces, then roll each piece out to a 12-inch circle. If you possess a lefse, or scored rolling pin used in preparing Norwegian pancakes, by all means use it. The breads will be much more attractive. Otherwise, you might use a fork to cross-hatch the surface.

Bake until crisp (about 4 minutes). The breads should not be overly browned. Cool on racks. Serve the breads whole, for guests to break into pieces. (These keep quite well if they are stacked, wrapped in plastic wrap, and stored in a cool, dry place.)

Silver-Dollar Blinis

It's been my experience that no matter how many of these I prepare, they all disappear. The solution is to whip up double the amount you think you might need. Warm any that outlast the hors d'oeuvre and present them with crystal bowls of sour cream and beach plum preserves (or Damson plum jam) to accompany coffee.

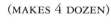

(MAKES 4 DOZEN)

> 1 package dry active yeast
> 1½ cups lukewarm milk
> 1½ cups all-purpose flour
> 3 eggs, separated
> ½ teaspoon salt
> ⅓ cup butter, melted
> Butter

In a large bowl, mix the yeast and the milk, and let stand for 10 minutes. Thoroughly beat in the flour, egg yolks, salt, and melted butter. Cover and let stand in a warm, draft-free place for 1½ hours. Beat the egg whites until they are stiff and fold into the batter. Heat a heavy nonstick skillet or griddle, rub it generously with butter, and drop the batter by teaspoons onto it. Brown on one side, turn, and lightly brown on the other.

Serve warm. If you prefer, cool the blinis, wrap them in foil, and refrigerate for up to 48 hours. To serve, preheat oven to 300 degrees F., arrange blinis on a baking sheet, and heat for 5 minutes.

Chocolate Squares

Rich! Rich! Rich!

(Makes 9 3-inch squares or 16 2 ¼-inch squares)

> 20 ounces semisweet chocolate
> 4 ounces unsweetened chocolate
> ⅓ cup each dark rum and warm water
> 8 jumbo eggs
> 1 cup granulated sugar
> 1½ cups heavy cream
> 1 tablespoon vanilla extract
> ½ cup finely ground black walnuts (if these are not
>   available, substitute blanched almonds)
> Confectioners' sugar
> 2 cups whipped cream

Preheat oven to 450 degrees F.

Pour boiling water one-inch deep into a pan larger than the cake pan and place it in the oven.

Butter and line with wax paper a 10-inch square, 2-inch deep cake pan.

Place the chocolate, rum, and water in the top of a double boiler over simmering water and stir until the chocolate is completely melted; the water should not touch the underside of the top. Transfer the chocolate mixture to a large mixing bowl. Add the eggs and sugar to the top of the double boiler and beat over simmering water until tripled in volume. Fold into the chocolate mixture. Cool 10 minutes.

Meanwhile, whip the heavy cream until it forms soft peaks and fold in the vanilla extract and the nuts. Carefully fold this mixture into the chocolate-egg mixture; immediately pour the batter into the prepared cake pan and set the pan in the hot-water bath in the oven. Bake 30 to 40 minutes or until a toothpick inserted into the center of the cake comes out clean.

Remove both pans from the oven and allow the cake to cool without removing it from the water bath. When the cake is cool, cover with plastic wrap and refrigerate for at least 1 hour. Just prior to serving, set the cake pan in warm water for a moment, then turn the cake out onto a cutting board covered with plastic wrap. Use a sharp knife to trim away ½ inch from the edges of the cake. Place a paper doily over the cake (the bottom is now the top) and sift confectioners' sugar over it. Discard the doily and arrange the cake on a fresh doily on a serving plate. Cut the cake into squares and serve with dollops of whipped cream.

Sweets for the Sweet Life

After the ball (or concert or film) is over, or to enliven a winter Sunday afternoon, stage a serious sampling of sweets with a series of awesome desserts that taste dangerously rich but actually treat your heart and figure right: snowflake-light Angel Food Cake with Pink Grapefruit Cream; it's sweetness is counterpoised with the ribbons of tart, pink grapefruit cream. Bread Slice Pudding with Port Wine Jelly. Moist, sugary Eggplant-Apple Cake with Jellied Lady Apples, one per customer. Jordan Almond Ring. Oat-Wafer Napoleons with Apricot Cream. Creamy Cranberry Pie. Old-Fashioned Fruited Wheat Bundt. Then, throw caution to the winds with one final dazzler: Devil's-Food-May-Care Mandarin Mint Cake, deliberately designed to put guilt back into gorging. As a finishing touch, use stick cinnamon to stir colored sugars into spicy herb teas or flavored coffees, then toast your tootsies by a blazing fire while you sip.

Menu

*Angel Food Cake with
Pink Grapefruit Cream*

*Bread Slice Pudding with
Port Wine Jelly*

*Eggplant-Apple Cake with
Jellied Lady Apples*

Jordan Almond Ring

*Oat-Wafer Napoleons with
Apricot Cream*

Creamy Cranberry Pie

Old-Fashioned Fruited Wheat Bundt

*Devil's-Food-May-Care
Mandarin Mint Cake*

*Black Walnut/Bittersweet-Chocolate
Pudding Cake*

Angel Food Cake with Pink Grapefruit Cream

Winter is the best time to try this ethereal sweet. Then artificial heat dries out excess moisture indoors, and angel food cakes are better behaved than when summer's open-window policy and resultant high humidity turns egg-white-lightened desserts tough and chewy. Split this pristine cake into three snowy layers and fill with tangy pink grapefruit cream. Frost with whipped cream, sprinkle with a mane of shredded coconut, and decorate with Christmas cherubim should your party fall close to the holidays.

> *1 1/2 cups egg whites*
> *1/4 teaspoon cream of tartar*
> *1 1/2 cups granulated sugar*
> *2 teaspoons vanilla extract*
> *1 cup cake flour*

Preheat oven to 375 degrees F.

Beat the egg whites until they are foamy. Beat in the cream of tartar and then 3/4 cup of the sugar, 1 heaping tablespoon at a time. When the meringue is stiff and glossy, sprinkle a few tablespoons of sugar over the top and fold it in by hand. Continue the sifting and folding in by quarter cups until all the sugar has been incorporated, then fold in the vanilla.

Sift the cake flour several times, then sift 1/4 cup over the meringue, and fold in gently but thoroughly, using a spatula. Continue the sifting and folding in until all the flour has been used. Do not overmix. Spread the batter in an ungreased 10-inch tube pan. Bake for 35–40 minutes or until the cake springs back when the top is lightly pressed with your finger. Cool the cake in the pan.

Pink Grapefruit Cream

(YIELD: ABOUT 2 CUPS)

> *1 1/2 cups freshly squeezed pink grapefruit juice*
> *1 1/4 cups granulated sugar*
> *2 tablespoons cornstarch*
> *2 egg yolks*

Mix the juice, sugar, and cornstarch until no lumps remain. Bring to a boil over medium heat, stirring constantly, and cook until the mixture is thick and clear. Beat the egg yolks in a heat-proof bowl, then beat in the *hot* grapefruit mixture. Return the grapefruit cream to the pan and stir for 2 minutes over *very* low heat. Do not allow the cream to come to a boil or it will curdle. Cool to room temperature and then chill.

Topping

> *1 1/2 cups heavy cream*
> *2 tablespoons granulated sugar*
> *2 cups coarsely grated coconut*

Whip the heavy cream until it is foamy, then continue beating until the cream is stiff while you sprinkle in the sugar.

To assemble the cake:

Cut the cake crosswise into 3 equal layers. Spread the bottom 2 layers with the cold Pink Grapefruit Cream. Top with the remaining angel food slice. Ice the top and sides of the assembled cake with the whipped cream topping. Sprinkle with the grated coconut. Refrigerate 3–4 hours. Serve cold.

237

Bread Slice Pudding with Port Wine Jelly

I love the mixture of sophisticated and homespun, particularly when it comes to desserts. I'm especially fond of preparing old-timey favorites in a slightly new way. Bread pudding is one of those comforting desserts that doting mothers used to serve to their children back in the days when food was meant to "stick to your ribs." Today, ribs are kept stylishly slim, and bread puddings follow that trend, too. Port wine jelly fancies up this dish, the number of egg yolks are reduced, and meringue lightens what once could be a somewhat heavy treat.

Incidentally, if port wine jelly is unavailable, substitute seedless red raspberry jelly, which is also delightful here.

(SERVES 8 TO 10)

3 eggs
½ cup granulated sugar
3 cups milk
⅓ cup dark rum
½ teaspoon each nutmeg, cinnamon, and allspice
24 slices good-quality white bread, with crusts trimmed
5 egg whites
¼ teaspoon cream of tartar
10 tablespoons sugar
Melted butter
1 cup port wine jelly

Beat the whole eggs, ½ cup of sugar, milk, rum, and spices until well mixed. Cut 16 slices of the bread into 1-inch cubes and place in a buttered soufflé dish. Pour about two-thirds of the egg-milk mixture over, stir to soak the bread cubes, and let stand for 15 minutes, stirring occasionally. The liquid should be fully absorbed.

Beat the egg whites until they are frothy, add the cream of tartar and 5 tablespoons of sugar, and beat again until the whites hold a peak. Beat in the remaining 5 tablespoons of sugar, a little at a time, until the meringue is stiff and glossy, and the sugar no longer feels gritty when a bit is rubbed between thumb and forefinger.

Preheat oven to 350 degrees F.

Gently fold two-thirds of the meringue into the moistened bread cubes. Cut the 8 remaining bread slices in half on the diagonal, soak them in the remaining egg-milk mixture, and lay them over the bread pudding in an attractive overlapping pattern. (Leave a small hole in the center to hold the port wine jelly.) Bake the pudding for 1 hour, then cool to room temperature.

To serve the pudding warm, pipe the remaining meringue around the edges and bake in an oven preheated to 425 degrees F. for 5–6 minutes, or until the meringue is attractively browned. If you are preparing the pudding more than 24 hours in advance of serving, fold all the meringue into the bread cubes and proceed as directed, substituting whipped cream for the meringue in the final step.

I press and shape one-fourth of a large slice of bread into a small cup, set it in an ovenproof dish, and bake along with the pudding until golden. While it's still hot, I brush it (and the top of the pudding) lightly with melted butter. At serving time, I fill the bread cup with a little port wine jelly, place it in the center of the pudding, and serve additional jelly on the side.

Eggplant-Apple Cake with Jellied Lady Apples

In summer, when most of us beware of friends bearing zucchini large enough to swallow the dog (and just when we were plotting to unload one of *ours* on *them*), it's hard to believe that come January we might long for one of these monster vegetables. Even though the zucchini bread craze is over, my "untrendy" family still enjoys it at teatime. So, in desperation last January when my zucchini ran out, I substituted eggplant, another moist vegetable, with surprising results. The cake was damp and fruity with tiny crackly seeds, reminiscent of a fig pudding a Dutch neighbor used to steam up around Christmas or New Year's when I was very young. The eggplant itself has a distinctive flavor—not so bland as zucchini—that complements the dried fruits and nuts. I like to decorate the cake with pieces of the glossy black eggplant skin to add a little mystery . . . no one can ever guess what it is. The candied apples are fun to eat and look rather pleasant, but they aren't essential.

(SERVES 8 TO 10)

> 1 medium-size eggplant
> ½ cup granulated sugar
> Water
> 1 cup tightly packed light-brown sugar
> ¾ cup boiling water
> 1 apple, grated
> 4 tablespoons butter, cut in pieces
> 2 cups all-purpose flour
> 1 egg
> 2 tablespoons brandy
> 1 teaspoon baking soda
> ½ teaspoon salt
> ½ teaspoon each powdered cinnamon and nutmeg
> 1 cup each walnut halves, muscat raisins, and halved candied cherries
> Jellied Lady Apples (see below) (optional)

Cut the eggplant in quarters lengthwise, then cut away all but ¼ inch of the flesh, leaving the skin undamaged. The object is to end up with 4 large, triangular pieces of the black skin of the eggplant, which you will use to decorate the top of the cake. (This step is a bit trying. Feel free to omit it and merely ice the cake if you prefer.) Cut the eggplant flesh into strips roughly the length and thickness of your middle finger, or about 3 inches by ¾

(continued)

inch. Bring the granulated sugar and 1 cup of water to a rolling boil, then continue to boil without stirring for 3 minutes. Add the eggplant skin and boil for 3 minutes more, separating the pieces of skin gently with a wooden spoon to keep them from sticking together. Carefully remove the pieces of skin 1 at a time and flatten them out on buttered wax paper or aluminum foil. Cool to room temperature.

Meanwhile, stir the brown sugar into the ¾ cup of boiling water and continue to boil for 3 minutes. Add the strips of eggplant and boil until syrupy (about 5 minutes), stirring occasionally. If the syrup begins to burn, lower the heat immediately. Cool to room temperature, then cut the eggplant into 1-inch pieces.

Preheat oven to 350 degrees F.

Place the eggplant pieces (not the skin) and the grated apple in a mixing bowl. Add the boiled syrup and 4 tablespoons of butter, and mix lightly. Add the flour, egg, brandy, baking soda, salt, and spices, and stir only enough to barely mix the ingredients. Stir in the nuts, raisins, and cherries. Butter a 7-inch or 8-inch ovenproof bowl (I used a stainless-steel mixing bowl) and carefully cut the eggplant skin into tapered ribbons to fit. Arrange these pieces shiny sides against the bowl. Spoon in the cake batter a little at a time, taking care not to disarrange the position of the eggplant skins.

Place the bowl in the preheated oven and bake for 60 minutes, or until a toothpick stuck in the center comes out clean. Remove from the oven, cool 5 minutes, then gently loosen around the edges with a dull knife. Place a plate over the top of the bowl, quickly turn it over, and turn the cake out. Use a cloth or a dull knife to scrape away any batter that might have oozed onto the strips of eggplant skin. But take care not to damage the glossy eggplant ribbons. I prefer the cake as is, but if you like you may ice it in between the eggplant ribbons. Surround with tiny candied apples if desired. The cake here is bedecked with an ornamental Christmas apple and a few Victorian glass leaves.

Jellied Lady Apples

(YIELD: 16 APPLES)

At one time I would have tinted these bright red. Now I prefer a more natural look, and no food coloring. Please yourself. I still occasionally include red and green candied cherries in a holiday dessert, but candied papaya cut in ⅓-inch cubes is also attractive and tasty.

> 16 *small lady apples*
> 2 *cups granulated sugar*
> ⅔ *cup light corn syrup*
> 1 *cup water*
> ¼ *teaspoon lemon juice*

Thoroughly wash and dry the apples. Mix the sugar, corn syrup, and water in a small, heavy saucepan. Cook over low heat, stirring constantly, until the sugar dissolves, then cook without stirring until the syrup reaches the hard-crack stage (300 degrees F. on a candy thermometer). If the candy threads are brittle when a little syrup is dropped into ice water, the hard-crack stage has been reached. Remove from the heat and stir in the lemon juice (and coloring if you use it). Keep the pan of syrup liquid by placing it in a pan of hot water, and dip in the apples, one at a time. Arrange on buttered foil until the syrup hardens.

241

Jordan Almond Ring

The trick here is not merely that Jordan almonds attractively circle the cake but that some are also finely ground and folded into the batter. The result is a crackly texture that is unusually tasty. The cake is also lovely when ground unblanched almonds are substituted for the ground candy-coated ones. But please don't omit the colorful whole Jordan almonds that decorate the top, or you'll miss a good deal of the drama.

(SERVES 10)

> 2 *cups whole Jordan almonds*
> ½ *cup (1 stick) sweet butter*
> 1¼ *cups granulated sugar*
> 3 *eggs, at room temperature*
> 2¾ *cups all-purpose flour*
> 1½ *teaspoons baking soda*
> ½ *teaspoon salt*
> 1¼ *cups buttermilk or sour milk*
> 3 *tablespoons Amaretto*
> 1½ *teaspoons vanilla extract*
> ¼ *cup minced candied lemon peel*
> *Lemon Icing (see below)*

Preheat oven to 350 degrees F.

Finely chop 1¼ cups of the Jordan almonds and set the rest aside. In the large bowl of an electric mixer, cream the butter until it is soft, then cream in the sugar, ¼ cup at a time. Beat in the eggs, 1 at a time, and continue to beat for 4 minutes.

(continued)

Sift together the flour, baking soda, and salt. Beat the dry ingredients into the creamed mixture, ½ cup at a time, alternately with the buttermilk or sour milk, mixing well after each addition. Stir in the Amaretto, vanilla, reserved chopped almonds, and lemon peel.

Pour the batter into a buttered ring mold and bake for 40–50 minutes or until a toothpick comes clean when it is inserted into the thickest part of the cake. Cool 15 minutes, then loosen both the outside edges and the center circle with a knife, and turn the cake out of the pan. Cool to room temperature, molded-side up, on a wire rack. Use a pastry bag fitted with a wide fluted tip to pipe the Lemon Icing attractively around the top of the cake. Arrange the remaining whole Jordan almonds in a pretty pattern over the icing.

Lemon Icing

(YIELD: 2½ CUPS)

> 3½ cups confectioners' sugar
> ½ cup (1 stick) butter
> ¼ teaspoon ground nutmeg
> Lemon juice, strained

Cream the sugar and butter. Beat in the nutmeg and just enough lemon juice to make a thick icing. Chill well.

Oat-Wafer Napoleons with Apricot Cream

Classic Pâte Feuilletée or Puff Paste, while delicious, is not only difficult to prepare but is ultra-high in butter content (one pound per recipe). I developed this more healthful oat-crust Napoleon (six tablespoons of butter per recipe) to please a friend who had to restrict his fat intake somewhat. He was still permitted the occasional dessert but was advised to show restraint. He swore he preferred this variation to the authentic item. The oat layers are best made the morning of your party.

(MAKES 10 TO 12)

Oat Layers

(MAKES ABOUT 30)

> 6 tablespoons sweet butter, melted
> ¼ teaspoon nutmeg
> 1¼ cups old-fashioned rolled oats
> 1 tablespoon all-purpose flour
> 1 tablespoon grated orange zest (the thin outside
>   skin of an orange excluding the bitter white pith)
> 1 teaspoon baking powder
> 1 egg
> ⅔ cup granulated sugar

Toss the butter, nutmeg, and oats in a large bowl. Sprinkle the flour, orange zest, and baking powder over, and mix well. Beat the egg and sugar together thoroughly and beat into the oat mixture.

Butter and flour the *bottoms* of 2 baking sheets (12 by 18 inches) and spread the batter thinly over both to within 1 inch of the edges of the pans. Bake for 15 minutes, then remove 1 pan and, while it is still warm, use a sharp knife to score the crust into rectangles 3 inches by 6 inches and then to carefully loosen and remove them with the help of a metal spatula. Place the oat wafers on a foil-covered flat surface to cool. Remove the second pan from the oven and, while it is still warm, repeat the scoring and loosening process.

Apricot Cream

(YIELD: 2½ CUPS)

> 1½ cups milk
> ½ cup light cream
> 2½ teaspoons potato starch
> ¾ cup apricot jam or preserves
> 2 egg yolks, beaten
> 2 envelopes unflavored gelatin
> ⅓ cup cold water
> ½ cup heavy cream, whipped

In a small, heavy saucepan, beat the milk, light cream, potato starch, apricot jam, and egg yolks until thoroughly mixed. Cook over low heat, stirring constantly, until the mixture thickens. Soften the gelatin in the cold water for a few minutes, and then stir it into the hot apricot cream until the gelatin dissolves. Chill until partially set. Beat the apricot cream briefly, fold in the whipped cream, and chill again until nearly but not quite set.

To assemble the layers:

> *Confectioners' sugar*

Spread one-third of the oat wafers with the apricot cream, top with a second oat wafer (use any damaged ones here in the middle), layer with more apricot cream, and top with perfect oat wafers. Repeat to make 10 Napoleons. Place the Napoleons briefly in the freezer to firm the cream quickly and neaten up any filling that might have oozed out over the edges. Transfer the Napoleons to the refrigerator and keep well chilled until just before you serve them. At the last moment, sift confectioners' sugar over the tops through a fine sieve.

Creamy Cranberry Pie

The tart creaminess of these pies makes a lovely finish to Thanksgiving or Christmas dinner, or a welcome change-of-pace dessert when presented with other, sweeter sweets. One pie that is cut into thin slivers provides ten guests a first-come-first-served treat. But even two pies will disappear in minutes once they are discovered.

(SERVES 8 TO 10)

> 1 recipe Pastry for a One-Crust Pie (page 259)
> ³⁄₄ cup granulated sugar
> 2 tablespoons arrowroot
> ²⁄₃ cup sour cream
> 2 eggs
> ¹⁄₄ teaspoon salt
> 1 cup apple yogurt
> 2¹⁄₂ cups cranberries, rinsed, dried, and picked over to remove
>   stems, and so forth
> ¹⁄₂ cup currant jelly

Preheat oven to 450 degrees F.

Prepare the pie pastry, roll it out, and fit it into a 9-inch pie shell. Do not stretch the dough. Crimp the edges and refrigerate the pie shell.

Beat together thoroughly the sugar, arrowroot, sour cream, eggs, and salt. Stir in the yogurt and cranberries, and turn the mixture into the chilled pie shell. Bake for 35–40 minutes. Remove from the oven and cool to room temperature. Melt the jelly over medium heat and pour it over the pie. Chill well.

Old-Fashioned Fruited Wheat Bundt

Moist and wheaty is how I remember Grandfather Nicholas's spicy fruit and nut cake. This is a treasure, flavored with pumpkin, banana, and grated apple, and laden with nuggets of walnuts, dates, and dried apricots. My version is updated by the inclusion of toasted and sweetened wheat germ.

(SERVES 8 TO 10)

> ¹⁄₃ cup butter
> 1 cup light-brown sugar
> 1 egg
> ¹⁄₄ cup sour milk or buttermilk
> ¹⁄₂ cup cooked pumpkin
> ¹⁄₂ cup grated peeled apple
> 1 small, very ripe banana, mashed
> 1¹⁄₄ cups all-purpose flour

¾ cup whole wheat flour

2½ teaspoons baking powder

½ teaspoon baking soda

1 teaspoon cinnamon

¼ teaspoon each powdered cloves, allspice, nutmeg, and salt

¾ cup toasted and sweetened wheat germ

1 cup each coarsely chopped walnuts, dried apricots, and dates

In the large bowl of an electric mixer, beat the butter until it is fluffy and light in color. Add the sugar 2 tablespoons at a time, beating thoroughly after each addition, until the mixture is smooth. Beat in the egg thoroughly. In another bowl mix the sour milk, pumpkin, apple, and banana.

Preheat oven to 350 degrees F.

Sift together the flours, baking powder, baking soda, spices, and salt, and stir into the egg mixture alternately with the milk-fruit mixture, until the batter is thoroughly mixed. Fold in the wheat germ, walnuts, apricots, and dates, and pour the batter into a well oiled and sugared 9-inch bundt pan. Bake for 1–1¼ hours, or until a toothpick inserted in the thickest part of the cake comes out clean. Cool for 15 minutes in the pan and then remove. Sprinkle with additional granulated sugar if desired.

Devil's-Food-May-Care Mandarin Mint Cake

Deep, rich, chocolate layers flecked with orange, spread with fudge, and decorated with mandarin segments and after-dinner mints. What could be more devilishly delicious?

(SERVES 10 TO 12)

½ cup (1 stick) butter

1 cup each light-brown and dark-brown sugar

½ cup dark corn syrup

3 eggs, at room temperature

4 squares good-quality semisweet chocolate

½ cup heavy cream

2 teaspoons lemon juice

2¼ cups cake flour, measured after *sifting*

2 teaspoons baking soda

½ teaspoon salt

1 cup boiling water

1 rounded teaspoon orange zest

2 teaspoons each vanilla extract and almond extract

Fudge Icing (recipe below)

1 6-ounce can mandarin orange segments, well drained

Thin after-dinner mints

In the large bowl of an electric mixer, cream the butter until it is fluffy and smooth. Beat in the sugars, 2 tablespoons at a time, until the mixture is smooth. Beat in the corn syrup

(continued)

until thoroughly incorporated. Beat in the eggs, 1 at a time, beating well after each addition. Melt the chocolate in the heavy cream, add the lemon juice, and then cool to room temperature. (If you're in a hurry, pop the pan into the freezer for 1–2 minutes.)

Sift the flour, measure it, and sift it again with the baking soda and salt. Stir the dry ingredients into the batter alternately with the chocolate cream, ending with the dry ingredients. Add the boiling water, orange zest, and vanilla and almond extracts.

Preheat oven to 375 degrees F.

Butter and lightly flour two 8-inch-square cake pans, pour equal amounts of batter into them, and bake for 25–30 minutes. Cool the layers in the pans for 5 minutes, then remove and place them on wire racks to cool.

Frost the top of 1 layer with cooled Fudge Icing and top with the remaining layer. Use a fancy nozzle to decorate the top of the cake with a thick layer of Fudge Icing. Decorate with mandarin orange segments and halved after-dinner mints. Chill until 15 minutes prior to serving.

Fudge Icing

¼ *cup granulated sugar*
4 *ounces unsweetened chocolate*
2 *ounces sweet chocolate*
¾ *cup heavy cream*
3 *tablespoons sweet butter*
1 *teaspoon almond extract*

Put all the ingredients except the almond extract in a small, heavy saucepan and cook over medium heat, stirring constantly, until the mixture forms a soft ball when a bit is dropped into a cup of cold water. Remove from the heat and beat in the almond extract. Cool to room temperature.

Black Walnut/Bittersweet-Chocolate Pudding Cake

This dense, moist cake is easily whirled up using the steel blade of a food processor. You may also use an electric mixer if you scrape down the sides of the bowl several times and add the nuts last.

(SERVES 10 TO 12)

> ½ cup sweet butter
> 8 slices homebaked or other firm-textured white bread
> 1 cup light cream, at room temperature
> 7 large eggs, at room temperature
> 3 large egg yolks
> 1 cup granulated sugar
> 6 ounces good quality bittersweet chocolate, melted in the top of a double boiler
> over hot, not boiling, water
> 1 cup black walnut meats, finely chopped

Cream the butter until it is fluffy and pale yellow. Soak the bread in the cream for 5 minutes, then beat it into the butter. Beat in the eggs and egg yolks, one at a time, alternately with the sugar. Beat in the chocolate and the nuts until well mixed.

Butter a tall 2-quart steamed pudding mold. Pour the mixture into the mold and cover first with aluminum foil and then the cover of the mold. Place in a kettle of boiling water that reaches three-quarters of the way up the side of the mold. Steam the pudding for 1 to 1½ hours or until it is firm to the touch. If necessary, add more boiling water to keep the water level constant. Immediately loosen the sides of the pudding with a sharp knife if necessary, and unmold onto a serving plate.

Note: If you do not have a pudding mold, you can improvise. Place the pudding in a buttered Bundt pan, cover with several thicknesses of aluminum foil, tie tightly with string, and proceed as directed above.

Menu

Caviar Parfait

Toast Points

Champagne

After all the concern and love you've lavished on friends, relatives, acquaintances, guests, guests of guests, and even on party-crashing strangers; after brunches, lunches, and dinners (little ones and large); after cocktails en masse and for two, cookouts and cook-ins, beach bashes and sleek city sit-downs; after you've planned, shopped, arranged flowers, rearranged furniture, cooked, cleaned, chatted, and charmed; after the blood, sweat, tears, euphoria, elation, cheers—in other words, after you've been the host or hostess with the absolute mostest for heaven knows how long . . . it's finally your turn!

Take time off to indulge yourself with a fantasy party. Mine involves a slinky marble bathtub, mountains of bubbles, orchids by the yard, candlelight, the finest champagne, and . . . caviar! If money is no object, fill up an oversized champagne flute with the real thing (and nothing but the real thing), grab a gold spoon, and overdo. On the other hand, if for you the price has to be right, consider a Caviar Parfait with strata of fresh black Beluga, golden-brown Osetra, and bright red saltwater salmon caviar, layered with sour cream and minced scallions, minced hard-cooked egg yolks and whites, topped off with a blush of orange freshwater salmon caviar. That's *really* entertaining! And who deserves it more than YOU?

Additional Recipes

Lobster Butter

Use this flavorful butter for canapés, to finish grilled or broiled fish, or in sauces.

(YIELD: ABOUT ½ CUP)

1 *lobster shell*
½ *cup (1 stick) sweet butter*
2 *tablespoons white wine or water*

Remove all traces of lobster meat from the shell. Place the shell on a baking sheet and dry it out in a slow oven for 35–40 minutes, or until it shatters and has the sound of broken china when you break it into pieces. Pound into pieces about ¼–½ inch and place these in the top half of a double boiler along with the butter and 2 tablespoons of white wine or water. Cook over boiling water until the butter melts, then allow the mixture to simmer for 15 minutes without letting it boil

Take a fine strainer, line it with damp cheesecloth, set it over a small bowl of ice water, and pour the hot butter through. Place the bowl in the refrigerator until the butter hardens, then lift the butter off the liquid, wrap it well in plastic wrap and then in aluminum foil, and refrigerate. Use the remaining liquid for fish stews or soups.

Mayonnaise

(YIELD: ABOUT 2 CUPS)

1 *egg, at room temperature*
2 *teaspoons Dijon mustard*
2 *egg yolks, at room temperature*
1 *cup olive oil*
½ *cup vegetable oil*
1½ *tablespoons white vinegar or lemon juice, slightly warmed*
Salt and white pepper to taste

Place the egg and mustard in a food processor fitted with the steel cutting blade and whirl them until they are well mixed. With the motor running, add the egg yolks, 1 at a time, waiting until the first is incorporated before you add the other. Mix the oils together and add them to the processor, ½ teaspoon at a time, beating continuously and waiting until each fresh addition has been well absorbed before adding the next ½ teaspoonful.

When one-half of the oil has been added, add the vinegar or lemon juice, then continue to beat in the rest of the oil in a very thin, steady stream, pausing occasionally to make sure it is all being incorporated. Whirl in the salt and pepper. If the sauce is not to be used right away, stabilize it by whirling in a teaspoon of boiling water. Cover tightly and keep chilled.

Hollandaise Sauce

(YIELD: ABOUT 1½ CUPS)

1 cup (2 sticks) sweet butter
6 egg yolks
4 teaspoons lemon juice
Salt and pepper to taste

Melt the butter in a small, heavy saucepan set over medium heat. Warm the container of a food processor or blender with hot water, then quickly drain and wipe dry.

Put the egg yolks, lemon juice, salt, and pepper into the warmed container, cover, and whirl until well mixed. With the blade still whirling, add the hot butter in a very thin stream through the opening in the top. Take care not to add the butter too quickly or the mixture may curdle. Serve immediately or transfer the sauce to a bowl or jar and keep it warm by setting it in a pan of warm water.

Crème Fraîche

(YIELD: ABOUT 3 CUPS)

1 cup sour cream
2 cups heavy cream

Put the sour cream in a wide-mouthed jar, then spoon in the heavy cream, 1 spoonful at a time, stirring well after each addition. As soon as the mixture is smooth and well blended, cover the top of the jar with cheesecloth, set the jar in a pan of warm water (80 degrees F.), and allow it to stand overnight. Stir, cover, and refrigerate.

Coconut Cream

(YIELD: ABOUT 2 CUPS)

1 small coconut (white meat only), grated
1 cup each hot cream and hot milk
½ teaspoon arrowroot

Soak the coconut in the hot cream for 15 minutes. Squeeze it through several layers of cheesecloth into a second bowl. Replace the coconut in the first bowl, soak it in the hot milk for 10 minutes, then squeeze through cheesecloth into the second bowl. Discard the coconut. Stir the arrowroot into ¼ cup of the coconut milk until smooth, add it to the rest of the coconut milk, and cook at a low boil, stirring constantly, until the cream thickens. Cool to room temperature, then chill.

Flavored Mustards

Chiffon Mustard Sauce

> 2 teaspoons Dijon mustard
> 1½ cups sour cream
> ½ cup heavy cream, whipped
> Salt and freshly ground white pepper to taste

Use the back of a spoon to work the mustard into the sour cream until smooth. Fold in the whipped cream, salt, and pepper. Chill well.

English Mustard Sauce

> 3 tablespoons dry mustard
> Dark beer

Place the mustard in a small dish and stir in enough beer to make a smooth sauce that has the consistency of heavy cream.

Fresh Tomato Sauce

(MAKES ABOUT 3 CUPS)

> 3 tablespoons butter or olive oil
> 1 carrot, scraped and grated
> 2 large onions, peeled and coarsely chopped
> 2 small cloves garlic, peeled and sliced
> 16 fully ripe tomatoes, peeled, seeded, and cut in eighths
> 2½ cups chicken broth
> Salt and coarsely ground black pepper to taste

Heat the butter or oil in a heavy stainless-steel pan. Add the carrot, onions, and garlic, and sauté until the onion is soft without letting it take on any color. Add half the tomatoes and cook over medium heat, stirring occasionally, until the tomatoes are quite soft. Add the broth and simmer the sauce for about 20 minutes, or until it thickens somewhat. Coarsely puree the sauce in a food processor or blender, return it to the pan, season to taste, and simmer until it is nicely thickened. Coarsely chop the remaining tomatoes, add to the sauce, and boil at high heat for 2 minutes.

Sauce Vinaigrette

(YIELD: ABOUT 1 CUP)

¼ cup wine vinegar
⅛ teaspoon salt
Generous pinch of freshly ground black pepper
¾ cup olive oil

With a wire whisk or in a food processor or blender, beat the vinegar and seasonings together until well blended. Add the oil and beat again.

Walnut Vinaigrette

Prepare Sauce Vinaigrette as directed above but substitute walnut oil for part of the olive oil and, if you like, add 1 tablespoon minced walnuts that have been blanched for a few minutes in hot water and relieved of their skins.

Mustard Vinaigrette

Prepare Sauce Vinaigrette as directed above but add 1 teaspoon of dry, or 2 teaspoons of prepared, French mustard when beating the vinegar and seasonings together. Proceed as directed.

Orange Vinaigrette

Prepare Sauce Vinaigrette as directed above but add 1 tablespoon fresh orange juice and 1 teaspoon grated orange rind when beating the vinegar and seasonings together.

Lemon Vinaigrette

Prepare as directed in Sauce Vinaigrette but substitute lemon juice for the vinegar.

Béchamel Sauce

(YIELD: 2 CUPS)

> 3 *tablespoons butter*
> 1 *small onion, peeled and thinly sliced*
> 3 *tablespoons all-purpose flour*
> 1 *cup each cold milk and heavy cream*
> ½ *teaspoon salt*
> *White pepper*

In a heavy saucepan, melt the butter over medium heat and cook the onion until it is just soft. Discard the onion slices and blend in the flour with a fork. When the mixture is smooth, remove it from the heat, and stir in the milk and cream all at once. Press out any lumps and stir constantly over medium heat until the sauce bubbles and turns creamy and thick. Strain, if necessary, and season to taste with salt and white pepper.

Rich Fish Stock

Delightfully flavorful as a base for fish sauces or soup, this stock may be prepared in advance, then refrigerated or frozen for future use. To clarify it for use in aspics, after straining, refrigerate it just long enough for any fat particles to rise to the surface, then skim these off.

(YIELD: ABOUT 8 CUPS)

> 2 *tablespoons butter*
> 1 *medium-size onion, coarsely chopped*
> 2 *medium-size carrots, thinly sliced*
> 2 *ribs celery, thinly sliced*
> 2 *pounds bones, heads (with gills removed), and trimmings from any*
>   *white-fleshed, non-oily fish*
> *Cooked lobster, shrimp, or mussel shells (optional)*
> 4 *cups white wine*
> 5 *cups water*
> 2 *sprigs parsley*
> *Salt*

In a large stockpot, melt the butter and add the onion, carrots, and celery. When the vegetables are soft but have not taken on any color, add the fish parts, cooked seafood shells, wine, and water, and bring to a boil. Reduce the heat, add the parsley, and allow the stock to simmer, uncovered, for 25 minutes. Add salt to taste and strain through several thicknesses of damp cheesecloth.

Your Own Yogurt

Before beginning the yogurt-making process, it's a good idea to have on hand a reliable thermometer (the floating dairy-type is best) and some means for keeping your yogurt at the proper incubating temperature (98 to 108 degrees F.) until it reaches the firmness you prefer. A four-cup electric yogurt-maker with automatic temperature controls is perfect (follow manufacturer's instructions), but an equally good substitute might be one of the following:

1. a pan of warm water set over the pilot light of your gas range; top the jars of yogurt with an inverted aluminum-foil pan to keep the heat in;
2. an electric frying pan filled to the depth of one inch with warm water and its temperature controls set to warm; be sure to cover the yogurt as above;
3. a pan of water set in a well-insulated gas or electric oven that has been preheated to 100 degrees F., then shut off.

(YIELD: 4 CUPS)

> 1 quart whole or skim milk, in any combination that suits your taste (the more butterfat the milk contains, the creamier the yogurt; milk low in butterfat produces a tangier yogurt)
>
> 2–3 tablespoons instant nonfat dry milk
>
> 2–3 tablespoons fresh, plain, unflavored yogurt, at room temperature, or any commercially packaged yogurt starter culture

To prepare the yogurt, put the milk and nonfat dry milk in the top of a double boiler. Bring the mixture just to the boiling point, then allow to boil, stirring constantly, for 30 seconds (this helps to produce a firmer curd). Remove from the heat and allow to cool. When the temperature of the mixture descends to 112–115 degrees F. on your thermometer (or, if you don't have a thermometer, if it feels slightly warm when you sprinkle a few drops on your wrist), stir in the unflavored yogurt or starter culture until thoroughly blended.

Pour into warm, sterilized 1-cup jars or glasses and cover lightly with sterile lids or screw tops. Allow to ferment in a warm place for 3–6 hours or, for a tangier yogurt, incubate it for as long as 10 hours.

As soon as the yogurt is set, refrigerate it and keep it for as long as 5 days. Reserve a small quantity of this first batch to use as a starter for the next; it should keep for about a week stored, tightly sealed, in a sterilized container in your refrigerator.

Sun-Dried Tomato Chutney

I may well be the only one who does not relish cooked sun-dried tomatoes. It seems to me that the salty-sweet flavor and interesting texture are much diminished when they are subjected to heat and moisture. That's why this tomato chutney is prepared in the conventional manner and then, at the last moment, enhanced by the unique qualities of the sun-dried variety. A variation on the theme.

(YIELD: ABOUT 2 PINTS)

> 10 *medium-size ripe tomatoes*
> ½ *cup vinegar*
> ½ *cup currants*
> 1 *large onion, peeled and chopped*
> 3 *large cloves garlic, peeled and minced*
> 1 *2-inch knob of fresh ginger, peeled and minced*
> 1 *cup each granulated and light-brown sugar*
> 1 *teaspoon each dry mustard and curry powder*
> ½ *teaspoon each ground cloves and salt*
> ½ *cup coarsely chopped sun-dried tomatoes*

Dip the tomatoes in scalding water and slip off the skins. Cut the tomatoes in quarters, remove the seeds, and coarsely chop. In a large stainless-steel, glass, or enamel saucepan, cook the tomatoes in ¼ cup of the vinegar until soft. Add all the remaining ingredients except the sun-dried tomatoes and cook, stirring frequently, until the mixture thickens. Cool to room temperature. Just prior to serving, stir in the sun-dried tomatoes.

Double-Crust Pie Pastry

(YIELD: ENOUGH DOUGH FOR A 2-CRUST PIE)

> 2½ *cups all-purpose flour*
> 1¼ *teaspoons salt*
> 7–8 *tablespoons (about 1 stick) chilled sweet butter*
> 7 *tablespoons chilled vegetable shortening*
> 7–8 *tablespoons ice water*

Sift the flour and salt together into a large bowl. Cut the butter and shortening into small pieces, tuck them down into the dry ingredients, and, using 2 knives or whirling the mixture for a few seconds in a food processor, cut them into the flour only enough for the mixture to resemble coarse meal.

Use a fork to stir in the ice water, 2 tablespoons at a time, until the dough comes away clean from the sides of the bowl and forms a ball. It's best to do this by hand so that you don't overwork the dough. Chill for at least 15 minutes before rolling out.

To roll out the dough, first divide it in half, then roll each half out in turn on a lightly floured pastry board, once again taking care not to overwork it. Fit the crust loosely into the pie plate without stretching the dough. Trim any ragged edges, leaving a 1-inch edge all around. Crimp the edges. Bake as directed in the recipe you are following.

Pastry for a One-Crust Pie

If the recipe you are making calls for only a single crust, prepare as above, then wrap the extra dough in aluminum foil and refrigerate or freeze it until needed.

Baked Pie Shell

Follow the directions for Pastry for a One-Crust Pie. Prick the bottom of 1 crust with a fork and flute the edges. Line the crust with foil and cover the bottom with 2 cups uncooked rice or beans. Chill for 30 minutes. Bake in a preheated 450-degree F. oven for 15 minutes. The rice and beans can be reused. Remove the foil and fill the shell.

Pastry for Tarts

(YIELD: ENOUGH FOR ONE 9-INCH OR SIX 3-INCH TARTS)

1½ cups all-purpose flour
6 tablespoons granulated sugar
Generous pinch of salt
7 tablespoons chilled butter, cut in small pieces
1 extra-large egg
Ice water

Combine the flour, sugar, and salt in a small bowl or the container of a food processor. Tuck the pieces of butter down into the mixture. Using 2 knives or the steel blade of a food processor, cut in the butter until the mixture resembles coarse meal. Add the egg, stir in quickly and lightly until well blended, press the mixture into a ball, and knead it lightly 3 or 4 times. If the dough does not hold together, sprinkle with a few drops of ice water and knead lightly 3 or 4 times more. Wrap in plastic wrap or wax paper, and refrigerate at least 2 hours before rolling out.

Preheat oven to 400 degrees F.

To roll out, first bring the dough to slightly below room temperature. On a lightly floured board, roll out to a thickness of ⅛ inch, taking care not to overwork the pastry. Line the pan or pans with the dough and prick all over. Bake for 7–10 minutes or until lightly browned. After taking from the oven, cool on a rack. Remove the crust from the pan and carefully spoon in the filling.

Kneading Bread Dough

Although a food processor is perfectly capable of doing the job, there's something wonderfully elemental and intensely satisfying about working dough with your own two hands—vigorously pushing, pulling, folding, and refolding it until it firms up and becomes a smooth, elastic mass, ready for baking.

Begin by sprinkling a pastry board, counter, or tabletop lightly with flour. Dust your hands with flour, turn the dough out onto the work surface, and pat the dough into a firm ball. With the heels of both hands on the edge of the dough push it firmly away from you, using sure, quick movements. Then pull up the far side of the dough with your fingertips and fold it toward you.

Rotate the dough a quarter-turn clockwise and repeat the pushing, lifting, and folding motion. Continue to rotate, push, lift, and fold. About halfway through the length of time specified in the recipe, turn the dough over and repeat the process.

Sausage-Making

Aside from the marvelous flavor, there are other advantages to preparing your own sausages. These may be seasoned to taste, with the amount of spices, herbs, salt, and pepper that conforms to your particular palate or diet. Also, these are *fresh* sausages, that is, made when you need them, preservative-free, not dried, smoked, or otherwise cured. Basic directions for sausage-making are as follows:

1. *Chopping or grinding the ingredients:* Use a sharp knife, a meat grinder, or a food processor to prepare the ingredients. (To make hand-chopping easier, partially freeze the meat beforehand. To ensure even chopping in your food processor, first cut the meats into 2-inch cubes.)

2. *Mixing the ingredients:* If you're not using a food processor, your fingers are the best tools for evenly distributing seasonings, and so forth. Any ingredient that must retain its texture also needs this tender, loving hand care. After mixing, let the flavors develop by refrigerating the mixture for 12–24 hours.

3. *Preparing the casings:* Because they stretch and shrink right along with the sausages, natural casings are best. Believe it or not, these aren't difficult to locate. Fine butcher shops nearly always carry them, as do many specialty food shops, as well as farmers and others who do their own butchering or make their own sausages. Natural casings usually come packaged in salt and require a few simple preparations before they are ready for use. Rinse the amount you'll need 1 at a time under running water, then slip 1 end of each over the end of the faucet so that the water runs through the full length. Soak in warm water for 30 minutes, arrange on paper towels (without overlapping), and cover with a damp towel until ready to use.

If casings are unavailable, divide the meat mixture in thirds and wrap in double-strength plastic wrap to form three large wursts. Tie each end and refrigerate. Just prior to serving, simmer, still wrapped, in a large pot of water. Cool slightly, unwrap, slice, and brown.

4. *Filling the casings:* Use the sausage-stuffing attachment that comes with your food processor or grinder, if you have one, and follow the manufacturer's instructions. If not, it's not too difficult to improvise by using a funnel with a fairly large spout (one that can fit into the casing) plus the handle of a wooden spoon to tamp the meat down. Hold the funnel in the crook of your arm, against your body, and slip a very damp casing over the spout.

Tamp the sausage mixture down to the end of the nozzle with a wooden spoon that has been dipped in ice water (to prevent it from sticking). Tie off the casing about 1 inch from the end, using strong thread or light string. (Never tie off beforehand or the air in the funnel will cause the casing to inflate.) Force the sausage mixture loosely into the casing; it will expand as it cooks.

5. *Cooking the sausages:* To avoid the "pop!" of split casings, prick sausages on all sides with a sharp needle and place them in a single layer in a pan just large enough to hold them without crowding. Add enough water or broth to reach halfway up the sausage sides, cover, and simmer for 5 minutes, then turn, re-cover, and simmer for 5 minutes more. Drain the sausages, discarding the water, and dry with paper towels. Add 2–3 tablespoons of vegetable oil to the pan and brown the sausages on all sides over low heat.

CREDITS

DINNERWARE AND LINENS, PAGES 31, 129, 174, 175, BY YVONNE YOUNG TARR

Acknowledgments

For you who so kindly dug into your butler's pantries, kitchen cabinets, storerooms, and cellars to find me that indispensable collectible, that unique antique, that treasured "what not": Thank you. For you who shared with me your antique shop showrooms, living room parlors, secret and not so secret gardens: Thank you, too. For you who tolerated lights, cameras, wires, food, drink, flowers, silver, candles, and packing baskets full of excelsior without so much as a grimace: Thank you so much . . . ERNESTINE LASSAW, LEE AND JORDAN GRUZEN, BARBARA HALE, MARILYN AND MURRY HILLMAN, CAROLE AND NORMAN MERCER, ANN SPANWELL, EMILY COBB, IAN WOODNER, AND BRAN FERREN.

263

Index

ABOUT THE AUTHOR

YVONNE YOUNG TARR has written twenty cookbooks and numerous magazine and newspaper articles as well as her syndicated columns, "The Quick Gourmet" and "The Diet Gourmet." Her books include the award-winning *The Great East Coast Seafood Book, The New York Times Bread and Soup Cookbook, The Ten-Minute Gourmet Cookbook,* and *The Great Food Processor Cookbook.* She and her husband, the sculptor William Tarr, live in East Hampton, New York, where they entertain splendidly.